M000190881

*The BTSOP Alumni Association would like to dedicate this work to Brother Justin Hopkins for his hard work in the kingdom of God and on this publication.*

# Contents

# Ephesians

*by*

*Donny Weimar*

## The City of Ephesus

Ephesus is the first and greatest metropolis of all Asia Minor. Having been the capitol of Ionia, she is now the capitol of Asia Minor – under the auspice of the Roman Empire. The city is flourishing with citizenry. The Temple of Diana is her limits and stands as one of the Seven Wonders of the World. This colossal idol was initially burnt down in 355 B.C. It took 120 years to build the new structure. The semicircular theater is 495 feet in diameter with a seating capacity of 24,500 people.

Paganism and beliefs in the dark arts of magic and sorcery dominated her religions. From the Jewish dispersion landed several Jews in the locale. Paul preached there for three months in Jewish synagogues. At present day, the city is now in ruins. The notorious Goths decimated the great temple in 262 A.D. It was very much a part of the first century Gentile religion in Asia Minor.

## The Founding of the Church at Ephesus

Paul is an integral part of the spiritual growth of the Ephesians faith. On his second missionary journey is spent a few days with the brothers and sisters there. Then again on his third journey he spent more than two years. In this important center of trade and population, Paul spoke "so that all they that dwelt in Asia heard the word of the Lord, both Jews and Greeks"

(Acts 19:8-10, 18-20). In the twentieth chapter of Acts we read of the account of the apostle's farewell address to the elders of the church at Ephesus. Revelation 2:1-7 presents the message of Jesus to this church.

## The Epistle

The letter opens with a common greeting to the church. In some ancient manuscripts "Ephesus" is not found in the scripts. This has led some to see the possibility that the letter was written to the church at Laodicea, as mentioned in Colossians 4:13-17. It may have been a circulated epistle that found its final rest at Ephesus. That the letter may have been circulated has inferred the truth that the Bible is applicable to all readers and churches of Christ. It was most likely written during Paul's two years of imprisonment (61-63 A.D.). Philippians, Colossians and Philemon were also written from the prison quarters.

## The Outline of Ephesians

I. The apostolic salutation (1:1-2)
II. The believer's position in grace (1:3-3:21)
    A. The seven elements of the believer's position (1:3-14)
    B. The prayer for knowledge and power (1:15-21)
    C. Christ exalted to be the Haed of his body, the church (1:22-23)
    D. The method of Gentile salvation (2:1-10)
    E. The Gentile position by nature (2:11-13)
    F. Jew and Gentile one body in Christ (2:14-18)
    G. The church a temple for the habitation of God through the Spirit (2:19-3:21)
        1. The church a mystery hidden from past ages (3:1-12)
        2. Parenthetic: the prayer for inner fullness and knowledge (3:13-21)
III. The walk and service of the believer as in Christ, and as having the Spirit (4:1-5:17)
    A. The walk to be worthy the position (4:1-3)
    B. The seven unities to be kept (4:4-6)
    C. The ministry gifts of Christ to his body (4:17-29)
    D. The purpose of the ministry gifts (4:12-16)
    E. The walk of the believer as a new man in Christ Jesus (4:17-29)
    F. The walk of the believer as indwelt by the Spirit (4:30-32)
    G. The walk of the believer as God's dear child (5:1-17)

IV. The walk and warfare of the believer as filled with the Spirit (5:18-6:24)
  A. The inner life of the Spirit-filled believer (5:19-20)
  B. The married life of Spirit-filled believers as illustrating Christ and the church (5:21-33)
  C. The domestic life of Spirit-filled believers as children and servants (6:1-9)
  D. The warfare of Spirit-filled believers (6:10-24)
    1. The warrior's power (6:10)
    2. The warrior's armour (6:11)
    3. The warrior's foes (6:12-17)
    4. The warrior's resource (6:18-24)[1]

**CHAPTER 1**

# Ephesians
### *by*
### *Daniel Ridinger*

---

## Ephesians 1:1-2: The Introduction

In verse 1, Paul begins the Ephesian Epistle by introducing himself as "an apostle of Jesus Christ…." This is Paul's customary method of introduction in many of his writings (cf. Rom. 1:1; 1 Cor. 1:1; 2 Cor. 1:1; Gal.1:1, 1, 2 Tim.1:1, and Titus 1:1). The term "apostle" refers to Paul's relationship to Jesus as His official representative who had been personally commissioned and sent on a mission. This also says something about Paul's authority as a messenger of Christ. The "signs, wonders and mighty works" (cf. 2 Cor. 12:2) which Paul did demonstrated that he was not inferior to any apostle, even though He considered himself "least of the apostles" (cf. 1 Cor. 15:9).

Paul addresses this epistle "to the saints which are at Ephesus, and to the faithful in Christ Jesus." Specifically, his letter is directed to the Ephesian brethren, "the saints which are at Ephesus", but generally, "to the faithful in Christ Jesus." The word "saints", found nine times in the Ephesian Epistle, refers to God's holy people who are sanctified, set apart, to serve Him (cf. Rom. 1:7; 1 Pt. 2:5, 9). The Catholic teaching that a saint is "a person formally recognized or canonized by the Church after death, who may be the object of veneration and prayers for intercession"[2] is foreign to New Testament doctrine. It is obvious that "the saints" to whom Paul wrote were living people. Too, the expression "in Christ" or its equivalent "…occurs one hundred seventy-six times in the Pauline writings, thirty-six times in Ephesians alone."[3] This term refers to the spiritual position of the Ephesian Christians.

Paul extends a customary greeting to the recipients in verse 2, "Grace to you and peace from God our Father and the Lord Jesus Christ." "Grace" is God's unmerited favor. God has given us what we need but not what we deserve with reference to salvation (cf. 2 Tim. 1:9). God has extended His "grace" to all mankind (cf. Titus 2:11). It is "by grace…through faith" that a person is saved (cf. Eph. 2:8). The results of salvation by grace is "peace" – tranquility of soul because one has been reconciled to God (cf. Eph. 2:14-17; Rom. 5:1, 2). Also, grace and peace are components of the closing salutation in this epistle (cf. Eph. 6:23, 24). The exact words "God our Father and the Lord Jesus Christ" are found in six other Pauline salutations (cf. Rom. 1:7; 1 Cor. 1:3; 2 Cor. 1:2; Phil. 1:2; 2 Th. 1:1; Phlm. 3).

## Ephesians 1:3-14: The Spiritual Blessings In Christ

Ephesian 1:3-14 is one long sentence in the original language. It is a "majestic statement of praise."[4]

According to verse 3 Paul says, "Blessed be the God and Father of our Lord Jesus Christ, who hath blessed us with every spiritual blessing in the heavenly places in Christ…" God has opened Heaven's window and showered His people with blessings from above – the greater blessings – spiritual blessings. Christians should be thankful to God and express genuine praise to Him for these blessings.

Observe that "every spiritual blessing" is located "in the heavenly places in Christ." The expression "in the heavenly places", literally "in the heavenlies", is found five times in the Ephesian Epistle and in no other New Testament writing (cf. 1:3, 20; 2:6; 3:10; 6:12). The words "in Christ" establish that these blessings are only in Jesus. This is equivalent to saying "in Christ's spiritual body" – His church (cf. Eph. 1:22, 23). There are no spiritual blessings outside of Christ. The only way that a person can access these spiritual blessings is to obey the gospel by acknowledging faith and being baptized into Christ (cf. 1 Cor. 12:13; Gal. 3:26, 27).

The nature of the greater blessings is set forth as being "spiritual, relating to the human spirit or soul. These blessings are part of "the riches of God's grace" (cf. verse 7). Paul elaborates more on these magnificent spiritual blessings in verses 4-14.

Election and adoption as God's sons are the first two spiritual blessings mentioned in verses 4-6. In verse 4, Paul refers to God's eternal plan of election, that is, "even as he chose us in him before the foundation of the world to be holy and without blemish before him in love." What God has done is revealed by the phrase "chose us in him." The word "chose" means "to pick or choose out for oneself."[5] When God did the choosing is indicated by the expression "before the foundation of the world." God "chose us" prior to throwing or laying down a universe into space – before speaking a material universe into existence which had no prior existence.[6] The reason why God "chose us" is in order that we might be "holy and without blemish in love." The translators of the ASV and KJV linked "holiness and blamelessness" to "love" in verse 4, "...that we should be holy, and without blame before him in love." If love comes at the conclusion of verse 4, then God's love is the basis of election. In the NASV and the ESV the expression "in love" is connected with verse 5. If love is linked to verse 5, then God's love explains why He foreordained us to adoption as sons. The reason for the difference is a punctuation problem that is difficult to resolve. The passage teaches that God's eternal purpose (cf. Eph. 3:11) – before the creation of the world – involved determining those in Christ to be the recipients of His spiritual blessings. They are the elect of God. The choice of God was not the selection of individuals, arbitrary or unconditional as some teach. "The election has to do with selecting or predetermining holy characteristics, not individuals."[7]

We encounter the doctrine of foreordination or predestination in verse 5, "having foreordained us unto adoption as sons through Jesus Christ unto himself...." The term "foreordained" is translated "predestinated" {KJV} and "predestined" (NKJV/ESV/NASV}. The word "foreordained" means "decide upon beforehand, predetermine."[8] "God set beforehand certain bounds, limitations or criteria to be met."[9] It does not mean that God arbitrarily determined that certain individuals would be saved and others lost.

Foreordination – predestination is taught in the Bible but not Calvinistic predestination. John Calvin taught, "All men are not created for the same end; but some are foreordained to eternal life, others to eternal damnation. So according as every man was created for the one end or the other, we say, he was elected, that is, predestined to life, or reprobated, that is, predestined to damnation (Calv. Inst., book 3, chapter 21, section 1)."[10] The Westminster Confession of Faith says, "III. By the decree of God, for the manifestation of His glory, some men and angels are predestinated unto everlasting life; and others foreordained to everlasting death. IV. These angels and men, thus predestinated, and foreordained, are particularly and unchangeably designed, and their number so certain and definite, that it cannot be either increased or diminished."[11] God has blessed mankind with free-moral agency, the ability to choose. Each accountable person has a choice with regard to election and salvation. It is God's desire that all people be saved (cf. 1 Tim. 2:3, 4; 2 Pt. 3:9). Jesus died in order that all sinners might be saved (cf. Jn. 3:16; 2 Cor.

5:14, 15). All people are invited to be saved (cf. Mt. 11:28-30; Rev. 22:17). God calls people through the gospel and belief of the truth to become the elect of God (cf. 1 Th. 1:4; 2 Th. 2:13, 14). The gospel is to be preached to the "whole creation" [every creature {KJV}] (cf. Mk. 16:15). Accountable people may choose to either obey God or disobey Him. Those who are obedient and remain faithful to God will be saved and ultimately, receive an incomparable eternal inheritance (cf. Mk. 16:16; Rom. 8:17, 18; 1 Pt. 1:3, 4). On the other hand, the disobedient will be cast into eternal Hell (cf. Mt. 25:41, 46).

The foreordination of God is in view of "adoption as sons" (verse 5b). God determined beforehand that those "in Christ" would be adopted as His sons. William Barclay commenting about adoption in the Roman world said, "The person who had been adopted had all the rights of a legitimate son in his new family and lost absolutely all rights in his old family. In the eyes of the law, he was a new person. So new was he that even all debts and obligations connected with his previous family were abolished as if they had never existed."[12] Adoption as sons pertains to the status and privileges that God bestows on members of His family which is "according to the good pleasure of His will to the praise of the glory of His grace, which He freely bestowed on us in the Beloved." (cf. verse 6)

Redemption is another spiritual blessing described in verse 7a, "In whom we have our redemption, through his blood…." Sometimes Christians sing "I've Been Redeemed", and that truth is clearly taught in this passage. The term "redemption" means "release from a captive condition…deliverance…the release fr. sin…that comes through Christ."[13] It has been cautiously estimated that 300,000-350,000 out of a population of about 900,000-950,000 were slaves in first century Rome at the time of Augustus. Furthermore, it has been calculated that Italy in the first century had around two million slaves out of a population of about six million at the time of Augustus. This means that about one out of three were slaves in first century Rome and Italy.[14] We are aware that slavery is still a social problem in many parts of the world; however, untold numbers of people are spiritually enslaved to sin and don't even know it. Jesus said, "…Verily, verily, I say unto you, Every one that committeth sin is the bondservant of sin." The practice of sin has bound their hearts and souls through the lust of the flesh, the lust of the eyes and the vainglory of life (cf. 1 Jn. 2:15-17). People are powerless to free themselves from sin's bondage. Thankfully, God sent His Son, Jesus, to be the Redeemer (cf. Is. 59:20) who would give His life as a ransom – the payment price (cf. Mk. 10:45; 1 Tim. 2:6) to free all mankind from spiritual slavery. Christians are the people whom Jesus has purchased out of the world for His own possession (cf. Acts 20:28; Tit. 2:14; 1 Pt. 1:18, 19). In Christ we are free from sin's bondage to serve God (cf. Rom. 6:17, 18). The price that Jesus paid, however, to redeem mankind was costly, that is, it "was through his blood." The only way that mankind could be redeemed was for Christ's precious blood to stain Golgotha's cross in death (cf. Mt. 26:28; Jn. 19:34; Rev. 1:5). The cross was a Divine necessity. Jesus' dual Nature, God-Man, enabled God to die in the flesh for our sins (cf. Heb. 2:14-18).

Closely connected to the effectiveness of Christ's blood is "forgiveness of our trespasses" (cf. verse 7b). "Trespasses" [sins {KJV/NKJV}] depict "... one making a false step so as to lose footing: a violation of moral standards, offense, wrongdoing, sin."[15] We should take sin seriously because God does not treat it lightly. The sacrifice that was demanded in order for God to forgive mankind attests to the horrendous nature of sin. Forgiveness, that is, remission of sins – Divine pardon, would have been impossible without Jesus' shed blood (cf. Heb. 9:22; 10:11). The Jews during the time of the law of Moses offered up untold numbers of blood sacrifices yearly. The Day of Atonement was a solemn annual occasion when Israel was reminded of their sins (cf. Heb. 10:3). The High Priest would enter into the Most Holy Place in order to atone first for his own sins and then again for the sins of Israel (cf. Lev. 16). The blood of all those yearly sacrifices, however, could not provide absolute forgiveness of sins (cf. Heb. 10:4). Each slain sacrificial animal pointed toward the coming of the Messiah and ultimate forgiveness (cf. Is. 53). Today, Christians have absolute forgiveness of our sins because of Jesus' sacrifice and His shed blood. God will never bring up even one sin for which we have received forgiveness (cf. Heb. 10:17, 18). We continue to have God's forgiveness as long as we keep on walking in the light (cf. 1 Jn. 1:7). Both redemption and forgiveness are "according to the riches of God's grace." Truly, in Christ "there is therefore now no condemnation..." (cf. Rom. 8:1).

According to verse 8, the "riches of God's grace" (cf. verse 7c) have been "lavished upon us, in all wisdom and insight" {ESV}. This speaks of the magnitude of God's grace. He has made His grace to abound – to overflow to those who are in Christ. The words "wisdom and insight" point to the fact that "God has provided the knowledge and ability to know and to do his will" which Paul takes up in the following verse.[16]

In verse 9, Paul says, "making known unto us the mystery of his will..." In antiquity, the word "mystery" was associated with the mystery cults. They had their secret rites and signs as do secret societies today. The secrets or mysteries were hidden from the uninitiated. Only the initiated – those to whom the mystery had been revealed knew the meaning to the secrets.[17] "In the NT mystērion signifies a secret which is being, or even has been, revealed, which is also divine in scope, and needs to be made known by God to men through his Spirit."[18] Paul uses the term "mystery" six times in Ephesians (cf. 1:9; 3:3, 4, 9; 5:32; 6:19). "Paul clarifies the mystērion...as the good news of salvation to the Gentiles, including their incorporation into the body of Christ, the church"[19] (cf. Eph. 3:1-13). He identifies the "mystery" with the Christ and the church (cf. Eph. 5:32) and with the gospel (cf. Eph. 6:19). God has revealed "the mystery" to us through inspired men (cf. Mk. 4:11; 1 Cor. 2:7; Eph. 3:5). Also, Paul teaches that we can understand the mystery of God (cf. Eph. 3:4; Col. 2:2). Making known the mystery is "... according to his good pleasure which he purposed in him." The term translated "good pleasure" means "state or condition of being kindly disposed, good will...state or condition of being favored, favor...."[20] The same expression is found in verse 5. The NASV renders it "according to His kind intention" in both places. God's love is involved in the mystery that has been revealed. The KJV and NKJV render words "in him" in verse 9 as "in himself." Reference is to God who was pleased to reveal his plan and to complete that plan in His Son.[21]

According to verse 10, God's purpose is to complete His plan in Christ, "unto a dispensation of the fulness of the times, to sum up all things in Christ, the things in the heavens, and the things upon the earth; in him, I say..." The word "unto" in the original language is eiv indicating purpose which is translated "with a view to" in the NASV. The term "dispensation" [oikonomia] is rendered "plan" {ESV} and "administration" {NASV}. Literally it means "responsibility of management, management of a household, direction, office" but also a "state of being arranged, arrangement, order, plan."[22] It is described as the "dispensation of that grace of God" (cf. Eph. 3:2) and "dispensation of the mystery" (cf. Eph. 3:9). Reference is to God's administration of His plan of salvation, the mystery that has been revealed. The "fullness of the times" refers "to the completion of the successive stages or periods of redemptive history."[23] It is the period spanning from Christ's birth (cf. Gal. 4:4) until He comes again. It is described elsewhere in the Scriptures as the "last days" (Acts 2:17), the "ends of the ages" (cf. 1 Cor. 10:11; Heb. 9:26) and the "end of times" (cf. 1 Pt. 1:20). We are living in the last dispensation of time, the present Christian age. God's plan is "to sum up all things in Christ, the things in the heavens, and the things upon the earth..." The expression "sum up" is translated "gather together in one" {KJV} and "unite all things" {ESV}. The context of the Ephesian Epistle indicates that God is uniting – reconciling both Jews and Gentiles in one body, the church, over which Christ is the Head (cf. Eph. 1:22, 23; 2:14-15; 5:22-33).

In verses 11-13, Paul says that Christians are God's heritage. Verse 11 states, "in whom also we were made a heritage, having been foreordained according to the purpose of him who worketh all things after the counsel of his will...." The expression "in whom" is equivalent to "in Christ" (cf. verses 3, 10, 12, 20). Most of the other versions render "made a heritage" as "obtained an inheritance." The better view seems to be "heritage." The word "we" (cf. verse 11) is set in opposition to the term "ye" (cf. verse 13). It seems that the "we" refers to Paul and Christians from a Jewish background as God's "heritage" or possession. They are described as those "who first trusted in Christ" (cf. verse 12, KJV/NKJV). This correlates with God's plan for the "mystery of the gospel" to be preached first to the Jews (cf. Lk. 24:47; Acts 1:8; Rom. 1:16). Furthermore, Paul says that this is in keeping with God's predetermined purpose and will (cf. verse 12).

Paul addresses the Ephesian Christians who were of Gentile parentage in verse 13, "in whom ye also, having heard the word of the truth, the gospel of your salvation, --in whom, having also believed, ye were sealed with the Holy Spirit of promise..." This verse teaches that the Lord's heritage is not confined only to Jewish Christians (cf. 1 Pt. 2:9, 10). The Ephesian brethren were now included in God's heritage because they too had been obedient to the gospel. The record of Paul's two-year evangelistic endeavor in Ephesus is found in Acts 19. He had personally proclaimed to them the "...word of the truth" which also is described as "the gospel of your salvation...." (cf. Eph. 4:21). Hearing "the word of the truth" was necessary in order for the formation of faith in their hearts (cf. Rom. 10:14-17). The word "believed" is a synecdoche, a figure of speech in which a part stands for all that is involved in becoming a Christian. It means that the Ephesians obeyed the gospel plan of salvation (cf. Acts 19:1-6; Eph. 2:8; Mk. 16:16; Jn. 3:36). Consequently, they were "sealed with the Holy Spirit of promise" when they obeyed the gospel. In ancient times crates, packages and sacks were sealed before being transported. The seal showed that the merchandise was intact, from whom the package was sent and to whom it belonged.[24] The "seal of the Spirit" identifies Christians as belonging to God (cf. Rev. 7:1-8). The Holy Spirit is given to Christians and indwells them in a non-miraculous manner (cf. Acts 5:32; Rom. 8:9-11; 1 Cor. 6:19, 20; 2 Cor. 1:21, 22). Paul admonished the Ephesians to, "...grieve not the Holy Spirit of God, in whom ye were sealed unto the day of redemption" (Eph. 4:30).

In verse 14, Paul describes the Holy Spirit as "an earnest of our inheritance...." The term "earnest" [arrabon] is translated "guarantee" in the NKJV/ESV and "pledge" in the NASV. 2 Corinthians 1:22 teaches that God has given Christians "the earnest of the Spirit in our hearts." William Barclay in commenting on the word "earnest" said, "The arrabōn was a regular feature of the Greek business world. It was a part of the purchase price of anything, a deposit paid in advance as a guarantee that the rest would in due course be paid. There are many Greek commercial documents still in existence in which the word occurs. A woman sells a cow and receives so many drachmae as arrabōn...Paul is saying is that the Holy Spirit is...the guarantee that some day we will enter into full possession of the blessedness of God."[25] The Holy Spirit "...is the down payment of the full manifestation of God's presence that Christians will come to know in the new heavens and new earth (cf. Rev. 21:3-4)."[26] The "earnest" is "unto [with a view to {NASV}] the redemption of God's own possession...." It seems that the words "unto the redemption of God's own possession...." indicate when God will take full possession of His people.

## Ephesians 1:15-23: The Prayer For The Ephesian Brethren

In verse 15, we observe the reason why Paul prayed for the Ephesian brethren, "For this cause I also, having heard of the faith in the Lord Jesus which is among you, and the love which ye show toward all the saint..." "For this cause" is translated "Wherefore I also," and "For this reason" in the KJV and ESV, respectively. Paul's prayer is based on the spiritual blessings in Christ (cf. verses 3-14). He informs the Ephesian Christians that he had heard about their "faith...and love...." The fact that Paul had "heard" should not be interpreted to mean that he was not well-acquainted with these brethren (cf. Acts 19; 20:17-38). Several years have passed since Paul preached in Ephesus. Also, Paul was in prison when he wrote the Ephesian Epistle. His knowledge about the circumstances of the Ephesian congregation came from reports of fellow-workers. He had heard about the Ephesian brethren's "faith in the Lord Jesus...." This reveals that the Lord was the object of their faith, just as our faith must be focused on Christ if we are to be pleasing to God. Also, Paul had "heard" about their "love which ye show toward all the saints..." Love and faith go hand in hand. Love is the outgrowth and outworking of faith (cf. Gal. 4:6; Ja. 2:14-17; 1 Jn. 3:16-18).

Paul was constant in prayer, thus reflecting his love and concern for the church. In verse 16, he writes that he ceases "...not to give thanks for you, making mention of you in my prayers..." He was sincerely grateful for the Ephesian brethren and regularly remembered them in his prayers. Being thankful for brethren and praying for them often was important to Paul and should be our concern, too (cf. Eph. 6:18; 1 Th. 5:17).

In verse 17, Paul prays that the Ephesian brethren would have a fuller knowledge of God, "that the God of our Lord Jesus Christ, the Father of glory, may give unto you a spirit of wisdom and revelation in the knowledge of him;...." Throughout the gospel narratives Jesus refers to God as His Father (cf. Mt. 7:21; 12:50; Jn. 20:17). The Heavenly Father is described as "the Father of glory...." – "the God characterized by glory" (cf. Acts 7:2).[27] Also, Jesus is called the "Lord of glory" which indicates a contrast to the indignity of the cross and the Majesty of its victim (cf. 1 Cor. 2:8).[28] Jesus shares in His Father's glory (cf. Jn. 17:5; 1 Tim. 3:16). Observe that Paul's first petition is that the Father give the Ephesian brethren "...a spirit of wisdom and revelation in the knowledge of him...." The word "spirit" is without the article and pertains to the human spirit, the rational part of man as opposed to the Holy Spirit. "The apostle did not pray that God would give to all the Ephesians the knowledge of the doctrines of the gospel by an immediate revelation made to themselves; but that he would enable them to understand the revelation of these doctrines which was made to the apostles, and which they preached to the world."[29] A similar thought is recorded in Colossians 1:9, "For this cause we also, since the day we heard it, do not cease to pray and make request for you, that ye may be filled with the knowledge of his will in all spiritual wisdom and understanding...." James teaches that wisdom will be given to the one who prays to God for it in faith, not doubting (cf. Ja. 1:5-8).

In verse 18, Paul continues, "having the eyes of your heart enlightened, that ye may know what is the hope of his calling, what the riches of the glory of his inheritance in the saints..." Paul's second petition is that the Ephesian Christians might understand three great truths about salvation in Christ. Two of these truths are mentioned in this verse and the third one in verse 19.

First, Paul mentions "having the eyes of your heart [understanding {KJV/NKJV}] enlightened..." Workman wrote, "These words...are a rather poetic restatement of what Paul means by give unto you a spirit of wisdom and revelation" (cf. verse 17).[30] Paul desired very much that the Ephesian Christians "know what is the hope of his calling...." The word "know" [οἶδα] means "to grasp the meaning of someth., understand, recognize, come to know, experience."[31] The Ephesian Christians in their unconverted condition had "no hope" (cf. Eph. 2:12). They now possess "hope" because of their obedience to the gospel call (cf. Eph. 4:4; 2 Th. 2:14). Biblical hope is "joyful and confident expectation of eternal salvation."[32] The hope of a Christian is described in different ways in the New Testament. Our hope is not of this world, but rather it is in Heaven (cf. Col. 1:5; Heb. 6:19, 20). It is a real and living hope (cf. 1 Pt. 1:3, 4). Paul wrote that it is "Christ Jesus" (cf. 1 Tim. 1:1). The "hope" that Christians have is made up of two elements, "desire" and "expectation." We desire eternal life with God, Christ and the righteous throughout the ages in Heaven, and we expect to receive it. This should encourage every Christian to be faithful to God regardless of hardships (cf. Col. 1:23). Secondly, Paul wanted the Ephesian brethren to "know... the riches of the glory of his inheritance in the saints...." The ESV/NKJV/NASV make the passage easier to understand, "may know...what are the riches of his glorious inheritance in the saints..." In verse 11, Paul mentions that Christians are God's "heritage" – possession. In verse 14, he refers to the Spirit as "the earnest of our inheritance", that is, the guarantee or pledge that we will receive it in full. In verse 18b, Paul is either referring to how precious Christians are in God's sight or to the riches of the Heavenly inheritance (cf. Rom. 8:18; Rev. 21:1-7).[33] Thirdly, in verse 19, Paul wants the Ephesian brethren to "know...what the exceeding greatness of his power to us-ward who believe, according to that working of the strength of his might..." God's power is necessary in order for hope to be realized and the inheritance to be obtained.[34] Paul used four synonyms relating to power in this passage: "power" [dunamis], "working" [energeia], "strength" [ischus], and "might" [kratos]. These terms reveal God's inherent "power" to accomplish His plan. Paul is saying that God is able to do what He has promised.

Verse 20 - "which he wrought in Christ, when he raised him from the dead, and made him to sit at his right hand in the heavenly place,...." Jesus knew that He would be crucified in Jerusalem for the sins of the world (cf. Mt. 16:21; Mk. 10:33; Jn. 3:14; 12:27; 13:1). His death was necessary in order to atone for the sins of all humanity and to fulfill all that was written about Him in the Law of Moses, the prophets and the psalms (cf. Lk. 24:44). Also, Christ knew that He would be raised from the dead on the third day (cf. Mt. 16:21; Mt. 20:18, 19; Jn. 2:19-22). The resurrection of Jesus and some of the post-resurrection appearances are recorded in all four of the gospel narratives (cf. Mt. 28:1ff; Mk. 16:1ff; Lk. 24:1ff; Jn. 20:1-21:25). Jesus' resurrection is a monumental event in the history of mankind (cf. Rom. 1:4), "the miracle of miracles" or "the crowning miracle." Paul informs us about the significance of Jesus' resurrection in 1 Corinthians 15:12-19. The emphasis is that without the resurrection Christianity is useless, our faith is futile, we are still in our sins, the dead in Christ are lost and we are to be pitied because of misplaced hope. Thankfully, Almighty God has demonstrated His Omnipotent power by Jesus' resurrection from the dead and His exaltation to the right hand of God's Throne (cf. Acts 2:33-36; Phil. 2:9-11).

Paul refers to the exaltation of Jesus in verse 21. God exalted Jesus "Far above all principality, and power, and might, and dominion, and every name that is named, not only in this world, but also in that which is to come:..." The phrase "Far above" relates to "rank, power." Jesus has been raised up to the highest place of honor (cf. Acts 2:33; Phil. 2:9) and has been given the greatest authority – "all authority in Heaven and on earth" (cf. Mt. 28:18). He has authority over both the spiritual and material realms. The only exception is God (cf. 1 Cor. 15:24-28). The "principality, and power, and might, and dominion" refer to created spiritual powers. These would refer to both good and bad created beings. In Eph. 6:12, Paul writes, "For our wrestling is not against flesh and blood, but against the principalities, against the powers, against the world-rulers of this darkness, against the spiritual hosts of wickedness in the heavenly places." The words "world rulers of this darkness" refer to earthly rulers who are the foes of righteousness. Also, Jesus is above "...every name that is named, not only in this world, but also in that which is to come..." (cf. Col. 2:10). Jesus has been exalted above not only all the heavenly created beings, but also "above...every name that is named, not only in this world, but also in that which is to come...." Jesus' name is "more excellent" than angelic beings (cf. Heb.1:4). The superior name of Jesus is Son (cf. Phil. 2:9-11; Heb. 1:5). Everything that Christians do is in view of Jesus' name (cf. Eph. 5:20; Col. 3:17).

In verse 22a, "...he put all things in subjection under his feet" is a restatement of verse 21. The term "subjection" means "to cause to be in a submissive relationship, to subject, to subordinate" (cf. Ps. 86).[35] Christ is the unquestioned Sovereign – the Lord of all (cf. Acts 10:36; Rom. 10:12). All angelic and human authorities are subject to Him (cf. 1 Cor. 15:27, 28). Verse 22b says, "...and gave him to be the head over all things to the church..." The resurrected Lord is the sole "head" of the church. Some believe that the term "head" refers to origin; thus, meaning that "Christ is divinely appointed as the source of the church's life."[36] Certainly, Jesus established the church (cf. Mt. 16:18) and purchased it with His own blood (cf. Acts 20:28; Eph. 5:25). The term translated "head" in the context of the Ephesian Epistle means, however, that Jesus is the Supreme Ruler the church (cf. Eph. 5:23, 24; Col. 1:18). He is the One who is "head over all things to the church–its worship, its laws, its plan of salvation, its moral standards, etc. No pope, bishop, church council, convention, synod, prophet, preacher, or anyone else dares to rob Christ of any of the authority God gave to Him."[37]

In verse 23, Paul reveals that the church "...is his body, the fulness of him that filleth all in all." The church is identified as "his body". Jesus has only one body for which He died and claims as His possession (cf. Eph. 4:4; 1 Cor. 11:12:13; Col. 1:24). Just as one's head and body are interrelated, so is the Head (Jesus) of the church to His body. The case of Saul of Tarsus' persecution of the church illustrates this point (cf. Acts 8:1-3; 9:1-22; 22:1-21; 26:1-23). "Saul, Saul, why persecutest thou me?" is the question that Jesus asked Saul on the Damascus road (cf. Acts 9:4; 22:7; 26:14). Saul was persecuting the church, but Jesus said that Saul was persecuting Him. Jesus cannot be separated from the church, His body. A vital spiritual union exists between the two. [Paul also mentions Jesus as the Savior of His body in Eph. 5:23.] Furthermore, in verse 23b the grandeur of the church is described as the fulness of Christ, that is, "...the fulness of him that filleth all in all."

Chapter 2

# Ephesians

*by*

*Foy G. Forehand*

---

## Introductory Remarks

Any and every study of Ephesians Two must include prime thoughts and concepts emphasized in this noble letter. The expression "in Christ," or its equivalent is seen throughout the letter and is manifestly significant. All spiritual blessings are "in Christ" (Eph. 1:3). To be in Christ is to be in His body, the church (Eph. 1:22-23); which body alone He will save in eternity (Eph 5:23b). God is to be glorified in this body (Eph 3:20-21). While there are many religious institutions in the world claiming some connection to Jesus, there is only one body of which He is the Head (Col. 1:18), and which has the Divine approval because it is built by Jesus Himself (Matt. 16:13-19). This one body is the eternal purpose of God (Eph. 3:10-11). It is everything God ever planned for mankind on this earth. In Chapter two of this letter to the Ephesians we find God's eternal purpose seen in mercy, love and grace (Eph. 1:1-10); and this eternal purpose is seen in the glorious peace in the eternal temple (Ephesians 2:11-22).

## Ephesians 2:1-10: God's Eternal Purpose Seen in Mercy, Love, and Grace

Ephesians 2:1 "And you did he make alive, when ye were dead through your trespasses and sins." These words follow the beautiful expression of the resurrection and exaltation of the Christ by the power of God (1:19-21). It is the power of God that makes an individual, who is dead in sin, alive. That power, 1 Corinthians 1:18; Romans 1:16, is the gospel message, the

New Testament, the last will and testament of the Lord Jesus Christ. These Ephesians had heard some preaching of Christ by Apollos (Acts 18:24-26), but because he knew ONLY the baptism of John, he had left disciples who were not in a saved relationship with God. When Paul came to Ephesus as described in Acts 19:1-7, he brought them "up to speed" with the full message of the Christ. They were then scripturally baptized (immersed) for the remission of their sins, and after Paul laid his apostolic hands on them they received miraculous gifts. In this way they were "made alive" in Christ.

The idea, "dead in sins," is a strange concept. The concept of death is variously misunderstood by materialists and spiritualists alike. To those without Biblical understanding the meaning of death usually takes the form of "annihilation," as with materialists; or "union with some elusive indefinable spirit world," by spiritualists. The word "death" signifies separation. One might be physically alive, but spiritually dead as the woman who gives herself to pleasure (1 Tim. 5:6). The concluding stanza of "Thanatopsis" by William C. Bryant suggests that one should be able to "wrap the draperies of his couch about him and lie down to pleasant dreams." "A Psalm of Life" by Henry Wadsworth Longfellow suggests "Life is real! Life is earnest! And the grave is not the goal; Dust thou art, to dust returnest, Was not spoken of the soul." Isaiah 59:1-2 clarifies this, concluding "your sins have separated between you and your God so that he will not hear." James, the half-brother of Jesus, is inspired to write in, "For as the body apart from the spirit is dead, even so faith apart from works is dead" (Jas. 2:26). These citizens of Ephesus were dead in sin; and by repentance they died to sin; and then these doubly dead men were buried in a watery grave, baptism (Rom. 6:3-5) and resurrected to walk in newness of life. In this way, God made them alive when they were dead in their trespasses and sins.

Ephesians 2:2 "wherein ye once walked according to the course of this world, according to the prince of the powers of the air, of the spirit that now worketh in the sons of disobedience." William Wordsworth commented in a poem, "The world is too much with us." How true. What is the "course of this world? According to Jesus in Matthew 7:13-14, it is the broad way that leadeth to destruction. Who is the prince of the power of the air? He is the same one the apostle Paul, by revelation and inspiration, designates "the god of this world" in 2 Corinthians 4:4; and John, by the same authority that Paul received, designates him "the old serpent, he that is called the Devil and Satan" (Rev. 12:9). What is "the spirit that now worketh in the sons of disobedience"? Perhaps a lion's share of effort should be expended on this point. Sectarians have been heard to say "We want to obey the authority of Jesus." They then do things regarding which they cannot show one word in the last will and testament of Jesus which will support their actions. The spirit, the attitude, which allows people to disobey Jesus while claiming to be obeying him is ubiquitous, it is everywhere. King Saul claimed, "I have performed the commandment of Jehovah" (1 Sam. 15:13). When Samuel questioned him he again retorted, "Yes, I have obeyed the voice of Jehovah," verse 20. Saul's concept of obedience is the same "spirit" that now worketh in the religious world in general, as "the spirit that now worketh in the sons of disobedience." In Matthew 28:20 Jesus commanded the apostles, and by contextual extension he commanded us, "teaching them to observe all things whatsoever I commanded you." Notice the spirit of observance, of submission, of humble obedience that is to be taught before any of the New Testament deeds can be taught and observed. Jesus did not say, "Teach them all things to observe." That was to be done for sure. We need to know what God has authorized; but the attitude, the spirit of humble submission is to be taught first. Commensurate with this point is that Jesus said, "what I commanded." Jesus has all authority in heaven and on earth (Matt. 28:18). Jesus did not say "Teach them to reject those things which I forbid." Many take this attitude, if the Scripture does not specifically forbid it I can do it. The spirit of disobedience is alive and well in the religious world around us. It is at work in the original manufacture of all denominations and in the proliferation of them. It is at work in those who attempt to shove a man-made mechanical musical instrument up in the face of Jesus when He said "sing" (Eph. 5:19; Col. 3:16; Heb. 13:15). Even in connection with the Lord's body this spirit of disobedience is seen in man-made organizations that are replacing the church in accomplishing pure and undefiled religion. The spirit of disobedience is seen in those who desire lax standards of morality to allow adultery to go unchecked; and to allow the use of beverage alcohol; and a host of other evil matters. We should, like the psalmist in Psalm 101:3, comport ourselves to "set no evil thing" before ourselves in any arena. By these few words we should learn to have a spirit of loving, humble, from the heart, submissive obedience to the last will and testament of Jesus Christ, and that obedience must be without addition, subtraction or substitution!

Ephesians 2:3 "...among whom we also all once lived in the lusts of our flesh, doing the desires of the flesh and of the mind, and were by nature children of wrath, even as the rest." In the movie, "Hot Millions," a question is asked about a computer manual, "Where is it supposed to live?" Can an inanimate object be said to live? An amazing hymn asks the pointed question "Where Livest Thou?" Some have suggested that one can NOT live in sin, but can ONLY commit sin. Beside the fact that the word "live" can have several usages, this verse makes it clear that these folks (and by common sense extension, modern people also) were then, and some are now, living in sin. The word "flesh" is significant. Those who hold the doctrine of "Original Sin," have in some instances made a false doctrinal commentary translating this Greek word "sarx" as "sinful nature." It is morally evil to mistranslate God's word. Study Hebrews 2:17 and you are struck with the fact that Jesus was made "IN ALL POINTS LIKE AS WE ARE" (emphasis mine, FGF). If we have a sinful nature, so did Jesus. If we are born with the guilt of Adam's sin, so was Jesus. If that is not blasphemy, I don't have a clue what would ever be blasphemy. The problem with humanity is each one has the choice to do "the desires of the flesh and of the mind." In John 7:17 Jesus made it clear that what an individual wills himself to do, then that is what he does; and if, that is IF, he wills to do God's will, he will know how to do so. The final expression in this verse has caused some people great difficulty: "...and were by nature children of wrath, even as the rest." How is it that one may be included in the "by nature" scenario? Among the problems faced, is the situation of Jesus. Was He "by nature" a child of wrath? Obviously not! The expression, "by nature" actually signifies the life of an individual who through constant choice and practice has come to have "evil" as his "second nature." That is, his constant practice of evil activities has brought about a nature devoted to evil, "even as the rest." This is necessarily true of any and every person who behaves badly throughout life.

Ephesians 2:4 "but God, being rich in mercy, for his great love wherewith he loved us." The contrast between the God, the one and only true and living God set forth in the Holy Bible and in it alone, the contrast between this God and all other so called gods is staggering. "God is love" (1 John 4:7-8). This word, "love," is never said of any creation of man which he calls god! God is perfect in all his attributes. God cannot lie (Tit. 1:2; Heb. 6:18). God's loving nature and His love are extolled throughout the Scripture (John 3:16, etc.). In His rich mercy, God makes it possible for an individual dead in sin to receive NOT the eternal punishment so richly deserved. However, God's love and mercy will not pardon anyone who rejects the terms and conditions God set for pardon. While God loves all His creation, Scripture makes it clear that only sentient humans are the object of saving love, mercy and grace. Salvation is never offered to angels that sin (Heb. 2:16; 1 Pet. 1:9-12). Salvation is never offered to animals. Salvation is never offered to children who are unable to make choices on the basis of good or evil. No plan of salvation is offered for children because they are not lost but are safe, as was Jesus (Heb. 2:17). The ending clause of the great old communion song "That Dreadful Night," is a sublime challenge to every Child of God, "Help each redeemed on to repeat, 'For me, He died for me!'"

Ephesians 2:5 "even when we were dead through our trespasses, made us alive together with Christ." As noted in verse one, dead in sin and trespasses is a figure of speech indicating a separation, a separation in this case from the Creator, from God. The expression, "even when" focuses the responsibility for this separation clearly and exclusively on the one who has sinned. Passages too numerous to catalogue emphasize the alienation which results from man's choice to sin against his God. Romans 5:6-8 clearly states this principle of alienation; and God's gracious love in effecting that reconciliation. A reconciliation which we do not deserve because we were self-made enemies of God: "(by grace have ye been saved)." The absolute majestic glory of God's grace cannot be, when done scripturally, overemphasized. Yet man has seen fit to distort this amazing characteristic of God into a grotesque caricature, changing God into a great cosmic Santa Claus, into a namby-pamby, spoiling, grandfatherly type who is unconcerned if his people do right or wrong and will somehow forgive every one unconditionally. Mere mortal men have been heard to say, "I am saved by grace alone, grace without definition." Astounding blasphemy. God Himself has defined His grace in Titus 2:11-12 as that which instructs us or teaches us the following: negatively, to deny "ungodliness and worldly lust;" and positively, to live "soberly, righteously and godly in this present world." The word "ungodly" is equal to impiety, and carries the significance of practicing religious activity not authorized in the New Testament. All unauthorized religious activity is ungodliness. That individual who is actually IN the grace of God will never consider using, much less actually use, or be involved in, any unauthorized religious activity. The phrase "worldly lusts" is the Divine definition of a life lived outside Divine authority. It is no coincidence that in the parallel letter to the Colossians, Inspiration states "...and whatsoever ye do, in word or in deed, do all in the name of the Lord Jesus..." (Col. 3:17) It is likewise significant that Inspiration caused Peter to write, "...I have written unto you briefly, exhorting, and testifying that this is the true grace of God: stand ye fast therein" (1 Pet. 5:12). If there is "true grace," then there is also "false grace." An interesting principle is that everything or concept of actual, real, value is always counterfeited. Man's doctrine of "grace" which does not include knowledge of God's word and strict compliance with God's last will and testament (in worship, in work, in daily living) is counterfeit grace and ends at the bottom of the broad way (Matt. 7:12-13), where everyone will face the judgment of Jesus Christ (2 Cor. 5:10), and those following the counterfeit grace will hear the eternally painful word, "Depart" (Matt. 25:41). The New Testament is the only expression of the saving grace of God on earth today. The apostle Paul said to the elders of this congregation in Ephesus, "And now I commend you to God, and to the word of his grace, which is able to build you up, and to give you the inheritance among all them that are sanctified" (Acts 20:32). Do not be deceived about the grace of God.

Ephesians 2:6 "and raised us up with him, and made us to sit with him in the heavenly places, in Christ Jesus." Inspiration reiterates the salvation process. When one is raised from the watery grave of scriptural New Testament baptism, that one is raised "to walk in newness of life" (Rom. 6:5). The abode of this "raised individual" then is a sphere, a realm, which Inspiration designates as "heavenly places." This is a spiritual realm though it is inhabited by those living in this physical world. In this spiritual realm we are at war with the "spiritual hosts of wickedness in the heavenly places" (Eph. 6:12b). This location is "in Christ." Those in this spiritual location are members of the body of Christ (1 Cor. 12:13; Col 1:18; Eph. 1:22-23; 5:23). Inspiration also defines this spiritual location as: "the kingdom of Christ and God" (Eph. 5:5); God's "kingdom and glory" (1 Thess. 2:12); the bride of Christ (Eph 5:22-23); "the house of God" (1 Tim. 3:14-15); "the church" (Eph. 1:22-23; Col. 1:18); and this church is God's "eternal purpose" (Eph. 3:10-11). No greater honor can be bestowed on a mere mortal human than being raised with Christ.

Ephesians 2:7 "that in the ages to come he might show the exceeding riches of his grace in kindness toward us in Christ Jesus." Divine riches are mentioned in this letter to the Ephesians in 1:7 and 18; 2:7; 3:8, and 16. These riches are important to God. The viewpoint of the world understands "riches" as being exclusively physical. Some people in this world have great physical riches and yet are impoverished in soul. This is not new. In Amos 8:6 we learn that some in Israel would "buy the poor for silver and the needy for a pair of shoes." All physical wealth is destined to be lost. It might be lost through financial reversals. It might be lost through government meltdown. It might be lost through death. It might be lost by the end of the world (2 Pet. 3:10-12). Jesus' words in Matthew 6:19-21 should be the watchword of every sentient creature on earth. Jesus asked a pertinent question, "If therefore ye have not been faithful in unrighteous mammon, who will commit to your trust the true riches?" (Lk. 16:11). True riches, what are these? True riches are anything and everything honorable, honestly, strictly and scripturally connected with God. All else is dross. These riches will actually be the benefit of eternity in Heaven following that great Judgment Day, that is, in the ages to come (Matt. 25:23).

Ephesians 2:8 "for by grace have ye been saved through faith; and that not of yourselves, it is the gift of God." Often, it is an unusual thing, as set forth in the book "Muscle and Shovel," often one must labor strenuously to see, understand, yea, perceive the OBVIOUS. Some teach a doctrine of salvation by "faith only." Scriptures is plain, that salvation is by faith. The eternal difference between "salvation by faith," taught throughout the Bible, and "salvation by faith alone" which is not found anywhere in the Bible is staggering! Yet, most religionists in the world today who claim some affinity with the Bible cannot see the difference. You are challenged, dear reader, to find one example of any individual who came to a correct, that is a saved, relationship with God who did so without obeying God's commands. What, then is the "gift of God" in this verse? It is the full combination of God's will (the New Testament) and man's loving, humble, submissive, from the heart obedience, to become saved, the entire package (Rom. 6:16-18). What about the expression "not of yourselves"? As obvious as it is to one who loves Scripture that this simply sets forth that no man ever has nor can he invent his own way of salvation, the explanation of revelation and inspiration in 2 Peter 1:21 is the perfect explanation, "For no prophecy ever came by the will of man: but men spake from God, being moved by the Holy Spirit." God's part is grace. Man's part is faith defined by Jesus in John 3:36 as obedience.

Ephesians 2:9 "not of works that no man should glory." Here Inspiration begins a contrast between Jewish compliance with the Old Testament law and observance of the New Testament law. "Not of works." What works? Leviticus 18:5 answers, "The sacrifices of the law." Likewise, Romans 10:5 states, "For Moses writeth that the man that doeth the righteousness which is of the law shall live thereby." That was the situation of the Jew under the Old Testament. Inspiration set forth that the apostle Paul had reason to glory as one who kept the law with a clear conscience (2 Cor. 11:21-22; Acts 23:1). Now Inspiration states pointedly, "...because by the works of the law shall no flesh be justified (Rom. 3:20). While many worldly minded religious people attempt to exalt Old Testament Israel over the New Testament "house of God, which is the church of the living God" (1 Tim. 3:15), Romans 2:28-29 make it abundantly clear that physical Judaism has no value in the New Testament dispensation. In fact, Ezra 6:62 and Nehemiah 7: 5 and 64 make it clear that without a indisputable official genealogy, no one can claim Jewish status. All genealogical records of Israel were destroyed by the Romans in 70 A. D. No man in the Christian dispensation can glory in his genealogy nor in the works of the Old Testament since Jesus' last will and testament was probated by Jesus Himself (Heb. 9:15-17; 10:9-10) and then its terms and conditions began to be preached on the first Pentecost after the resurrection of Jesus as recorded in Acts 2; which conditions are in force until the end of the world (Matt. 28:20).

Ephesians 2:10 "For we are his workmanship, created in Christ Jesus for good works, which God afore prepared that we should walk in them." As amazing as it is, many religious people cannot understand that many different KINDS of works are found in the Bible, especially in the New Testament. When one looks through the pages of the New Testament he finds: "works of the law" (Rom. 3:20); "works of the flesh" (Gal. 5:19-21); "works of human invention and merit" (Titus 3:5); extremely religious people of whom Jesus said, "ye that work iniquity" (Matt. 7:22-23); religious works "to be seen of men" (Matt. 23:5); evil works of darkness (John 3:19); and while this list could be extended, this is sufficient to clarity that there are some works which not only will NOT save, but these works will condemn. On the other hand Inspiration is pointedly clear that some KINDS of works not only are included in the salvation process, but it is on the basis of these works that each individual will face the judgment of Jesus Christ. Consider: "good works which glorify the Father" (Matt. 5:16); righteousness work (Acts 10:35), which, interestingly enough, according to Romans 1:16-17, is obeying the gospel of Christ; "the work of the Lord" (1 Cor. 15:58); "godly sorrow worketh repentance unto salvation" (2 Cor. 7:10); obedient work for salvation (Phil. 2:12); "work of faith," that is, work which is itself faith (1 Thess. 1:3); and again, the works required by God before God's grace is applied are many and varied but each one falls under the category of "obeying the gospel (2 Thess. 1:6-9). In every judgment scene one can find in the Holy Scriptures, each individual is judged on the basis of the individual's work. Consider this carefully. Why will God judge on the basis of an individual's works? The simple truth is, regardless of what the individual claims, or professes, he does what he actually and truly believes. Therefore judgment (Rom. 2:6) is on the basis of an individual's "works," compared or contrasted with the words of Jesus (John 12:48). Regarding these works God has prepared, Inspiration insists that we should walk in them. Should is an interesting word. We find in Philippians 2:10 "that at the name of Jesus every knee should bow." This is what should be, but each individual has a choice in this life to either obey or disobey Jesus' word. Those who choose foolishly in this life by not obeying the gospel will find that they shall bow in the judgment, but then it will be too late (Rom. 14:11-12).

## Ephesians 2:11-22: God's Eternal Purpose Seen in the Glorious Peace in the Eternal Temple

This second section of chapter two is amazing. Jesus is "the prince of peace" (Isa. 9:6-7). In this "holy mountain" which is "the house of God" (Isa. 2:1ff) men beat their swords into plowshares and their spears into pruning-hooks. Materialists of different sorts insist that this must be world peace enforced by Jesus with a rod of iron in his earthly, materially focused kingdom. Ephesians two shows that such a concept is a Devil's lie.

Ephesians 2:11 "Wherefore remember, that once ye, the Gentiles in the flesh, who are called Uncircumcision by that which is called Circumcision, in the flesh, made by hands." The word "wherefore" connects the following, verses 11 through 22, with the previous ten verses. As part of God's eternal purpose, He provided Jews with the written Law, and left Gentiles without a written law to prove that no man could save himself apart from the blood of Jesus Christ. A time existed when God recognized two categories of people: Jews and Gentiles. At that time God had made a covenant with physical national Israel and with them alone (Ex. 34:27-28; Deut. 5:1ff). While based on the Ten Commandments, it actually included the entire Old Testament. To these "Gentiles" (a designation still possible because Jerusalem and the genealogical records had not yet been destroyed when the Letter to the Ephesians was penned) Inspiration commands, "Remember." Remember THAT time. Remember THAT circumstance. Remember the Gentile situation while the Old Testament was in force. Remember!

Ephesians 2:12 "that ye were at that time separate from Christ, alienated from the commonwealth of Israel, and strangers from the covenants of the promise, having no hope and without God in the world." By even a cursory examination of the Old Testament one finds proof that Gentiles were still a matter of concern to God. Consider the Old Testament minor prophets of Jonah and Nahum as clear examples of this truth. The Gentile problem was that they had no written covenant as did Israel. No written covenant existed, regarding which, a Gentile could go to it and show by comparison that his life was righteous. Yet the system designated "The Patriarchal Dispensation" was in force from Adam to the Cross of Jesus Christ. In Romans 2:14-15, Inspiration clarifies how Gentiles "without the law," by their basic moral living, showing these moral principles in their daily living, ultimately were justified by the blood of Christ. Nonetheless, between the Jew and the Gentile, during the time of the Old Testament, God placed a barrier designed to keep the genealogy pure from Abraham, through Judah and David, to Jesus, the Messiah. While this barrier, "the law of commandments contained in ordinances," was in force, Gentiles were without God in the world. What reason might anyone have for going to a system that excluded them, left them separate from Christ, without God in the world and according to Galatians 5:4, actually to be severed from Christ and fallen away from grace? Why do it? Yet today some do it in an attempt to justify the use of man-made musical instruments, for lighting candles, for burning incense, for vestments (special clothes) worn to elevate a false priesthood composed of mere mortal men above others of like passions. Why? Indeed!

Ephesians 2:13 "But now in Christ Jesus ye that once were far off are made nigh in the blood of Christ." A certain "rock" group recorded a song many years ago entitled "That Was then, This Is Now." A gospel preacher, with substantially more experience than I, taught a group of young preachers, "Remember this concept: 'T' 'C'"! Then he explained, "Things change." "At that time," as it was when the Old Testament was in force, that was then. "But now" in the "fullness of the times" (Gal. 4:4), the time of the New Testament, God's last will and testament, "NOW," those described prophetically by the apostle Peter in Acts 2:39 as those who are "far off," "NOW," for us it is different. We who were estranged are made nigh in the blood of Christ. Amazing!

Ephesians 2:14-15 "For he is our peace, who made both one, and brake down the middle wall of partition, having abolished in his flesh the enmity, even the law of commandments contained in ordinances; that he might create in himself of the two one new man, so making peace." God's eternal purpose is realized in this ending, this fulfillment, this conclusion of the Old Testament. The Jewish world of Paul's day had difficulty with this concept. Israel and Judah had gone into captivity because they forsook the Old Testament to worship idols. They had been disciplined by God to have a respect for God's word. Were they now to give up everything they had held so dear for generations? God dealt with this difficulty through the Letter to the Hebrews. The Old Testament inheritance had been the "Promised Land." Now, the inheritance is changed to one that is "incorruptible, and undefiled, and that fadeth not away, reserved in heaven" (1 Pet. 1:3). This is the "one hope" (Eph. 4:4). This is the one and only inheritance (Matt. 25:34). Regarding any single inheritance there can be one and only one legal instrument to transfer the inheritance from the testator to the heir. Hebrews 9:15-17 makes it clear that the New Testament has the death of the Testator, Jesus Christ, to empower and enforce this will. Hebrews 10:9-10 states unequivocally that the first "will" had to be taken away so that the second "will" could be established. With this clarified, it should be easy to understand that every "testament" which came before the New Testament came too early; and every claimed or supposed "testament" which came after the New Testament came too late. Should we, then, leave the only "WILL" which can procure for us the eternal inheritance and go to a "will" which never applied to us, and which could not provide the ultimate inheritance even for those who were under it? In Acts 15:10, Peter clearly states that it, the Old Testament, was a burden "which neither our fathers nor we were able to bear." Some of the Jewish Christians of the first century might have gone back to it, but no one today can go back to it for we were never under it.

Ephesians 2:16 "and might reconcile them both in one body unto God through the cross, having slain the enmity thereby." Perhaps no word in the English language is as beautiful as that contained in the concept of reconciliation. Jesus said, "...go thy way, first be reconciled to thy brother,..." (Matt. 5:24). Great pain has been inflicted on the souls of humans because of ruptured relationships. Some relationships are ruptured by anger; others by depraved actions; others by religious error; and who knows all the other causes which might apply? Jesus also made it clear that the dividing line of the truth may not be compromised; and will make enemies of even the closest family members, Matthew 10:34-39. When one is apostate from the truth, from the beautiful bride, body, church, kingdom of the Christ, how can reconciliation be effected? If it is not in the apostate repenting and returning to the "one body," it can not happen. Any apparent reconciliation is counterfeit and vain; even as Jesus described those who worship according to man's doctrines (Matt. 15:8-9). Oh! But to be reconciled to Christ and to others of "like precious faith" (2 Pet. 1:1) in the "one body" is eternal joy. Eternal enmity, that is hatred, exist between the truth and error. Such has always been true! "Know ye not that friendship with the world is enmity with God?" (Jas. 4:4). The business of being reconciled to God was effected through the apostolic ambassador office as set forth in 2 Corinthians 5:20-21. As Jesus promised those who were his chosen apostles, John 14:24-25; 16:12-13, that they would be guided by the Holy Spirit into all truth, so today we have this "word of reconciliation" in the New Testament of our Lord and Savior Jesus Christ and in it alone.

Ephesians 2:17 "and he came and preached peace to you who were far off, and peace to them that were nigh." As the angels heralded the song at Jesus' birth, "Peace on earth," and He, Himself fulfilled those Old Testament prophesies, so now through, and only through, the terms and conditions of the New Testament, we can now have "the peace of God, that passeth all understanding" (Phil. 4:4). Therefore, now, as the fulfillment of God's promise to Abraham in Genesis 12:1-4, in Christ, "all families of the earth" may be blessed.

Ephesians 2:18 "for through him we both have our access in one Spirit unto the Father." Access to God the Father is an amazing and encouraging thought. Jesus said, "I am the way, and the truth, and the life: no one cometh unto the Father, but by me" (John 14:6). Man, even "religious" man, claims that many ways are available for access to the Father. Jesus taught that two and only two ways are available in this life: the broad way leading to destruction wherein the vast majority of humanity voyages through this life; and the straitened way which leads to life, entered at the narrow gate, regarding which gate only a few will even find it (Matt, 7:13-14). Jesus also made it clear that when we pray to the Father it must be done by the authority of Jesus Himself, "in my name," (John 16:23-24). Jesus has left us a new and living way, purchased and dedicated by the blood of Jesus (Heb. 10:19-22), and we now may boldly approach the throne of grace. Initial obedience to the gospel described as "having our hearts sprinkled from an evil conscience: and having our body washed with pure water" (Heb. 10:22); or as Peter so pointedly wrote in 1 Peter 3:21, "...doth now save you, even baptism, not the putting away of the filth of the flesh, but the interrogation of a good conscience toward God,..." must be the correct narrow gate for each individual to enter as it is the "new birth" (John 3:3-5; 1 Pet. 1:22-25). Is this one of the good works God has prepared for the saved? No! A thousand times, No! In scriptural New Testament baptism God alone is operating and the individual is totally passive. "...having been buried with him in baptism, wherein ye were also raised with him through faith in the working of God, who raised him from the dead" (Col. 2:12). Only by entering at this gate "into Christ" (Gal. 3:27) does one become saved and then and only then are the "good works" of the life of a Christian available, and those works ARE mandatory for one to remain saved. Inspiration states, "To him therefore that knoweth to do good, and doeth it not, to him it is sin" (Jas 4:17).

Ephesians 2:19 "So then ye are no more strangers and sojourners, but ye are fellow-citizens with the saints, and of the household of God." To the Jewish mind, every Jew was a brother and every one else was a stranger. In the stage musical which was made into a movie, "Fiddler On The Roof," the "Sabbath prayer" included the words "keep us from the stranger's ways." While the Old Testament was in power for Israel (again it is emphasized that it was for Israel only), all Gentiles were "strangers." Thank God for the New

Testament by which any and every human on the face of the earth can be changed from a "stranger" into a "fellow-citizen with the saints." Thank God that His eternal purpose, the church of Christ, is open to all. As the words of one of our hymns states, "even the vilest may now enter in." Thank God! The household of God, His family, is now open, and no greater privilege or honor could be bestowed on a man than this. No wonder with excitement and amazing wonder the beloved John wrote, "Behold what manner of love the Father hath bestowed upon us, that we should be called children of God; and such we are" (1 John 3:1)!!!

Ephesians 2:20 "being built upon the foundation of the apostles and prophets, Christ Jesus himself being the chief corner stone." In Matthew 16:18 Jesus said "I will build my church." Did Jesus have a plan? Most folks in the religious world, falsely called Christendom, never consider such a question. What difference does it make? Many a man thinks he has a better idea than Jesus had. The apostles and New Testament prophets were not the foundation but were instrumental in laying the foundation. What foundation did the apostles and prophets lay? In 1 Corinthians 3:11, Inspiration states flatly and without equivocation that the one foundation is the Christ. From Acts two when the twelve apostles "spake in other tongues as the Spirit gave them utterance," throughout Acts and in every place where they went, these men preached Jesus Christ and him crucified. The great commission (Matt. 28:18-20; Mk 16:15-16; Lk. 24:47) and the apostolic application of Jesus' command was the same in every place (1 Cor. 4:17). Not only must we today have the correct foundation, but the building itself must be according to the pattern set forth in the New Testament. Some attempt to muddy the water by asking "Which congregation" should we emulate? The problems at Corinth are usually used to deride God's beautiful pattern. Those problems were not allowed to stand, but Inspiration corrected them, demanded, and still demands compliance with the divine pattern. The Divine pattern includes: the terms of entrance into the household of God; avenues or acts of worship authorized by Jesus; and correct living as fellow-citizens with the saints, summed up in Colossians 3:17, "And whatsoever ye do, in word or in deed, do all in the name of the Lord Jesus, giving thanks to God the Father through him."

Ephesians 2:21 "in whom each several building, fitly framed together, growth into a holy temple in the Lord." No amount of earthly wisdom can match the spectacular beauty and glory of this temple. Each local autonomous congregation, under the oversight of a properly ordained and qualified plurality of men designated elders/pastors/bishop, fitly framed together in preparation for that final call to the eternal kingdom where the eternal inheritance will be had by every faithful member of the body: this is this holy temple in the Lord. The spiritual location of this temple on earth is "in the Lord." The growing aspect of this kingdom is seen in Isaiah's prophecy (9:6-7) where, regarding the Prince of Peace, Inspiration states, "of the increase of his government and of peace there shall be no end." By revelation and inspiration the apostle Peter concludes his second epistle in 3:18 with the command, "But grow in the grace and knowledge of the Lord and Savior Jesus Christ." Growth is one of many hallmarks of the churches of Christ.

Ephesians 2:22 "in whom ye also are builded together for a habitation of God in the Spirit." A temple is, by definition, a place where religion is practiced and the adherents of the religion access their god or gods. It is a dwelling place of deity. Every organization which has a temple or shrine is, that is, it IS a religion; and if it is not the body of Christ it is a false religion. Followers, members, of these false religions can not have heaven as their home after this life. While some "fraternal" organizations make public claims that they are not religions, the fact that they have temples proves that they are religions. With whom would I rather dwell? In the body of Christ, the holy temple of God in the Spirit? Or would I rather attempt to sucker God with a man-made counterfeit temple?

God's eternal purpose has been seen in grace, mercy and love in Ephesians 2:1-10; and in the glorious peace in the eternal temple in 2:11-22. The churches of Christ (Rom. 16:16) is everything God ever planned for mankind on this earth in preparation for eternity in Heaven. Learn this message of truth. Believe it. Obey the gospel to enter it. Live faithfully in it so that Heaven will be your home following the great judgment. In this spiritual location be the habitation of God in the Spirit.

CHAPTER 3

# Ephesians

*by*

*Aren Haggard*

## Ephesians 3: Introduction

Reading through Chapter 3 of Paul's letter to the Ephesians without understanding certain elements of the text is likely to leave you scratching your head. Not because Paul fails to be clear about his role in the mystery of Christ, or in his desire that the Ephesian church would comprehend the love of our Lord and Savior, rather because in the middle of a prayer, Paul interjects a parenthetical statement, a spontaneous explanation of the mystery of Christ and the grace that was bestowed upon him to preach it, which spans some twelve verses from verse 2 through verse 13. With that information your journey through this text should be considerably easier.

## Ephesians 3:1-12: The Church a Mystery Hidden From Past Ages

Ephesians 3:1 "For this reason I, Paul, a prisoner for Christ Jesus on behalf of you Gentiles." Here Paul begins what would be his second prayer for the church as Ephesus recorded in this letter, the first of course being found in Chapter 1.

Paul had a wonderful habit of praying for all the churches out of his deep concern for their faithfulness and wellbeing (Eph. 1:16, Col. 1:9, 2 Co. 11:28). When he could have retreated inward to focus on his own, often-perilous circumstances, Paul was diligent to look outward and upward and encourages his fellow Christians to do the same.

Twice in addressing the Ephesians, Paul refers to himself as a prisoner of Jesus (3:1, 4:1). He also acknowledges his imprisonment in Chapter 6 referring to his role as "an ambassador in chains"(6:20). This accurately describes both his physical condition as a prisoner in Roman custody as well as his spiritual stance in Christ on behalf of the gospel and the Gentiles.

In Acts Chapter 22 while Paul is preaching before an angry Jewish mob in the temple, it was his statement regarding his departure to the Gentiles to begin ministering to them that would be the catalyst for his imprisonment and subsequent journey through the Roman legal system.

Ephesians 3:2 "assuming that you have heard of the stewardship of God's grace that was given to me for you." It is at this point, in true Pauline fashion, that our text takes a slight, but related, detour in order to explain in greater detail the mystery delivered to the hands of the apostles and prophets such as Paul.

Our author has made this grace a central figure in the last two chapters, and describes it as a means by which we obtain acceptance and redemption (1:6,7), not through our own works but through the precious gift of Christ (2:5-8). It is revealed to us that the grace of God is not only shown in the forgiveness of sins, but more specifically in the inclusion of the Gentiles in God's scheme of redemption (2:11-18), saving both Jew and Gentile in the one body of Christ, which is the true mystery of the Gospel.

Paul refers to his responsibility in the Gospel as a stewardship, something valuable that had been entrusted to his care. Paul recognized that one day God would judge him on how well he managed the gospel that was given to him (1 Co. 4:1-4). Therefore he made it his aim to present every man perfect in Christ through his stewardship (Col. 1:24-29).

In similar fashion every Christian is a steward of what God has given to us individually (1 Pet. 4:10), and we too will be judged on our service in the kingdom and our proper use of what we have been given to manage both in talents and resources (Mt. 25:14-30).

Ephesians 3:3 "how the mystery was made known to me by revelation, as I have written briefly." Paul has already made mention in Chapter 1 of this revelation of the mystery (1:9). His point here is not only that the mystery had been disclosed, but also that the vehicle of disclosure was special revelation directly from God. As Paul said in his letter to the Galatians: "11 For I would have you know, brothers, that the gospel that was preached by me is not man's gospel.[a] 12 For I did not receive it from any man, nor was I taught it, but I received it through a revelation of Jesus Christ" (Gal. 1:11, 12).

For Paul, the Gospel he received was not gossip but the inspired and revealed mystery of God. He wants to make it clear that God has directly given into his care something uniquely special and that they should listen to him as someone with firsthand knowledge.

Ephesians 3:4 "When you read this, you can perceive my insight into the mystery of Christ." Not only is Paul saying that the unique and direct revelation of the mystery will be obvious, he says very plainly that if you read this, that is the information in this letter, you can know what I know! God had given Paul a mystery not to hold onto, but to reveal.

What an amazing concept to ponder. The Bible is 66 books of insider information given by God to choice individuals to record on our behalf. If we want to gain insight into the most amazing truths our God does not force us to scour hieroglyphics in an ancient Egyptian tomb or obtain enlightenment through some ascetic process He simply says, "read this."

Ephesians 3:5 "which was not made known to the sons of men in other generations as it has now been revealed to his holy apostles and prophets by the Spirit." While we can be certain that there are countless prophecies about the Messiah, redemption and fulfillment of promises throughout the Old Testament, one thing well hidden in regards to the Gospel, was the mystery that not only would the Gentiles be saved, they would become one spiritual body with Israel (2:16, 4:4).

With great clarity, the Holy Spirit under this new dispensation has brought into focus that which was previously unseen. With mention of the Holy Spirit, the apostle not only reiterates the special revelation of the Gospel, but also gives clear credit to who revealed it. Paul places great emphasis on the work of the Holy Spirit in man's redemption throughout Ephesians. In this letter Paul reveals that the Holy Spirit is the one who:

- Seals us for the return of Christ (1:13, 4:30)
- Gives us access to the Father (2:18)
- Strengthens us (3:16)
- Should fill every Christian (5:18)

Ephesians 3:6 "This mystery is that the Gentiles are fellow heirs, members of the same body, and partakers of the promise in Christ Jesus through the gospel." This mystery is that the Gentiles are fellow heirs, members of the same body, and partakers of the promise in Christ Jesus through the gospel.

For centuries God worked especially through the Jewish people. Paul explains this well in his description in his letter to the Romans: "4 They are Israelites, and to them belong the adoption, the glory, the covenants, the giving of the law, the worship, and the promises. 5 To them belong the patriarchs, and from their race, according to the flesh, is the Christ, who is God over all, blessed forever. Amen" (Ro. 9:4-5).

It has been revealed however that it was not God's goal to continually work primarily through the Jewish people, or uniquely save them apart from the rest of humanity. Through Christ on the cross peace was made and the wall of separation between Jew and Gentiles was removed (2:14-16).

Now in Christ, through the mystery of the cross, there is one inheritance (1:11-18), one body (2:16.4:4) and one promise for all whether Jew or Gentile (4:4).

Ephesians 3:7 "Of this gospel I was made a minister according to the gift of God's grace, which was given me by the working of his power." Paul acknowledges with great humility that the gospel was not only a gift to humanity but a gift of amazing grace towards him. Not only was he saved by it, but he was called to be an apostle of it, him of all people! Oh how deep and wide the grace and wisdom of God must be! Notice Paul's own words on this matter in Galatians 1:13-17: "13 For you have heard of my former life in Judaism, how I persecuted the church of God violently and tried to destroy it. 14 And I was advancing in Judaism beyond many of my own age among my people, so extremely zealous was I for the traditions of my fathers. 15 But when he who had set me apart before I was born, and who called me by his grace, 16 was pleased to reveal his Son to me, in order that I might preach him among the Gentiles, I did not immediately consult with anyone; 17 nor did I go up to Jerusalem to those who were apostles before me, but I went away into Arabia, and returned again to Damascus."

Daily Paul basked in the reality of God's grace, whether in prison or free, shipwrecked or preaching in the marketplace, because Paul knew how many Christians suffered at his hands, and what a phenomenal thing God was doing by allowing him to proclaim the Gospel. Paul saw himself as a living example of just how gracious God can be: "12 I thank him who has given me strength, Christ Jesus our Lord, because he judged me faithful, appointing me to his service, 13 though formerly I was a blasphemer, persecutor, and insolent opponent. But I received mercy because I had acted ignorantly in unbelief, 14 and the grace of our Lord overflowed for me with the faith and love that are in Christ Jesus. 15 The saying is trustworthy and deserving of full acceptance, that Christ Jesus came into the world to save sinners, of whom I am the foremost. 16 But I received mercy for this reason, that in me, as the foremost, Jesus Christ might display his perfect patience as an example to those who were to believe in him for eternal life" (1 Tim. 1:12-16).

Ephesians 3:8 "To me, though I am the very least of all the saints, this grace was given, to preach to the Gentiles the unsearchable riches of Christ." As was recently mentioned in 1 Timothy, Paul openly deemed himself the chief sinner, and here the "very least of all the saints". Paul is not merely being self-deprecating here, or looking for any sympathy, he is displaying on paper what he was confronted with every time he preached and wrote the words of God.

We would all do well to have a similar attitude of humility. We must all be careful not to think more highly than we ought to think about ourselves (Ro. 12:3), remember that we too were dead in our trespasses and sins (2:1) and always consider ourselves lest we also be tempted (Gal. 6:1).

To the lowly servant Paul was granted the privilege to preach to the Gentiles "the unsearchable riches of Christ". What an awe-striking image! Imagine a treasure hunter like Indiana Jones peering into the cavernous depths of a never ending cave after a long expedition seeing nothing but piles of gold and jewels and relics as far as the eye could see.

Spiritually this was how the apostle Paul portrayed Christ to the Gentiles. A treasure trove of mercy, grace, righteousness and truth all for the taking! Often in his parables Jesus referred to the kingdom of God in similar fashion, as a treasure hidden in a field and a pearl of great value (Mt. 12:44-46)

Ephesians 3:9 "and to bring to light for everyone what is the plan of the mystery hidden for ages in God who created all things." It was Paul's mission and purpose to reveal the mystery of God's eternal plan to unite both Jew and Gentile in Christ. The God who "created all things" also created this fantastic plan of salvation and kept this secret of all secrets until after the death of his only begotten Son.

Proverbs 25:2 says: "It is the glory of God to conceal things." Why did God conceal such wonderful news? Some have said that He kept this plan to save all of humanity through Christ a secret in order to spoil the plans of Satan (who knew scripture well as we see in Luke 4), something he certainly accomplished through Jesus' death at Calvary (1 Jn. 3:8).

Ephesians 3:10 "so that through the church the manifold wisdom of God might now be made known to the rulers and authorities in the heavenly places." While all that we might want to know on this subject simply cannot be known on this side of eternity, what this passage seems to indicate is that what God is doing through salvation on the earth is revealing something to the heavenly realm. 1 Peter 1:12 tell us that even angels desire to look into the working of Gospel.

So what are they learning about God's infinite wisdom through the church and the Gospel? It's possible that the heavenly beings looked on at the big issues such as Satan and evil, and after the creation of the world and all that is in it, us human beings and our massive sin problem and wondered what God would do.

God in His manifold wisdom manages to save humanity and destroy the works of Satan, namely sin and death, in one fell swoop through Christ on the cross. Now that message of Good News is lived out and shared through the church. We as the church are the living, breathing, sealed and redeemed proof of the Gospel.

Ephesians 3:11 "This was according to the eternal purpose that he has realized in Christ Jesus our Lord." The plan to send Jesus was not written in the mind of God whenever Satan rebelled, or in the Garden of Eden when Adam and Eve sinned. God knew He would redeem humanity to Himself through Christ "before the foundations of the world" (1:4). This idea in many ways is beyond our limited human comprehension. We would do well to remember the words of God in Isaiah: "8 For my thoughts are not your thoughts, neither are your ways my ways, declares the Lord. 9 For as the heavens are higher than the earth, so are my ways higher than your ways and my thoughts than your thoughts" (Is. 55:8-9).

This truth is easily recognizable in considering the mystery of the Gospel and God's "eternal purpose that He has realized in Christ Jesus our Lord."

Ephesians 3:12 "in whom we have boldness and access with confidence through our faith in him." We have great boldness and confidence through our faith in Christ that should permeate our walk with Him. We should be bold in our proclamation of the Gospel (1 Thess. 2:2), in prayer (Heb. 4:16) and as we consider the day of Judgment (1 Jn. 4:17) all because of our place in Christ. If we continue to be faithful to our Lord we can even have boldness and confidence in the face of death trusting that we will receive the crown of life (Rev. 2:10).

As the Ephesians contemplated the sufferings of Paul and their own potential tribulations they would need unshakable boldness and confidence that they have access to the Father through Christ, that very present help in time of trouble (Ps. 46:1).

## Ephesians 3:13-21: The Prayer for Inner Fullness and Knowledge

Ephesians 3:13 "So I ask you not to lose heart over what I am suffering for you, which is your glory." As Paul told the church at Thessalonica, "that no one be moved by these afflictions. For you yourselves know that we are destined for this." (1 Thess. 3:3). The last thing he wanted was for his sufferings as an apostle of Christ to cause them to lose their faith and walk away, especially because he was suffering for them, for their glory.

For their glory has in mind for the furtherance of the Gospel revealed both to Jew and Gentile, for the teaching they received from the apostle Paul and the encouragement they received through his faithfulness even in the most difficult of circumstances.

Ephesians 3:14 "For this reason I bow my knees before the Father." Now we continue where Paul began in verse 1, his prayer for these Gentiles. He bowed his knees in humble and earnest prayer for his brethren. While there is no official prayer stance throughout scripture, the posture of Paul's heart is worthy of emulating. We see in him a great reverence for God and deep concern for his fellow saints.

Ephesians 3:15 "from whom every family in heaven and on earth is named." While the ESV renders here "every family", an equally good and likely clearer translation is used in the NKJV, "the whole family". We are not only one family in Christ on this earth, but one with all the faithful in heaven as well.

As far as our naming is concerned this refers to us being named as children in the family of God. When we are identified, it is because of our mutual association as sons and daughters to our Father."

Ephesians 3:16 "that according to the riches of his glory he may grant you to be strengthened with power through his Spirit in your inner being." Paul's prayer is that God through his infinite wealth would strengthen the Ephesians through the power of the Holy Spirit. Much time in discussion is taken up in volumes elsewhere on the subject of "how" the Holy Spirit does such a thing. Our concern here is not with the "how" of God, but rather in trusting that He will and does.

His prayer of spiritual strength for the church is connected to his desire for them to have a deeper comprehension of the love of Christ as we will see in proceeding verses.

Ephesians 3:17-19 "so that Christ may dwell in your hearts through faith—that you, being rooted and grounded in love, may have strength to comprehend with all the saints what is the breadth and length and height and depth, and to know the love of Christ that surpasses knowledge, that you may be filled with all the fullness of God." The indwelling of Christ through the Holy Spirit is essential to the Christian. If Christ does not dwell in our hearts through faith, according to Romans 8:9 we do "not belong to Him."

It seems according to verses 17-19 of this chapter, that part of Christ dwelling in us and us being "filled with all the fullness of God" has to do with our comprehension of the love of Christ. That is, the more of His love we comprehend, the more of Him can live in us. The more of Christ that lives in us, the more faithful endurance we possess. As Paul says in Philippians 4:13, "I can do all things through Christ who strengthens me."

While we can never fully realize the love of Christ for us, we must make it our daily aim to comprehend more and more as we continue our transformation to become more like Him.

Ephesians 3:20 "Now to him who is able to do far more abundantly than all that we ask or think, according to the power at work within us." Paul illuminates two powerful truths here. One is our inability in prayer to convey exactly the right petition. After all Joshua asked for the sun to stand still, not the earth, and yet God understood what he meant and gave him what he needed. We seldom have just the right words to say, but we trust in our God who is perfect in all His ways to do the right thing.

The other is that no matter our thoughts and prayers, that God's ability is far above what we would ever even think to ask Him. So whatever it is you are asking God for, know that He can do far beyond that.

Paul expresses to God that he trusts Him to give the church at Ephesus exactly what they need.

Ephesians 3:21 "to him be glory in the church and in Christ Jesus throughout all generations, forever and ever. Amen." It all comes back to God. We must seek to be for His glorification in all that we do. If we will make this our aim we will find heaven as our home and draw others to God along the way with the mystery of God's grace and love through His Son Jesus Christ.

## Chapter 4

# Ephesians

*by*

*Jonathan Maner*

ଓଃ୬

## Ephesians 4:1-3: The Walk to be Worthy the Position

Ephesians 4:1 "I, therefore, the prisoner of the Lord, beseech you to walk worthy of the calling with which you were called." Therefore – Paul makes an allusion back to the previous chapter's discussion. Previously, he had discussed the mystery and glory of Christ, how the Gentiles were now "fellow heirs" (3:6), and the working of God's love in the life of the Christian. Finally, at the end of the chapter, in verses 20-21 Paul cannot help but praise God for His glory and magnificence. It is based upon this fact that Paul makes the statement he is about to proclaim in the remainder of the verse.

"...the prisoner of the Lord" – Paul writes while shackled in Rome (Acts 28:30-31). This is the second time Paul refers to himself as a prisoner in the book of Ephesians, the other being in 3:1. In the prison epistles total, Paul refers to himself as a prisoner some ten times. Since Paul was currently in dire circumstances, mention of such a fact would lend weight to the rest of the verse. Could we give the same exhortation sitting in a prison cell today?

"...beseech you to walk worthy of the calling with which you were called" – The Greek word utilized by Paul for "beseech" is the word "parakaleo" and carries with it several sub-definitions in Thayer's Greek Lexicon. I will highlight just a few I feel will aid our understanding of the passage: "to admonish, exhort; to beg, entreat, beseech; to strive to appease by entreaty; to console, to encourage and strengthen by consolation, to comfort." (Thayer, E-Sword) Paul strongly desired that the Christians in Ephesus walk (live their lives) in such a way that they were worthy of the name of Christ. The word "worthy" is the Greek word "axios" from which we derive our English word "axis" from ("the line about which a rotating body, such as the earth, turns"). In essence, might Paul be suggesting a form of balance in our lives as Christians? In order for things to be balanced, our order and knowledge need to be matched. The "called" in this verse is a reference to Christians. Paul alludes to this idea more fully in Rom. 8:28 when he says "...to those who are called according to His purpose". How are Christians "called"? Christians are called by obedience to the will of God through the Gospel (2 Thess. 2:14).

Ephesians 4:2 "with all lowliness and gentleness, with longsuffering, bearing with one another in love." "With all lowliness and gentleness..." – Paul begins a vivid description of what a walk worthy of the calling of Christ is in verse two. Lowliness has to do with modesty in regards to self-opinion. Humility is really what is at the forefront of the entire definition, it seems. There is no room for arrogance in Christianity; it is a plague and hindrance to the furtherance of the Gospel and the cause of Christ. This idea is consistent with other accounts of Biblical teaching (Prov. 16:18-19; Matt. 18:4; Phil. 2:3-8). "Gentleness" means mildness and meekness. In fact, the KJV rendering of the word is "meekness". The root word is the same for this usage and the one by our Lord in Matt. 5:5. Considering that "lowliness" and "gentleness" are connected by a conjunction in this verse, it is proper to study them together to grasp the full picture of Paul's writing in this verse. The conjunction "and" is an indication that the two words go together and are connected as far as ideology is concerned. That is, to say, you cannot have lowliness without gentleness and you cannot possess gentleness without lowliness.

"...with longsuffering" – What a lesson that needs to be learned today! With the "hustle and bustle" of everyday life and technology that allows us to more and more impatient every year, the need grows more and more for us as human beings to implement this principle of Christianity. "Longsuffering" is another word for "patience". Endurance and perseverance is required when it comes to the walk of a Christian. If you recall, "longsuffering" is one part of the fruit of the Spirit (Gal. 5:22). Suppose that God was never longsuffering toward us; could we possibly be breathing the air we are today and living in such comfort? I would venture to say that we would not. However, God is longsuffering, therefore, we are to be longsuffering! (Psa. 86:15)

"...bearing with one another in love" – As Christians, we need to lift one another up. Sometimes, one may have the challenging position of being a "pillar" to another individual who may be facing spiritual difficulties in their life (Gal. 6:1-2), but if we forcibly stay strong with abounding love in our hearts for one another, we will maintain the perfect bond of unity those of like precious faith share in Christ (Eph. 1:3).

Ephesians 4:3 "endeavoring to keep the unity of the Spirit in the bond of peace." Paul writes of labor and toil in regards to preserving this tie between brethren. The unity that Christians share is "of the Spirit" or from the Holy Spirit. Therefore, it is a Divine Institution made possible only by the working of God. What a wonderful truth for the Christian to be able to say "I can take part in something that was implemented by God Almighty"! I found it interesting when researching the word "bond" to find that it can even have reference to "ligaments by which the members of the human body are united together" (Thayer). This unity of the Spirit comes full circle with peace. Without peace, these "ligaments" become ruptured and torn, therefore, the body (Eph. 1:22-23) is not able to function properly. I don't think it would be out of character to say that peace is the glue that holds us members together. All of this, of course, having its roots and foundation in Christ and His Word.

## Ephesians 4:4-6: The Seven Unities to be Kept

Ephesians 4:4 "And now, we come to what would probably be described as the most important section of Scripture in all of the book of Ephesians. One of the most striking things about these next few verses is Paul's effort to maintain a simple thought process. Why would Paul do this? Because what we have in verses four through six are called the "Seven Non-negotiables." Basically, there are seven things Christians absolutely cannot disagree on: one body, one spirit, one hope, one Lord, one faith, one baptism, one God and Father of all. It is these seven things that are paramount to the life of a Christian and soundness of faith. No variation is available; we must agree on these matters to hold up unity the way God intended.

"There is one body and one Spirit" – the "body" is a reference to the church, which is the collection of those who have obeyed the Gospel (Col. 1:24; Acts 2:47). It is of utmost importance we understand that there is only one of these bodies. It would be completely illogical for there to be one head, Christ (Col. 1:18) and be several bodies. To assert there are multiple bodies of true believers is to assert that God tolerates disunity among His people. We know, unequivocally, that God does not advocate such. There is only one church; the church established on Pentecost in Acts chapter two with Christ as its head. It is said there are some 41,000 denominations in existence today. This is a far cry from God's intended plan! "one Spirit" is a reference to the Holy Spirit. The late Avon Malone said in his commentary "There is one

Spirit – one animating person or principle activating the body. The Spirit guided the apostles into 'all truth' (John 16:13). Therefore we have in 'the apostles' teaching' (Acts 2:42) 'all things that pertain to life and godliness' (2 Pet. 1:3)" (Malone 57). Following the one Spirit involves following explicitly the teachings in which He guided the writers of the Bible to pen (2 Tim. 3:16-17; 2 Pet. 1:20-21). Following the Bible is following God; plain and simple.

"...just as you were called in one hope of your calling" – The "call", as we have already discussed is through the Gospel. With that call and adherence to its commands, comes the greatest retirement package in the entire universe: heaven. All Christians' ultimate hope should be to spend eternity with God. Abiding by the "ones" reaps great benefits (Rev. 2:10b; Gal. 6:7). The Hebrew writer describes this hope as an anchor of the soul (Heb. 6:19). I am reminded of the encouraging and powerful words of Priscilla J. Owens in her song "We Have An Anchor":

> We have an anchor that keeps the soul
> Steadfast and sure while the billows roll,
> Fastened to the rock which cannot move,
> Grounded firm and deep in the Savior's love.

Ephesians 4:5 "one Lord, one faith, one baptism." "One Lord..." – The only true ruler and master of our lives is none other than Jesus Christ. Jesus Christ told us very explicitly in Matt 6:24 that no one can serve two masters. Therefore, our gaze should be completely fixated on Jesus Christ, the Author and Finisher of our faith (Heb. 12:2). Nobody is more deserving of our loyalty and adoration as He.

"...one faith" – As far as our relationship with the Creator is concerned, there is only one way to please Him: His way. Faith, as defined in Heb. 11:1, carries substance and evidence with it. It is not some blind leap in the dark as skeptics would say and it is not some warm, fuzzy feeling in the pit of one's stomach. It is fact handed down to us by God. Guy Orbison, Jr. says in relation to this section, "the term faith, here refers to the standard we follow. The One New Man follows the same standard of teachings. There are not many faiths and we may not choose the faith of our choice. Faith is a system of beliefs handed down to us from God (Jude 3)" (Orbison, Jr. 37).

"...one baptism" – The Greek word in use by Paul in this particular verse is "baptisma" and its definition as defined by Thayer is "immersion, submersion". The word it is derived from is "baptizo". Strong defines "baptizo" as "to make whelmed (that is, fully wet)". The evidence is mounting for the case that baptism is not sprinkling our pouring as some in the denominational world practice today, but is a complete deluge of the body in water. This ONE baptism is for the remission of sins (Acts 2:38) and is vital for soul salvation (Mk. 16:16). Through baptism, we are reconciled to God (2 Cor. 5:18). Let us not pervert the simple truth the Bible teaches on this matter.

Ephesians 4:6 "one God and Father of all, who is above all, and through all, and in you all." "one God and Father of all" – Every person, no matter what position, gender, color, etc. they are, can all trace their ultimate origin back to God. God is the Creator of the entire universe. In reference to Christians, He assumes the title of Father and we are His children (1 Jn. 3:1). It is only Christians who can truly call God their "Father" (Jn. 1:12). This is the very last of the "ones" being discussed by Paul, and it is a fitting end to this section. We must never forget that God is a "jealous God" (Ex. 20:5) in the sense that He wants exclusivity when it comes to our worship and spiritual service.

"...who is over all" – a specific passage comes to mind when I think of this section: Dan. 4:25. Our one God extends His authoritative reach into the kingdoms of this world. He is in control of His creation. Not in the sense that He supernaturally imposes His will upon mankind (which I believe He does not – Mk. 16:20; 1 Cor. 13:8-10) but that He exhibits power over the earth through His providence (cf. Est. 4:14).

"...and through all" – God allows His children to do His will in this life, therefore, in a sense, He is working through them. God never trumps our free will to choose whether or not we would carry out His precepts, but through every Christians personal choice to serve Him and apply His law, there comes the reality of God working through His creation to accomplish His will.

"...and in you all" – As Christians, we possess many of the attributes that God possesses (ones that we are able to possess, of course e.g. love, patience, joy, kindness, etc.) in this way, God is in us. Orbison, Jr states it in this way, "...the same genetic code found in the Father now exists in us. Therefore, we should look like our Father...we are begotten of Him. Therefore, we think like Him and have the same objectives that He has" (Orbison, Jr 38).

## Ephesians 4:7-11: The Ministry Gifts of Christ to His Body

Ephesians 4:7 "But to each one of us grace was given according to the measure of Christ's gift." Paul highlights that each and every person that is a

Christian receives this grace. The words are encouraging because it displays the mindset that God does not simply look upon His body of believers as a collective, but notices every single person that is part of His fold and realizes their value. Grace is simply receiving something we do not deserve. "According to the measure of Christ's gift" means that we were granted this grace based upon His will and desire, in a perfect fashion (in accordance with Christ).

Ephesians 4:8 "Therefore He says: "When He ascended on high, He led captivity captive, And gave gifts to men."" Paul begins by making a reference to Psa. 68:18. The first part of the verse speaking of Jesus Christ and His ascension into heaven (Acts 1:9). To use Avon Malone's thoughts on this verse, when Jesus Christ ascended into heaven, He defeated evil (captivity; Rom. 7:23). In the most basic sense, Jesus captured captivity (Gen. 3:15) and His ascension was the "final nail in the coffin", so to speak. It was at this time that Jesus Christ gave gifts to men. We are not to assume that this is a reference to supernatural gifts, but simply to certain abilities in which can be used in order to build up the body, edify and serve the Lord. This is certainly a lesson that must be taught and preached today: we must make use of the talents that God has given us for His glory. To waste our talents is like a teacher who teaches secular schooling Monday through Friday and yet, refuses to offer their services to teach Bible class on Sunday!

Ephesians 4:9 "Now this, "He ascended"—what does it mean but that He also first descended into the lower parts of the earth?" Before Jesus ascended, He had to first descend onto the earth. Oh, how truly special this notion really is! Paul goes into great detail about the gravity of this in Philippians 2:5-11. In utter humility, Jesus left a more glorious form in heaven in order to become a man (a lesser form) so that He could be our perfect example and sacrifice (Heb. 4:15; Titus 2:14)! Paul writes that it is naturally implied that if Jesus ascended, he must have descended."

Ephesians 4:10 "He who descended is also the One who ascended far above all the heavens, that He might fill all things." Paul continues to expand on the Jesus' ascension by discussing to what extent Jesus ascended. In short, Paul writes that it was magnificent and glorious with the phrase "far above all the heavens" – a reference to Jesus' exaltation. This is consistent with Phil. 2:9 where Paul writes that "...God has highly exalted Him and given Him the name which is above every name". Other passages, also, speak to this very same idea (Acts 2:33; 5:31). His ascension (along with every other aspect of His life) was to fulfill the will of the His Father (Matt.

3:15; Lk. 2:49). Further, Jesus said Himself that He came to fulfill the law (Matt. 5:17).

Ephesians 4:11 "And He Himself gave some to be apostles, some prophets, some evangelists, and some pastors and teachers." "And He Himself gave some to be apostles…" – Further extending His discussion on the "gifts" from verse eight, He now describes some of the gifts that were extended to people of the church, during that time. The first of these is "apostles" – Paul describes what is His current position (Eph. 1:1) and the position of the other eleven appointed by Jesus Christ (Matt. 10:1-4).

"…some prophets" – The Greek word used here prophets, as defined by Thayer, is "one who, moved by the Spirit of God and hence his organ or spokesman, solemnly declares to men what he has received by inspiration, especially concerning future events, and in particular such as relate to the cause and kingdom of God and to human salvation". It would seem, then, that this would have been a spokesperson for God. During that time, it would have been in a supernatural sense, considering that the church was still quite young. However, the need for prophets like those of old today has vanished, considering that we have the full revelation of God available to us in our hands: The Bible (1 Cor. 13:8-10; 2 Pet. 1:3).

"…some evangelists" – An evangelist is simply what we would consider, in our modern times, to be a preacher. Timothy filled this role (2 Tim. 4:5). The Greek word suggests a bringer of good tidings. No doubt, those who preach the Gospel are ones who bring good tidings (Rom. 10:15).

"…and some pastors" – The Greek word used here for "pastor" (poimen) is the same word used during Peter's exhortation to fellow elders in 1 Pet 5:2 when Peter tells them to "feed" the flock. This has the notion of shepherding, which is what pastors are to do! The same term is used in Acts 20:28 when Paul is meeting with the Ephesian elders in Miletus. Therefore, one must conclude that a pastor is the same as an elder, bishop, or presbyter. The title "pastor" does not belong to regular preachers of the pulpit. Unless, of course, the local preacher fits the qualifications for an elder (1 Tim. 3; Titus 1) and accepts the position to be an elder.

"…and teachers" – It seems there is always a need in the church for sound teachers. Particularly, growing up in a small congregation, I know the need all too well. I submit to you that the impact these teachers have/will have on youth and adults alike is far reaching and invaluable to the work of the Lord. Paul recalls Timothy's "genuine faith" in 2 Tim. 1:5 and attributes it to two superb female teachers: his grandmother Lois and his mother Eunice. A good teacher is not one to be taken for granted!

## Ephesians 4:12-16: The Purpose of the Ministry Gifts

Ephesians 4:12 "for the equipping of the saints for the work of ministry, for the edifying of the body of Christ." Finally, Paul wraps up the discussion on gifts by telling what the purpose of these gifts are. They are not for personal gain or to advance one's clout in the community, they are to bring glory to God! In order to finish a task that has been appointed to a person, they are in need of tools and resources to get them through said task successfully. As such, these are for our equipping, to add to the Christian arsenal. These tools need not be flaunted in an unworthy manner or used for something superficial, but are for the "work of the ministry". In turn, Paul expounds a little bit more and says they also edify (build up, promote) His Kingdom (1 Cor. 14:26).

Ephesians 4:13 "till we all come to the unity of the faith and of the knowledge of the Son of God, to a perfect man, to the measure of the stature of the fullness of Christ." Reflecting back on a discussion I had with my mentor, Guy Orbison, Jr. I'd like to mirror his thoughts in regards to this passage. The word "till" in this passage is not a reference to time as we would think, but the idea Paul achieves here is "for the purpose of". The gifts were given to attain the unity of the faith (Jude 3) and that coincides with spiritual maturity. The knowledge of the Son of God has to do with our cognizance and familiarity with Jesus Christ. All of this, helps us grow into a "perfect man"; not in the sense that we are sinless, but that we are spiritually mature and abiding in a faithful walk with Christ.

Ephesians 4:14 "that we should no longer be children, tossed to and fro and carried about with every wind of doctrine, by the trickery of men, in the cunning craftiness of deceitful plotting." Paul wanted the Ephesians to be everything that God wanted them to be. Paul's desire was for them to be the opposite of those in Athens who "...spent their time in nothing else but either to tell or hear some new thing" (Acts 17:21). It makes us think about those of whom the Hebrew writer mentioned who needed "milk and not solid food" (Heb. 5:12-13). The Ephesians needed to have their feet firmly planted in the Gospel of Christ so they could withstand trickery and the cunning craftiness of deceitful plotting that men so often do. The same rings true for Christians today; with the existence of so much error and falsehood, the time has never been as prevalent as now to pick up our Bibles and start studying.

Ephesians 4:15 "but, speaking the truth in love, may grow up in all things into Him who is the head—Christ." "but" is the word of contrast Paul uses in conjunction with verse fourteen to show what is the opposite of the gullible and easily twisted Christian. It starts with one who speaks the truth. Jesus Christ said the truth is what "make[s] us free" (Jn. 8:32) and that God's word is truth (Jn. 17:17). Therefore, if we hope to set others free from certain spiritual death (Rom. 6:23), then we must speak God's word! God's word is found in nothing else but the Bible (2 Tim. 3:16-17). However, Paul writes it is not enough for Christians to simply speak the truth, but the method about which we speak that truth is in love. Love ought to be the motivation for everything we do in this life, for God is love (1 Jn. 4:8). It is through this love that we are able to grow up in our faith and fulfill our necessary functions in the body with Christ at the head of it all."

Ephesians 4:16 "from whom the whole body, joined and knit together by what every joint supplies, according to the effective working by which every part does its share, causes growth of the body for the edifying of itself in love." Paul makes masterful use of imagery in this verse as he weaves a picture of the church (body) and its members composing it (joints, etc.). Every single part of a human beings body has some form of function. If it did not, than God would not have put it there! So, it is up to the Christian to make use of the talents in which God has given them in order to fulfill their much needed function within the body. A body cannot function at full capacity unless its members are working appropriately. When things are functioning as they are supposed to, then the body grows! However minute we think some tasks may be, it does not change the fact that God finds them important, or else why would Paul use language as "effective working"? Let us all find our place and get to work, for the fields are "white already to harvest" (Jn. 4:35).

## Ephesians 4:17-29: The Walk of the Believer as a New Man in Christ Jesus

Ephesians 4:17 "This I say, therefore, and testify in the Lord, that you should no longer walk as the rest of the Gentiles walk, in the futility of their mind." Paul was calling for a separation from the heathen ways and thought process that many of the Gentiles possessed. It is presumptuous to assume from this verse that Paul was prejudice toward the Gentiles, as he preached to them on many occasions and even scorned Peter for having prejudice toward Gentile brethren (Gal. 2:11-13). The idea Paul is setting forth is not walking in a worldly manner, but in a godly manner. The general categorization of this Gentile behavior was in the futility of their mind. The KJV rendering of "futility" is "vanity". The Greek word means "what is devoid of truth and appropriateness; perverseness, depravity; frailty, want of vigor."

Ephesians 4:18 "having their understanding darkened, being alienated from the life of God, because of the ignorance that is in them, because of the blindness of their heart." Darkness is the natural opposite of light, which is what a Christian is called to walk in (1 Jn. 1:7); to invite darkness into our understanding is to invite evil, confusion and wrongdoing in. This darkness takes full form in that it alienates (separates) us from God (Isa. 59:1-2). Paul, in a very vivid way, is describing the futile mind of the previous verse and gives two reasons for the alienation: 1.) ignorance; 2.) a blind heart. Ignorance is the plight of the futile mind and, contrary to popular belief, what you don't know CAN hurt you (2 Thess. 1:8). The slippery slope continues with the blind heart. The "issues of life" spring from the heart (Prov. 4:23), so when one does not guard it, it loses its spiritual "vision."

Ephesians 4:19 "who, being past feeling, have given themselves over to lewdness, to work all uncleanness with greediness." "who, being past feeling…"What an infinitely sad statement to be made in regards to a group of people. The level of immorality had reached such a point in the lives of these people that they had stopped feeling remorse for the things in which they had done. It is as if the people were devoid of consciousness, at this point (1 Tim. 4:2).

"…have given themselves over to lewdness" - Letting themselves go, they turned to the logical end for such a state of corruption: lewdness. This word means "unbridled lust, excess, licentiousness, lasciviousness, wantonness, outrageousness, shamelessness, insolence".

"…to work all uncleanness with greediness" – Paul concludes his description of the Gentiles by describing the state of their impurity. This impurity goes right along with greediness. Almost to suggest that the Gentiles are not satisfied with level of immorality they have slipped in but are thirsty for more. May we never be described in such a way.

Ephesians 4:20 "But you have not so learned Christ" I prefer the ESV rendering "But that is not the way you learned Christ" to the NKJV because I feel it is simpler to understand and still captures the spirit of what Paul is writing. After treading on the dark territory of the previous three verses, a ray of light shines forth when Paul says that the Christians at Ephesus have not walked in that way. Despite the enticing nature of the Gentile lifestyle, they dared to walk in a different direction (2 Cor. 6:17)."

Ephesians 4:21 "if indeed you have heard Him and have been taught by Him, as the truth is in Jesus." Orbison, Jr. states that the verse "is a first class conditional sentence in Greek, affirming the reality of the condition. 'If,' then carries the idea of 'since' this is true." (Orbison, Jr. 44). From this verse, we can know that the Ephesians had developed faith, since it comes from hearing (Rom. 10:17) and they had been taught in the correct manner; this is truthfully. Could Paul write the same thing of us today?

Ephesians 4:22 "that you put off, concerning your former conduct, the old man which grows corrupt according to the deceitful lusts" From this verse until the end of the chapter, Paul launches into what is deemed by Bill Burk as the "clean up/fill up" section of Ephesians chapter four. It is very similar to Col. 3:5-12 – the twin epistle to Ephesians. Christianity is not just about cleaning up your life and not doing the former sinful actions you were guilty of, but also about filling up your life with spiritual wealth, as well. Paul paints an image of casting off (putting away) an old man. This old man has gone the way of the sinner. He has given into the lusts of the world, whether it is of the flesh, eyes or pride of life (1 Jn. 2:16). The lust is deceiving, meaning that it is never really what it seems to be. Twisted and wretched by the world, the old man's dire need is to be cast off, knowing that continuing to go in this way only leads to more and more spiritual agony.

Ephesians 2:23 "and be renewed in the spirit of your mind." The Biblical heart is usually a reference to the mind. As we have already mentioned before, the issues of life spring from the heart and, if we hope to be renewed, it starts with change of mind and thought process. Essentially, this is the idea of repentance, to change our mind towards a change of action. The renewal only comes when we have cast off the old man (Acts 3:19). Adam Clarke puts it nicely when he says, "The mind is to be renovated; and not only its general complexion, but the very spirit of it; all its faculties and powers must be thoroughly, completely, and universally renewed." (Clarke)

Ephesians 4:24 "and that you put on the new man which was created according to God, in true righteousness and holiness." I like to think of it as the wearing of an old garment. This old garment of sin is dirty, it has holes, and smells. With obedience to the Gospel, the old garment is shed and a brand new garment is purchased is better in every single way. The conditions for attaining the garment is obedience to the Gospel (Acts 8:36-38). The new garment is none other than Christ (Gal. 3:27). This "new man" is not of the devil, but of God Almighty and was sculpted according to the plan that He has laid out for His creation. The new man does not possess feigned righteousness and holiness, such as the Pharisees had (Matt. 23:37), but genuine righteousness and holiness."

Ephesians 4:25 "Therefore, putting away lying, "Let each one of you speak truth with his neighbor," for we are members of one another." The "clean up" process continues with another staple to Christianity, and that is ridding yourself of the lying tongue. Ten verses earlier, Paul already mentioned speaking the truth in love (V. 15) and while this idea is fresh on the mind of the reader, Paul revisits it. The Greek word for "lying" in this verse is pseudos and is defined as "conscious and intentional falsehood; in a broad sense, whatever is not what it seems to be; of perverse, impious, deceitful precepts" (Thayer). Remember, lying is listed amongst the seven things that God hates (Prov. 6:17). Paul bolsters his statement by quoting a portion of Zech. 8:16. The picture of the human body is furthered as Paul describes the saints who make up the church as "members" and how we "of one another" in the sense that we share fellowship with each other (1 Jn. 1:7). Part of this relationship is that we are accountable to one another. If the body is to stay in proper, working order than we must be in sync.

Ephesians 4:26 "Be angry, and do not sin": do not let the sun go down on your wrath." Another aspect of cleaning up our lives and putting off the old man of sin is cutting wrath and rage that leads to sinful behavior. Paul quotes from Psa. 4:4. Anger, in and of itself, is not a sinful emotion to experience. However, anger that leads to sin is absolutely and totally unauthorized. Even Jesus experienced anger in His lifetime (Mk. 11:15-17), but the separating factor is He never let it get out of control and He never sinned (Heb. 4:15). The same rings true for us today.

"...do not let the sun go down on your wrath," – The guiding thought through this section of the verse is the idea of solving problems as quickly as possible. Implementing this principle into my personal life has been one of the most rewarding (albeit exhausting) practices I have ever had to do. I'm sure we can all think of times when we have "let something cool off" only to build up resentment in our hearts or not even solve it at all! This should not be the case. Trust me when I say, solving the problem then and there, however long it takes is worth it in the end and will make you feel scores better.

Ephesians 4:27 "nor give place to the devil." The NASB rendering of the passage might lend a little more understanding to our discussion when it says, "and do not give the devil an opportunity". Since we are putting away our former lives of sin, we do not give the devil a place in which he would have some kind of ground to ensnare us or trap us. Christians stray away from the things that could lead them to participate in acts not in line with God or His will.

Ephesians 4:28 "Let him who stole steal no longer, but rather let him labor, working with his hands what is good, that he may have something to give him who has need." "Let him who stole steal no longer…" – the idea of stealing in the original language means to "commit a theft or take away by theft" (Thayer, E-Sword). Christians should never be in the business of acquiring something that does not belong to them. The idea is to reform your former self in regards to the categories in which you struggle with in your life. The same idea would apply to any sin! The fruit of repentance is to quit partaking in the sin!

"…but rather let him labor, working with his hands what is good" – Paul says to do the opposite of stealing and that is to acquire the things you have by the sweat of your brow – work for it! Barnes says, "Let him seek the means of living in an honest manner, by his own industry, rather than by wronging others." (Barnes, E-Sword).

"…that he may have something to give him who has need" – we labor ourselves so that we can give back. Inevitably, we will run into people who have needs they cannot fulfill themselves. Our laboring with our hands helps them in that manner. The help can be profitable in the sense that it could strengthen our relationship with our Christian brother, or it could even win the non-Christian to Christ! We may never know the value.

Ephesians 2:29 "Let no corrupt word proceed out of your mouth, but what is good for necessary edification, that it may impart grace to the hearers." "Let no corrupt word proceed out of your mouth" – the meaning of "corrupt" in the original language means "of poor quality, bad, unfit for use, worthless" (Thayer, E-Sword). Of course, the implications of this were certainly different in ancient in reference to what was considered corrupt or not corrupt, but the principle stays true today. These are words that profit ones spirituality positively, and do not reflect it negatively. We think about what Paul said to the Colossians (Col. 4:6) and it is the same idea here. Rotten words have no place in Christian life.

"…but what is good for necessary edification" – Paul says, rather than letting corrupt words exit your mouth, words that are a reflection of God should come out of your mouth. The idea is words that promote one's spiritual growth, and does not hinder it. Far be it from us to partake in unfruitful speech. Building others up spiritually is a central goal of Christianity – it must be done!

"….that it may impart grace to the hearers" – this is the result of the edifying speech: grace. Grace is, very simply, receiving a gift we do not deserve. So, when we partake in speech that is godly in nature, than we are figuratively giving another person a gift; we are profiting them!

## Ephesians 4:30-32: The Walk of the Believer as Indwelt by the Spirit

Ephesians 4:30 "And do not grieve the Holy Spirit of God, by whom you were sealed for the day of redemption." "And do not grieve the Holy Spirit of God…" – How does one grieve the Holy Spirit of God? We grieve the Holy Spirit when we do not cast off our former life and put on the new man that is created according to God! (4:24) to counteract this grieving, we must instead display the fruit of the Spirit in our lives!

"…by whom you were sealed for the day of redemption" – Alluding back to chapter one and verse thirteen, we are sealed with the Holy Spirit when we obey the Gospel. This "sealing" refers to a signet or impression made by the seal that shows ownership by a king. When Jesus returns (the day of redemption) it will have importance during that time (Burk, BTSOP Notes, 7)

Ephesians 4:31 "Let all bitterness, wrath, anger, clamor, and evil speaking be put away from you, with all malice." Bitterness – this word means has to do with extreme wickedness or "bitter" hatred (Thayer, E-Sword; Vine's, 68)

Wrath – This word denotes "anger forthwith boiling up and soon subsiding again" (Thayer, E-Sword); Strong's Bible Dictionary says it can mean passion (as if breathing hard); so, basically what we have is a boiling anger towards another person

Anger – the idea is desiring for the ruin of another person; this is a reference to a violent anger, and not the normal and expected emotion every single person experiences in their life. The Psalmist says "be angry and do not sin…" (Psa. 4:4) and so did Paul earlier in this chapter.

Clamor – The idea seems to be arguing with another in a wrongful manner. To mimic Gary Hampton's thoughts, "If you have ever seen two, or more, people in a shouting match, you have seem clamor." (Hampton, E-Sword)

Evil Speaking – the phrase "evil speaking" could also be translated as "slander" (NASB). It is the Greek word "blasphemia" to which we get our word "blasphemy". It is speaking about another person in such a way that it tears down their character or good name. The purpose is malicious, of course.

"...to be put away from you with all malice" – This continues with the "clean up" aspect of our lives we've been discussing these past few passages. The NKJV rendering of the passage is confusing because it makes it seem as if Paul is telling the church at Ephesus to put away all of this things with malice, but malice is spoken of negatively in Titus 3:3. I prefer the ESV and NASB because it is more clear and accurate: "Let all bitterness and wrath and anger and clamor and slander be put away from you, along with all malice." (NASB). Malice has to do with ill-will and the desire to injure another (Thayer, E-Sword)

Ephesians 4:32 "And be kind to one another, tenderhearted, forgiving one another, even as God in Christ forgave you." "And be kind to one another..." – Kind carries the idea of being mild and pleasant (as opposed to harsh, hard, sharp or bitter) (Thayer, E-Sword). Certainly, our kindness is a reflection of how much we love each other. When we are kind to one another, we all accomplish more. If we are to be unified in this great body of Christ, we must STRIVE to live that way. One of the key ingredients to that formula is kindness.

Tenderhearted – We must have compassion for one another, as well! The hard hearted person doesn't seek to live in such a way that they will be in harmony with their brethren, but at odds. The tenderhearted person strongly seeks the best spiritually for the other person.

"...forgiving one another, even as God in Christ forgave you" – If we do not grant one another pardon after an individual has asked for forgiveness, we are at odds with this passage. So often we claim to forgive another person but never act as if they were deserving of that forgiveness. Such an attitude is not Christ-like! As such, the reason why we forgive is because we were first forgiven by God! Let us examine ourselves in this manner and ask, "Am I forgiving in the same way Christ would?" and if the answer is "no", it's time for us to change.

**CHAPTER 5**

# Ephesians

*by*

*Mark Teske*

ℭℨ

## Ephesians: Introduction

The great book of Ephesians reveals God's plan for His church in the eternal purpose. The fifth chapter of this excellent epistle continues the thoughts concerning the, which has been the subject under discussion ever since Ephesians 4:1. In the first three conduct of the church chapters, R.C. Bell notes that the subject under discussion is the calling of the church. He later notes that the final 15 verses of the book discuss the conflict of the church, where he lays forth the "whole armor of God."

Chapter 5 fits squarely in the middle of the discussion of the conduct of the church. Throughout this section of Scripture, Paul is inspired to use the concept of walking to describe the Christian life. "Walk the walk and don't just talk the talk" is not an inspired phrase, but it succinctly grasps the thought that Paul is trying to convey here. He encourages us to walk worthily (4:1), to walk in love (5:2), to walk as children of light (5:8), and to walk circumspectly (5:15) all the while avoiding the vain walk of the Gentiles (4:17).

## Ephesians 5:1-17: The Walk of the Believer as God's Dear Child

Ephesians 5:1 "Be ye therefore imitators of God, as beloved children" "Therefore" refers back to chapter 4, where Paul has just discussed numerous sins that the child of God should put away. He has just commanded them to be kind and tenderhearted toward one another. He completes the thought with the admonition to forgive one another as God in Christ has forgiven us

(Eph 4:32). It's immediately after this admonition of forgiving as God has forgiven that we're commanded here to be imitators of God.

In just a few short words, Paul summarizes much of what the Christian's life should be – an imitation of God. While short and simple, it is profound in its meaning and challenging in its application.

One of the most rewarding (and sobering) parts of parenthood is seeing your child act just like you. While it is pleasing when their imitation is flattering or leads them to great accomplishments, sometimes we can be embarrassed when the behavior is less than what we would like for others to see in us. The reality of the extent of influence you have on this young soul requires some serious self-examination as to how you live your life. Any faults or shortcomings in the way we live could last much longer than we are on this earth.

However, when we are imitating God, our role model is perfect in every way and is truly worthy of our imitation. How do we know how to imitate God? Jesus is the exact image of the invisible God (Colossians 1:15) and whoever has seen Him has seen the Father (John 14:9).

Ephesians 5:2 "and walk in love, even as Christ also loved you, and gave himself up for us, an offering and a sacrifice to God for an odor of a sweet smell." The word "walk" is used often in Scripture as a euphemism for the way that we live our lives. In the previous chapter, we were already encouraged to walk worthy of the calling with which we were called (Eph 4:1) and to avoid the vain walk of the Gentiles (Eph 4:17). The references to walking in this section of Scripture continue with this admonition to walk in love.

The word translated "love" twice in this verse, ἀγάπη, comes from the same root word as "beloved" in the previous verse. The continual repetition of this great and challenging word helps us to understand the main point that the inspired author is trying to help us understand. A selfless decision to look out for the best interest of others despite any personal cost to ourselves – that is the emphasis of true agape love.

The expectation isn't just that we'll walk in love, but that we'll walk in love the way that Christ Himself walked. His walk included great personal sacrifice – in His emptying Himself (Phil 2:7), learning obedience through suffering (Heb 5:8), being subjected to an illegal trial by His brethren (Mat 26:59), determined by the legal authority to be innocent (Luke 23:4), but was then scourged (Mat 27:26), abused (Mat 27:27-31) and crucified (Mat 27:32-54). All of this sacrifice was motivated completely and entirely out of love (John 3:16).

As we contemplate our own personal walk of love, any sacrifice that we have to make for others absolutely pales in comparison to the sacrifices of Jesus. Some would dare shy away from obedient service when it results in a mere inconvenience or the remote possibility that some personal sacrifice on their part might be necessary. This should never be the case! We should instead base our decision to serve obediently just as Christ did – without consideration for our own personal cost.

Ephesians 5:3 "But fornication, and all uncleanness, or covetousness, let it not even be named among you, as becometh saints." Beginning in verse 3, the inspired apostle begins to provide us a deeper understanding of just what it means to walk in love. There are certain actions and activities that one must put away when we rise out of the watery grave of baptism (Rom 6:1-4) and the inspired apostle is helping us to understand some of those things.

Fornication (Greek πορνεία) relates to any sexual activity that does not take place in the setting that God had designed – the marriage bed. Sexual activity within marriage was designed by God (Gen 2:24-25) and is honorable (Heb 13:4). However, whenever those activities are taken outside of that relationship, the result is sin. This particular sin, while very personal in its nature, has dire consequences that will permeate a family or even an entire society with its ugliness if it is not held in check.

The word that is translated "uncleanness" in the ASV or "impurity" in the ESV is the Greek word ἀκαθαρσία. This particular word is also used in the Septuagint to describe the state of being ceremonially defiled. In its New Testament usage, it is often paired with covetousness, as Jamieson, Fausset & Brown note: "Uncleanness" and "covetousness" are taken up again from Eph 4:19. The two are so closely allied that the Greek for "covetousness" (pleonexia) is used sometimes in Scripture, and often in the Greek Fathers, for sins of impurity. The common principle is the longing to fill one's desire with material objects of sense, outside of God."[38]

"As becometh saints" is a very meaningful phrase when we understand the true meaning of the word "saints". The original Greek word, ἅγιος, has the same root as the word that we translate as "holy", which means to be set apart for a special purpose. A proper understanding of the word "saints" would be "those who have been made holy". Thus, we should live our lives in such a way as to show evidence that we are indeed set apart from the world for a particular purpose, and thus we are different from the world around us. While we live in the midst of a society that revels in fornication, uncleanness and covetousness, as Christians we rise above such activity and live our lives in imitation of Christ, which separates us from those activities.

Ephesians 5:4 "nor filthiness, nor foolish talking, or jesting, which are not befitting: but rather giving of thanks." The list continues in this verse and contains more things which we are to avoid. Filthiness, αἰσχρότης, includes obscenities, indecent behavior and filthy speech. Foolish talking is closely related, but covers more ground than just the obscene. Jesting refers to coarse jesting, vulgar speech, dirty talk. This is not a prohibition from Christians engaging in humor of any sort, but only the type of humor that deals with inappropriate subjects.

However, we should instead use our voices to give thanks to our God. Regarding this subject, James was inspired to write: "but the tongue can no man tame; it is a restless evil, it is full of deadly poison. Therewith bless we the Lord and Father; and therewith curse we men, who are made after the likeness of God: out of the same mouth cometh forth blessing and cursing. My brethren, these things ought not so to be. Doth the fountain send forth from the same opening sweet water and bitter? Can a fig tree, my brethren, yield olives, or a vine figs? neither can salt water yield sweet" (Jam 3:8–12).

Ephesians 5:5 "For this ye know of a surety, that no fornicator, nor unclean person, nor covetous man, who is an idolater, hath any inheritance in the kingdom of Christ and God." Paul is inspired here to show the conclusion of a life filled with these sins. If we engage in these activities, there is no room for us in the Kingdom. When we fail to imitate Christ in the things that we do, we can lose our inheritance.

Often in Scripture, covetousness is compared to idolatry (e.g. Col 3:5). Covetousness is an inordinate desire for that which belongs to another – a desire for that which has been created rather than for the Creator. This is a form of idolatry, as Scripture warns time and time again (Mat 6:24, I John 2:14).

The continued practice of the sins listed above will prevent souls from making it into heaven. While these sins are tolerated in the sin-sick world in which we live, as Christians we need to be as far away from these sins as we can possibly get. Who in their right mind would casually play around with a deadly poison that is toxic to the body? How much more should we avoid these sins which are toxic to our eternal souls!

Ephesians 5:6 "Let no man deceive you with empty words: for because of these things cometh the wrath of God upon the sons of disobedience." The clear warning is given here for us to beware of false teaching regarding these subjects. It may be hard for us to believe that some would try to "excuse away" such sinful activities through their false religious teaching, but that is often done. This can be seen in the Calvinistic doctrine of "once saved, always saved" that teaches that no matter what sins a person continues to willfully commit, they cannot lose their salvation. This can be seen when some try to justify couples living together to "get to know each other" prior to marriage to ensure that they are compatible and won't divorce later. This can be seen when some try to justify the practice of homosexuality. This can be seen by those who would ignore the clear teaching about marriage, divorce and remarriage (Matthew 19:9). There is no shortage of examples where people attempt to justify sins with their empty words.

The proper response of every Christian to any sin that they commit should be godly sorrow (II Cor 7:9-10). As a result of this godly sorrow, repentance takes place and the Christian puts the sin to death and determines to walk in a new direction (Rom 6:1-4).

Ephesians 5:7 "Be not ye therefore partakers with them." In this passage, having fellowship with those who practice these evil deeds is prohibited. What is being prohibited here is being a "partaker" (συμμέτοχος) or one who shares with them. Paul very clearly helps us to understand in I Cor 5:9-13 that in order to not associate with everyone who commits these types of sins we would need to go out of the world. However, there is a big difference between associating with someone who is caught up in sin and partaking in that sin with them. In his letter to the Romans, Paul makes the point clearly when he states after listing numerous sins, "those who practice such things are deserving of death, not only do the same but also approve of those who practice them" (Rom 1:32).

This significant difference was sadly never understood by the Pharisees (Mat 9:10-13), who accused Jesus of being a sinner Himself because He ate and associated with sinners and tax collectors.

Ephesians 5:8 "for ye were once darkness, but are now light in the Lord: walk as children of light." The illustration of light and darkness is one that is familiar to any Bible student (e.g. Mat 5:14-16; Luke 2:32; Luke 11:33-36; John 1:4-9; Rom 2:19; I Thess 5:5; I John 1:7-10). Darkness is the dwelling place of sin, doubt and error while light is associated with holiness, hope and truth. Darkness is where we used to be, but when we became a Christian we came into the light. The change in our relationship with God occurred when we obeyed the Gospel.

The last section of the verse could be restated like this, "Since you're now a child of God, behave like one!" When we put off sin at our conversion, our life has changed completely. The sins that used to ensnare us are now an abomination to us. We now walk with the knowledge that our sinful activity is what sent Christ to the torture of the cross and we want to remove ourselves as far away from those awful choices as we possibly can.

Ephesians 5:9 "(for the fruit of the light is in all goodness and righteousness and truth)." The fruit of the light described here is similar in thought to the fruit of the Spirit which is described in Gal 5:22-23. Being a child of light requires that we obtain and retain certain qualities in our lives which are manifestations of the changes that have taken place within our heart.

Goodness (ἀγαθωσύνη) is the quality of having uprightness in our heart and our life. It's more than just making a feeble effort to be "good enough". Rather, goodness shows a consistency in our actions – doing the right thing every time and avoiding the wicked thing every time. One who exhibits goodness is one who is constantly seeking to do what is right just because it is honorable and pleasing to God. He finds each and every sin to be repulsive merely for the reason that it is sin.

Righteousness is the quality of always seeking to do that which is right. Truth in this context is grounded in the idea that the determinations that we make as to what is good and what is right isn't based upon our personal opinion, but rather upon the objective standard that God has set for morality.

Ephesians 5:10 "proving what is well-pleasing unto the Lord." The word that is translated "proving" (δοκιμάζω) is a word that means to examine, test and discern. Knowing what is pleasing to the Lord sometimes requires considerable effort on our part. Effort is required in study of His word and the instructions that He has left for us. Effort is required in practical, personal application of those instructions into the situations that we find in our life. Effort is required in actually following through and doing that which we know is right to do. However, when these efforts are consistently applied, Christian maturity is what occurs within our life (Heb 5:14).

Ephesians 5:11 "and have no fellowship with the unfruitful works of darkness, but rather even reprove them." Similar to the thought in verse 7, we should not be in partnership or have fellowship with the sinful acts of darkness. The abhorrence and repulsion that we should feel toward all sin would prevent us from taking up residence in the close proximity of them.

We can see this progression toward sin illustrated in the life of Lot. When he separated from Abraham, he "pitched his tent toward Sodom" (Gen 13:12). By the time of the battle of the kings in the very next chapter, Lot and his family are said to be living in Sodom (Gen 14:12). Finally, when the angels have come to Sodom to destroy it, they find Lot sitting in the gate – which is a place of prominence for the elders of the city (Gen 19:1). In a city that was so overcome with wickedness that the Lord was compelled to destroy it, Lot had become quite comfortable living in such close proximity with wickedness. While he escaped with his daughters, his wife and his sons-in-law were all destroyed on that day.

In addition to avoiding the sins ourselves, we should also warn others of them. The word translated "reprove" (ἐλέγχω) means to keep it from being hidden and secret, expose it, and warn others about it. While pointing out the sins of others is not "politically correct" in today's society, it yet remains a command. We need to be sure to lovingly convince them, using the word of God, that the actions being committed are indeed wrong.

Those who engage in sin do not wish for the light to expose their evil deeds (John 3:19) and often make accusations against those who would dare challenge their sinful choices. Their self-described sins of "being judgmental" or "intolerant" are to their minds much worse than the true sins which sent the Son of God to the cross.

Ephesians 5:12 "for the things which are done by them in secret it is a shame even to speak of." While we are commanded to reprove the sins in verse 11, verse 12 lets us know that it is shameful to speak about these things. Clearly this is not a total prohibition from ever mentioning these sins, as such would be a clear contradiction of the previous verse.

It is shameful to speak of these things in several ways. First, sin is ugly and repulsive and as Christians it would be better if we could go through our lives and never have to speak of these things. We need to make sure that we feel this way about every sin, and not just those select few sins that we find especially distasteful.

Second, sin should never be mentioned casually without thought for its consequences and its cost. We should feel great shame if we ever speak of any sin and we fail to reprove as we mention it. Too many Christians have been an improper example by laughing at the sins of another or even pay money to watch others portray examples of sin as a form of entertainment.

Third, some sins are so repulsive that they should not be considered by anyone. In the Old Testament, we have the example of parents burning their infants to death in a fertility ritual to the idol Molech. They were sacrificing their children in a worthless and selfish attempt to improve their own financial well-being. In discussing this, God tells Jeremiah, "I did not command them, nor did it come into My mind that they should do this abomination, to cause Judah to sin" (Jer 32:35). If such things are so horrible that they never came into God's mind, they should never come into our conversations.

Ephesians 5:13 "But all things when they are reproved are made manifest by the light: for everything that is made manifest is light." As we reprove sinful things for the benefit of ourselves and others, we shine our light upon them. Subject to that light, others can see their nature and benefit by it.

The last part of the verse can be difficult to understand at first. Jameson, Faussett & Brown explain the section very well: "The devil and the wicked will not suffer themselves to be made manifest by the light, but love darkness, though outwardly the light shines round them. Therefore, "light" has no transforming effect on them, so that they do not become light (Jn 3:19, 20). But, says the apostle, you being now light yourselves (Eph 5:8), by bringing to light through reproof those who are in darkness, will convert them to light. Your consistent lives and faithful reproofs will be your "armor of light" (Ro 13:12) in making an inroad on the kingdom of darkness."[39]

Ephesians 5:14 "Wherefore he saith, Awake, thou that sleepest, and arise from the dead, and Christ shall shine upon thee." This verse further explains the difficult passage of verse 13. It shows that it is the person who needs to awake and arise and that Christ is the one who is shining. Verse 14 isn't a direct quotation of any Old Testament verse, but Paul never makes such a claim. Some passages that are similar are found in Isaiah at 29:16, 51:17, 52:1 and 60:1.

Ephesians 5:15 "Look therefore carefully how ye walk, not as unwise, but as wise." Another admonition on the way that we walk – this time we are told to walk carefully. Some versions translate ἀκριβῶς as "circumspectly", looking all around in every direction to ensure that you know where you are and what's going on around you. Other translations of the word include "diligently", "accurately" and "closely."

A wise walk is a walk in which a person is effectively and consistently applying the truths of God's word into their life. Diligence is required to walk in a careful manner, ensuring that God's word is followed as closely as possible. To ignore His commands, which are for our benefit (Deut 10:13), is to choose to walk in darkness when we have the light switch in our own hands.

Ephesians 5:16 "redeeming the time, because the days are evil." Redeeming the time, meaning to make the most of our time. The emphasis here is on the importance of using the time that we have in a proper manner. Nobody has the power to make more than 24 hours in a day, so we need to be careful about how we use those hours that are continually passing away. We need to focus ourselves on spiritual matters, discerning right from wrong, choosing to do what's right and helping others to do the same.

Wickedness surrounds us. The days are evil. Satan knows that the limited time that he has until the Judgment day are all that he has left for eternity and he won't slow down or give up in his efforts. As a result, we need to be continually in the spiritual battle and not stop to rest until our job here on this earth is done.

Ephesians 5:17 "Wherefore be ye not foolish, but understand what the will of the Lord is." "The fear of the Lord is the beginning of wisdom" states Psalm 111:10. The person who shows wisdom is the one who spends their time and effort in the most important pursuit possible – preparing themselves for eternity. Some spend their time doing things that are indeed temporary and will vanish away (James 4:14) when they are burned up (II Pet 3:10).

For us to understand (συνίημι) the will of the Lord, we must not only know it, but know how to practice it. Jesus highlighted this point in Luke 12:47 when He said, "And that servant who knew his master's will but did not get ready or act according to his will, will receive a severe beating." It takes more than mere knowledge, it also requires preparation and action on our part.

## Ephesians 5:18-20: The Inner Life of the Spirit-Filled Believer

Ephesians 5:18 "And be not drunken with wine, wherein is riot, but be filled with the Spirit." The first part of this verse commands us not to be in the process of getting drunk (μεθύσκω) with wine. In the original language, the second person plural, present tense, imperative, and passive voice are used. The progressive passive, which would best translate this sentence into modern English did not even exist until 1825. This resulted in a less-than-precise translation in the classical English translations. The sense of the progressive passive is that it is the process of getting drunk that is being forbidden rather than just the possible outcome of total drunkenness. For more information on this subject, I recommend Louis Rushmore's book Beverage Alcohol.

Ephesians 5:19 "speaking one to another in psalms and hymns and spiritual songs, singing and making melody with your heart to the Lord." This verse is one of the classical passages dealing with singing in the New Testament and closely parallels Col 3:16.

The singing described here can be contrasted with the pagan feasts of the day in which the drunken participants would sing their drinking songs. The Christian song is completely different. There is a communication that occurs among those who are singing – their hearts and minds are engaged in the activity. The passage indicates through the active, plural reflexive that the songs are sung by everyone and they are sung to everyone. There is no way for an individual to obey this command without both singing and being sung to.

The content of the songs are specified. They are spiritual in nature – psalms, hymns and spiritual songs. The instrument to be used is also specified – the heart. Where God has been specific in a command as to what He wants, it necessarily excludes everything else. Just like we have no authority to choose our worship songs from the secular "Top 40" of the day because God has been specific as to what type of songs He requires, we cannot change the instrument from the heart to something that God has not specified.

Ephesians 5:20 "giving thanks always for all things in the name of our Lord Jesus Christ to God, even the Father." The parallel with Colossians 3 continues, as this verse is parallel to Col 3:17. The attitude of thankfulness is something that should always accompany the Christian.

## Ephesians 5:21-33: The Married Life of Spirit-Filled Believers as Illustrating Christ and the Church

Ephesians 5:21 "subjecting yourselves one to another in the fear of Christ." While we are to submit to one another, this passage is not teaching the necessity of a communal lifestyle. Rather, the details of this submission will be laid forth in the coming passages. Paul will discuss submission to one another (5:21), in marriage (5:22-33), children and parents (6:1-4) and slaves and masters (6:5-9).

Jesus taught submission throughout His ministry here on the earth. One of the most dramatic examples of this is when he submitted to the will of the Father in His prayer in the Garden of Gethsemane (Matt 26:36-42). Jesus explained that his job was to do the will of the Father who sent him and accomplish his work (John 4:34). Scripture clearly tells us that Jesus was submissive to his parents (Luke 2:51). If deity in the flesh can humble Himself and be submissive, certainly we can be submissive in accordance with God's commands.

Ephesians 5:22 "Wives, be in subjection unto your own husbands, as unto the Lord." From here through the end of the chapter, Paul begins a dual discussion of both marriage and the church (Eph 5:32). In keeping with the context of the book, the subject of the church is a key part of this passage.

Paul is helping us understand the very nature of God's design for the home and at the same time provides some very profound teaching about Christ and the church.

The text in verse 22 is very clear and self-explanatory, yet the teaching of this verse is denied, neglected and abused by many. God established marriage and the family with a clear order in mind from the very beginning. Oftentimes when discussing roles within marriage (e.g. Matt 19:3-9; I Tim 2:13) reference is made back to the first 3 chapters of Genesis, when all was established. This shows us that the ordered relationship between husband and wife is our design by our very natures and not subject to the culture in which we live.

Just because a woman is to be in subjection to her own husband does not imply that the wife is in any way inferior to the husband. They are equals, but they take on different roles within the family. As we see in the coming verses, as the proper role of the husband is described, the challenges of this role of leadership in the family are quite daunting.

She is to submit to her husband "as unto the Lord." This simile raises the expectation to a very high level and it is repeated again in verse 24. Our submission to our spouse should parallel our submission to the Lord. The word "Lord" (κύριος) or "master" itself implies submission on the part of the one using the phrase. Jesus asked in Luke 6:46, "And why call ye me, Lord, Lord, and do not the things which I say?"

Ephesians 5:23 "For the husband is the head of the wife, as Christ also is the head of the church, being himself the saviour of the body." The essence of the relationship is beginning to take shape here. The husbands and Christ are both shown to be heads in their respective areas, while one of the responsibilities that come with that is laid forth. In Koine Greek κεφαλή (headship), when it refers to the relationship between people, always means authority and not "source" as some have argued. This usage is the same in English, as well.

As Christ sacrificially gave of Himself to be the savior of the church, so also the husband must give of himself sacrificially to be the spiritual head of his family. His concern needs to be for the spiritual growth and progress of his own family over his own personal needs and desires. Just as Christ's headship over the church doesn't vary from culture to culture, the husband's headship over the family doesn't change, either.

Just as the role of submission is often denied, neglected and abused, so also is the role of leadership often denied, neglected, and abused. Far too many families have fathers who are shirking their responsibility of spiritual leadership. Rather than being sacrificial, they are selfish. Rather than leading, they are lacking. As a result of the failures of these husbands, their role is either left undone or the broken pieces are picked up by the wife as she attempts to do both jobs herself.

Ephesians 5:24 "But as the church is subject to Christ, so let the wives also be to their husbands in everything." This verse is complimentary to the thought given in verse 23. While verse 23 commands the husbands to be heads of their families, verse 24 commands wives to be in subject to their husbands.

Ephesians 5:25 "Husbands, love your wives, even as Christ also loved the church, and gave himself up for it." Husbands are to ἀγαπάω (agapao) their wives. This type of love is a decision that has been made to look out for the best interests of another, despite any personal cost or hardship. This is the type of love that God had for the world in John 3:16. While the cost to God was quite significant, the decision was made that our salvation was in our best interest, so the sufferings were endured. This is the type of love that a husband is to have for his wife.

The addition of this type of love adds depth to the role of leadership in the home. When a husband wants what is in his wife's ultimate best interest and is willing to sacrifice whatever is necessary to achieve that end, you have the perfect recipe for the home. What woman wouldn't want to follow a man who is constantly looking out for her rather than looking out for himself? This type of relationship leads to mutual respect and a proper sense of worth.

Ephesians 5:26 "that he might sanctify it, having cleansed it by the washing of water with the word." Here the inspired writer is talking again about Christ and the result of His giving Himself up for the church. Sanctify (ἁγιάζω) comes from the same Greek root word as "holy". To sanctify something is to make it holy, to set it apart for a particular purpose. Christ has cleansed us through His sacrifice.

Cleansing through the washing of water is a familiar concept throughout the New Testament. It is clearly a reference to baptism (Acts 2:38; Acts 22:16; Rom 6:3-4; I Pet 3:21). In the many passages such as we have here in Ephesians, the act of baptism is described as the method through which we are cleansed from our sins and made holy.

Ephesians 5:27 "that he might present the church to himself a glorious church, not having spot or wrinkle or any such thing; but that it should be holy and without blemish." Paul is inspired to lay forth some of the great blessings of being cleansed by the blood of Christ in baptism. We, the church, can now be presented before God in a glorious way. Remember when Isaiah was before the presence of God, he said: "Woe is me! for I am undone; because I am a man of unclean lips, and I dwell in the midst of a people of unclean lips: for mine eyes have seen the King, Jehovah of hosts" (Isa 6:5). Isaiah was not able to be in the presence of God in a sinful state. However, as Isaiah had his sin removed (Isa 6:6-7) and was able to be in God's presence, so also when our sins have been washed in the blood of Jesus we can be in the presence of God.

Ephesians 5:28 "Even so ought husbands also to love their own wives as their own bodies. He that loveth his own wife loveth himself." R. C. Sproule comments beautifully on this verse, "One of the most wonderful parts of the marriage ceremony is the vow that we take to cherish one another. To cherish one another means to hold one another in the highest esteem and to place an infinite value on one another."[40]

Our bodies require constant attention and maintenance. We need a steady supply of oxygen, water, food and other essentials to keep our bodies alive. In the same way, a marriage requires a steady supply of love, encouragement and understanding in order to stay healthy and alive. Women were created with a greater need for these things than the man, thus husbands need to go out of their way to ensure that their wife receives all that she needs.

Ephesians 5:29 "for no man ever hated his own flesh; but nourisheth and cherisheth it, even as Christ also the church." Once again, when we consider what Christ has selflessly done for the church, any inconvenience that we encounter when we are nurturing and cherishing our wife pales in comparison. We will happily supply everything she needs to not only survive, but also to thrive and prosper.

In a similar light, we can see how Christ has nurtured and cherished the church. He planned and designed it before the foundation of the world (Eph 1:4; 3:10-11). He provided us with everything that we need (II Pet 1:3), including leadership to watch for our souls (Heb 13:17), fellowship with Christians to encourage us (Heb 10:24) and correction when it is needed (Jam 5:19-20). Truly, He has made provision for our spiritual needs while here on this earth.

Ephesians 5:30 "because we are members of his body." Just as a husband cares for his wife as if she were his own physical body, so also Christ cares for His church because we are His body. Paul is beautiful in his weaving together the two topics under consideration here.

Ephesians 5:31 "For this cause shall a man leave his father and mother, and shall cleave to his wife; and the two shall become one flesh." This passage, a quotation of Genesis 2:24, is also quoted by Jesus as He discusses marriage

(Mat 19:5; Mar 10:7). Obviously, this passage has great significance to the marriage relationship, where both parties separate from their respective parents and form a new family.

In context, the passage is equally applicable to becoming a part of the church, the bride of Christ. When we become a child of God at baptism (Act 2:47), we leave the person where we were and begin a new life (Rom 6:1-4). The commitment that we make in becoming a child of God is life-long, just as the commitment in marriage.

Ephesians 5:32 "This mystery is great: but I speak in regard of Christ and of the church." Paul explicitly states for us here that he is writing by inspiration about the church in this section. It can be properly concluded from this statement then that marriage was designed to be a type of the church. The dual teaching that has been done since verse 22 makes even more sense when this fact is laid forth so clearly.

Ephesians 5:33 "Nevertheless do ye also severally love each one his own wife even as himself; and let the wife see that she fear her husband." This verse provides a summary of the final 11 verses of the chapter. Husbands are to love their wives and wives are to respect (φοβέω) their husbands.

## Chapter 6

# Ephesians

*by*

*Landon Rowell*

## Ephesians: Introduction

R. C. Bell once wrote, "Imagine the first reading of this epistle in the assembly of the Ephesian church. A letter from their loved and trusted apostle, who was a prisoner in faraway Rome, was a memorable event. Tensely, every member listened to every line. As the reader came to the passage naming husbands and wives or parents and children or masters and slaves (likely many were slaves), how agape with interest each respective group drank in every word of its special message! Did some earnest husband speak right out: "Brother, please read that again"?[41]

Paul, having dealt with the husband wife relationship in Ephesians chapter five, continues his relationship exposition in Ephesians chapter six. He will cover the Parent/Child, Master/Slave, and Christian/God relationship. What powerful statements on relationships that are made in this great chapter, keeping in mind that these relationship sections are drawing from Paul's theme statement, "submitting to one another out of reverence for Christ."[42] As Dummelow stated, "It is a worthy conclusion to this immortal Epistle!"[43]

## Ephesians 6:1-4: Parent Child Relationship

Ephesians 6:1 "Children, obey your parents in the Lord, for this is right." This is the parallel to Colossians 3:20 where Paul takes a similar outline as he has done here in dealing with relationship.

The Greek word for children is "τέκνα" which usually signifies younger children or those that are not Christians. However considering Paul previously addressed Christian husband and wives and after this section will address

Christian masters and slaves it seems apparent here, to this writer, that he is writing to those old enough to be Christians. Couple that with the fact that he is writing to children that should not only listen but have a compelling reason to listen ie they will be in sin without adhering to Paul's statements, it appears to be specifically to children that are Christians.

God has always expected children to be obedient and respectful to their parents. There are two basic reason for this. (1) The family dynamic is only successful if everyone knows their role and follows it. It will become dysfunctional without everyone doing their part. (2) When children learn obedience and respect for others it will be an easy transition therefore to learning obedience and respect for God. This second reason is naturally the most important. That is why God, under the Old Law, took this so seriously: Deuteronomy 21:18-21 "If a man has a stubborn and rebellious son who will not obey the voice of his father or the voice of his mother, and, though they discipline him, will not listen to them, 19 then his father and his mother shall take hold of him and bring him out to the elders of his city at the gate of the place where he lives, 20 and they shall say to the elders of his city, 'This our son is stubborn and rebellious; he will not obey our voice; he is a glutton and a drunkard.' 21 Then all the men of the city shall stone him to death with stones. So you shall purge the evil from your midst, and all Israel shall hear, and fear." How many children being raised in the church today would still be alive if we were still under the Old Law? Something every parent should think about, considering the obvious gravity God puts into it.

Paul, inspired by God, places a critical phrase in this verse that is connected to obey, "in the Lord." As brother Wacaster writes, "It is an adverbial phrase that specifies the "realm" of obedience, namely in those things that are pleasing to God. A child is not to go contrary to the will of God in an effort to obey his parents."[44] Under the Law of Moses God so closely allied this idea that in Leviticus 19:3 He ran this truth together, "Every one of you shall revere his mother and his father, and you shall keep my Sabbaths: I am the LORD your God." If either of these were broken under the Mosaic Law it was grounds for death.

Ephesians 6:2 "Honor your father and mother" (this is the first commandment with a promise)." Honor is of higher value than obedience. One can physically "obey" many expectations God has but without honor that obedience is far from proper. For example many children will do what their parents want them to do such as the dishes, take out the trash, laundry, etc. but if they are doing it for any reason other than respect and honor it is not being done right. With that in mind let us not forget that respect and honor toward parents is not natural it is a learned character trait gleaned by parents that not only teach but train their children as we will see in a moment (6:4).

"...this is the first commandment with a promise." This statement has caused much controversy for many. There are two basic explanations for this. (1) It is the first with a specific promise. (2) It is the first to children and it contains a promise. Both are possible but this writer prefers the latter to the former.

Ephesians 6:3 "that it may go well with you and that you may live long in the land." This is a quote from Deuteronomy 5:16 and Exodus 20:12. When one looks to those passages one will see God granting long days (life) in the promised land of Canaan to those children that honored their parents. Here Paul takes that Old Testament promise and continues the application to the present yet without the limitation to Canaan. The apostle clearly is "adapting the promise in spirit to a wider area."[45] Children that honor and respect their parents and learn from their wisdom and maturity will generally live a healthy and prosperous life.

Keep in mind that this promise is not specific or individual but general. There have been plenty of children that have lived short lives by no fault of their own. However the general rule is that children who adhere to their training (Proverbs 22:6) will live long productive lives.

As a side note there is nothing wrong with desiring to live a long life on this earth as a long lived life is a blessing from God. It blesses us by (1) allowing us to prepare for eternity longer (2) allowing us to be more useful longer (3) allowing us to study God's Word and His works longer.

Ephesians 6:4 "Fathers, do not provoke your children to anger, but bring them up in the discipline and instruction of the Lord." As my mother used to joke around and say "the Bible says Fathers do not provoke your children, not mothers." This particular verse is one I think far too many fathers have overlooked through the years. It is the responsibility of fathers not only to keep from provoking their children but to raise them by training them and instructing them in the ways of the Lord. Herein we see yet another example of God proclaiming the leadership that men are to be involved in. The spiritual wellbeing of the family is the father's responsibility.

The Greek word for provoke is "παροργίζετε" and has been translated by some as "exasperate." Joseph Thayer properly defines it as, "to rouse to wrath, to provoke, exasperate, anger."[46] This particular word carries an idea of intent to anger. Notice "Where ὀργή itself is used thus, it is generally interchangeable with θυμός... But θυμός is preferred for the passionate rage which boils up suddenly, Lk. 4:28; Ac. 19:28, even though ὀργή seems by derivation to be particularly well adapted to express this... This term, however, contains an element of awareness and even deliberation absent from θυμός."[47] Thus the idea is fathers do not deliberately cause your children to become full of wrath.

Brother Wacaster had this to say, "There is a tendency on the part of parents to become impatient with their children when their children annoy them or disturb them... The apostle has touched on one of the greatest dangers that a parent faces in child rearing. It is that of causing the child's temperament to be soured, and thus making them feel that the parent is acting under the influence of anger rather than concern for the child's good" (Wacaster 467).

The Greek word for discipline is "παιδείᾳ" and "primarily denotes 'to train children,' suggesting the broad idea of education."[48] The NKJV better translates this as "training." This is the positive side of raising children and yet this is where a lot of parents fail. What I mean is that they teach their children many things about God, righteousness, sin, and so on and so forth but they fail to actually train them. As way of example, my son was going through a phase where when you would ask him to do something he would answer by saying "no." One day after I asked him to do something and he responded thusly I got frustrated and in no uncertain terms made my displeasure known concerning his response. My wife quickly stepped in and told my son to explain why he said that. He responded that he was simply trying to do what "mom" had asked first. She then explained to him a better way of telling me or her his concern without saying "no." My wife at that moment "trained" my son. I was about to "teach him a lesson" whereas my wife trained him. Parents must train their children which is not only giving their kids knowledge but also showing them how to apply that knowledge and gain wisdom. Many of our precious children that have been raised in the church are falling away because they have been taught their parents faith but have not been trained to have their own.

The Greek word for instruction is "νουθεσίᾳ" and literally means "a putting in the mind." This is the negative side of raising children in that it deals with the warnings. We are to warn our children of sin, unrighteousness, darkness, and hell. The idea is not to scare them into righteousness but simply make them aware of the dangers of unrighteousness. Jesus instructed or admonished when he said, "And do not fear those who kill the body but cannot kill the soul. Rather fear him who can destroy both soul and body in hell" (Matthew 10:28).

Some have objected to parents training their children in religion. It is suggested that this will somehow leave the children without independence and able to make their own choices. There is a problem with their logic however in that they only apply such logic to religion. Notice these same people train their children in math, language skills, science, sports, etc. and yet they do not consider these to leave a child with little to no independence. This alone shows the fallacy in their argument, and all that is necessary to trample such a destructive and illogical thought.

## Ephesians 6:5-9: Master Slave Relationship

Ephesians 6:5 "Bondservants, obey your earthly masters with fear and trembling, with a sincere heart, as you would Christ." It has been estimated by many that under Roman rule the slave to freeman ratio was at minimum one to one and during certain emperors as much as three to one. Thus we find the need for Paul to deal with such situations. This writer agrees with Brother Walker's thoughts on the Bible and slavery. He writes, "The Bible does not directly oppose or condemn slavery. It does, however, regulate it in such a way as to bring about its demise."[49]

The Greek word for bondservants is "δοῦλοι" and means slave. Vines explains, "originally the lowest term in the scale of servitude, came also to mean 'one who gives himself up to the will of another." This word is found 126 times in the ESV and 127 in the KJV. Keep in mind Romans considered slaves no different than "beasts" and/or "property."

"obey your earthly masters" This is that which has been constant each and every time this subject is addressed (I Peter 2:18; I Timothy 6:1-2; Colossians 3:22-25). Slaves were to show their masters the Christian way in their work ethic. They were to go the extra mile and whatever was asked of them they were to do their best.

"according to the flesh" This is not in the ESV but is found in other translations. Slaves were to obey their masters in all things earthly and physical but they were not to consider themselves in subjection to their masters concerning spiritual matters. Where master and slave were Christians there should be an understanding of equality in Christ. Remember how Jesus handled those that asked to be the greatest in the kingdom "...The kings of the Gentiles exercise lordship over them, and those in authority over them are called benefactors. 26 But not so with you. Rather, let the greatest among you become as the youngest, and the leader as one who serves."

"with fear and trembling" One will first consider this as threatening but when one looks closer they will see that the idea here is not of being scared of their masters but of honor and respect towards them. When the slave honors and respects the master this brings honor and respect to the slave. Every slave could do far more for the cause of Christianity by submitting than by rebelling.

"with a sincere heart" Here we have the motives behind the obedience by which the slave was to have toward his/her master. Not every master was going to treat their slaves in such a way that they were pleased to serve them faithfully. However Christian slaves were not to be obedient based on the treatment of their master but rather on their love for Christ and being a light to their master that God would be glorified. As Paul ended this powerful verse "as you would Christ."

Ephesians 6:6 "not by the way of eye-service, as people-pleasers, but as bondservants of Christ, doing the will of God from the heart." We have here a reiteration for emphasis. The doubling up here shows it is of great importance.

"eye-service" is the idea of working hard only when the master or those over the slave are looking. If the master leaves the work is not done as diligently. This is unacceptable behavior for Christians.

"people-pleasers" This is the idea of only doing that which the master finds necessary with little to no concern for quality. Several phrases have come about with this idea of being people-pleasers such as doing just enough to "pass the muster" or "I did good enough to pass government work." These fall short of doing the best one can do.

"but as bondservants of Christ" Here we see once again that Christians are slaves of Christ. Some don't like the idea of being called a slave however being a slave to a great master was not really a bad thing. Under the Old Law a slave could, after a set amount of time, choose to stay a slave or receive his freedom. Many who had great masters chose to stay slaves (Exodus 21:1-6). We sing a song relating to that idea titled "Peirce My Ear."

Ephesians 6:7 "rendering service with a good will as to the Lord and not to man." It would appear this is an extension to the end of verse six and should read thusly, "doing the will of God from the heart, rendering service with a good will as to the Lord and not to man."

I like what Barns states on this verse, "…he should regard his lot in life as having been ordered by Divine Providence for some wise and good purpose; and until he may be permitted to enjoy his liberty in a quiet and peaceable manner…he should perform his duties with fidelity, and feel that he was rendering acceptable service to God."[50]

Ephesians 6:8 "knowing that whatever good anyone does, this he will receive back from the Lord, whether he is a bondservant or is free." This has been the promise of God since sin barged in and man fell for it (Genesis 3).

"knowing that whatever good anyone does, this he will receive back from the Lord" There is a basic reality that slaves that do good and work hard would most likely find their masters pleased with them but that doesn't appear to be the focus of Paul here. The focus looks past this life and into the life to come where the righteous will be rewarded by being with God for eternity. I'm reminded of what God told the Christians in Rome "And we know that for those who love God all things work together for good, for those who are called according to his purpose" (Romans 8:28). There is a place prepared (John 14:1-4) for those that do the works they were created for in Christ Jesus (Ephesians 2:10) and that place is heaven (Revelation 4).

"bondservant or is free" We find an addition to more than one class of servant now. The slave which has been under consideration up to this point and now the hired servant. I think it should be pointed out here that these principles obviously should be applied today to those that are hired and work at a company. Those hired today should do their best and work their hardest. Christians should be the gold standard of dedication to one's job. It is sad to hear of Christians that use "sick days" for vacation days or are chronically late to work. There should never be a time where a Christian is fired for not doing their job unless that job has tried to interfere with spiritual matters. Some common work related things that Christians should never do are things like missing worship services, being unethical i.e. stepping on someone while going up the corporate ladder, advancing immorality like selling alcoholic beverages, abortion pills, etc... Outside of spiritual matter conflicts, Christians should be held in the highest esteem for their work ethic.

Ephesians 6:9 "Masters, do the same to them, and stop your threatening, knowing that he who is both their Master and yours is in heaven, and that there is no partiality with him." Here we find Paul shifting from instructing slaves to instructing masters.

"Masters, do the same to them" We find here that God holds masters to the same expectations he does slaves. Masters are to be hard workers who are ethical and moral. They are not to simply act like they care for the slaves but actually care for them and treat them like they would want to be treated (Matthew 7:12).

"stop your threating" A most powerful truth being seen here in that it shows that even though some masters were Christians the master slave mentality was still common. That being that slaves were property and not human beings. "Lipscomb noted, "The spirit that threatens is a bitter, dictatorial one, lacks kindness and consideration, and greatly exasperates and embitters the servant" (Wacaster 476). Christianity brought something new "respect for all human life." Coffman expressed this clearly when he stated, "Behind a commandment like this lay the infinite dimensions of those tremendous new value judgments which were brought to mankind from above by Jesus Christ the Lord. The infinite value of human life!"[51]

"knowing that he who is both their Master and yours is in heaven" Sobering words to everyone especially masters who were having to change their mentality toward slaves. The God of heaven whom they were serving was the same God of the salves whom they owned and therefore making both slave and master servants of Christ.

"there is no partiality with him" Jews were notorious concerning their disdain for Gentiles. One only has to look to the book of Jonah to see this clearly revealed. However Christianity ushered in the new covenant that had been promised where both Jew and Gentile would have the spirit poured out on them (Joel 2:28; Acts 2:17). Peter observed this truth when he went to Cornelius' house and explained "Truly I understand that God shows no partiality, but in every nation anyone who fears him and does what is right is acceptable to him" (Acts 10:34-35).

## Ephesians 6:10-20: Soldier Officer Relationship

Ephesians 6:10 "Finally, be strong in the Lord and in the strength of his might." Here we see Paul putting some final thoughts on his treaties concerning relationships.

"be strong in the Lord and in the strength of his might" There is only one strength that can overcome Satan and his army and that is the strength that comes from the Lord. "Any attempt to combat Satan while remaining outside of the Lord is both foolish and fatal" (Wacaster 477). As Paul wrote to the church at Philippi "I can do all things through him who strengthens me" (Philippians 4:13). Brother Roy Deaver wrote, "The christian does not feel that he is strong within himself. He does not have an attitude of human self-sufficiency. He realizes well his weaknesses, limitations, and inabilities. In the realizations of these, he strives to be strong in the Lord. He has committed himself to be used as an instrument for righteousness. He believes the Lord will and does work through him to accomplish His will. He looks to the Lord as the source of his strength. He knows that God is all-powerful, and that there is mighty power available to those who believe."[52]

Ephesians 6:11 "Put on the whole armor of God, that you may be able to stand against the schemes of the devil." What a powerful direct statement of fact. With God's armor we can stand against Satan we can withstand anything he does.

"Put on" We, as children of God, have a responsibility placed upon us if we want to "stand in the might of His power." We have to put the armor on. Today there are many who are "waiting for God to put their armor on them." James notice this type of behavior and in his inspired letter he wrote concerning it. "

"whole armor of God" The Greek word for "whole armor" is πανοπλίαν and means "all armor, full armor" (Vines Vol. 2 pg. 38). This includes not only the suit that covers the body but also the weapons one uses for offense and defense. Every Christian must make certain they are not spiritually exposed in any way but fully armed. Arming oneself with anything other than God's armor is ludicrous. We cannot defeat Satan without God nor can we defeat Satan without using the tools God has given us.

"that you may be able to stand against the schemes of the devil" The Greek word for schemes is μεθοδείας meaning "to follow up or investigate by method and settled plan" (Thayer pg. 395). This word is found only here and Ephesians 4:4 and is also where we get our English word "method" from. Satan has a method to his madness. He by no means is haphazard in his attempts to tempt and deceive us. He is cunning and designs his attacks like a roaring lion (II Corinthians 2:11; I Peter 5:8). Satan "never tells the story nor paints the picture like it really is" (Deaver pg. 116). This is symbolically depicted in Revelation 12. The whole chapter has Satan moving from one plan of action to another. What a fascinating scene and jolt to Satan to discover all his plans are folly against God Almighty. We can stand up and drive back Satan no matter his plan if we have prepared ourselves for the battle.

Ephesians 6:12 "For we do not wrestle against flesh and blood, but against the rulers, against the authorities, against the cosmic powers over this present darkness, against the spiritual forces of evil in the heavenly places." Has there been a more eerie sentence than this? Why do we need to be strong in the Lord and His might putting on His armor because we are in a battle!!!

"For we do not wrestle" The Greek word for wrestle is πάλη, which is only found here in the New Testament, means "to engage in intense struggle, involving physical or nonphysical force against strong opposition—'to struggle, to fight'" (Louw & Nida Vol. 1 pg. 495). Thayer's vividly describes this word as meaning, "a contest between two in which each endeavors to throw the other, and which is decided when the victor is able...[to] hold him down with his hand upon his neck" (Thayer's pg. 474) (brackets mine).

"against flesh and blood" This phrase simply signifies humanity. The Christian warfare is not against other humans it is against Satan and his messengers. Satan will use humans (Ephesians 4:14) but our war is not against those humans but their master the devil.

"but against the rulers" These rulers/principalities, Greek word ἀρχάς, appear to be the hierarchy of the demonic world. Notice that this description is in the plural not singular and as such would lean away from describing Satan only and more towards Satan and his messengers. Adam Clarke stated these were "Chief rulers; beings of the first rank and order in their own kingdom."[53] Thayer describes these rulers as "demons holding dominions entrusted to them in the order of things" (Thayer pg. 76). Brother Wacaster contends "that Paul is speaking here of evil powers that have sway over the world" (Wacaster 480).

"authorities" Once again we get a glimpse into this demonic hierarchy. This Greek word, ἐξουσίας, has to do with the office these rulers have, hence their authority. Thayer described this word as "the leading and more powerful among created beings superior to man, spiritual potentates; used in the plur. of a certain class of angels... used also of demons: in the plur., Eph. 6:12; Col. 2:15" (Thayer pg. 225). Kittel and associates had this to say concerning the word, "Formally, NT usage is closest to that of the LXX. exousía is God's power, the power given to Jesus, or the power given by Jesus to his disciples... It may also denote a sphere of dominion, e.g., the state (Lk. 23:7), the domain of spirits (Eph. 2:2), or the spiritual powers (1 Cor. 15:24; Eph. 1:21; Col. 1:16; 1 Pet. 3:22)" (Kittel pg. 239).

"cosmic powers over this present darkness" The ESV, in this author's opinion, does not translate this well. The Greek word for cosmic powers is "κοσμοκράτορας" and is more accurately translated world ruler or age ruler. Due to the two possibilities, world or age, there has been some speculation as to the meaning here. Was Paul talking about a specific period of time, as the ESV ostensibly suggests, or was he talking about the sinful world in general? Considering the context and generality of not only the other descriptions but also the complete text it seems to this author that Paul is pointing to this sinful world. The ASV & LEB have the better, "...against the world rulers of this darkness..."

The point is Satan and his demons or messengers are the rulers of this old sinful world and as a result this world has become full of darkness. As Christ pointed out, "And this is the judgment: the light has come into the world, and people loved the darkness rather than the light because their works were evil" (John 3:19). Lipscomb to this point added, "These evil spirits reign over the existing state of ignorance and alienation from God. That is, the world in its apostasy is subject to their control..."[54]

"spiritual forces of evil" Once again Paul is stipulating to the fact that Christians are at war against the spiritual not the physical. This spiritual force is comprised of all sorts of forces of evil. Satan's mind is so deprived that he is able to even "invent evil" (Romans 1:30).

"in the heavenly places" The Greek phrase "ἐν τοῖς ἐπουρανίοις" is found five times in the New Testament each of which are in this magnificent epistle (Ephesians 1:3, 20; 2:6; 3:10; 6:12). What we learn from this is that this phrase is meant to be a descriptive term for the realm where the spiritual good and evil operate. Thus it cannot be made to be exclusively a realm of the good or evil.

Ephesians 6:13 "Therefore take up the whole armor of God, that you may be able to withstand in the evil day, and having done all, to stand firm." How could anyone upon hearing of the enemy and his rule, authority, power, and forces of evil not want to get dressed and ready for battle and yet day after day people all over the world wake up and go about their day spiritually naked.

"the whole armor of God" see verse 11.

"be able to withstand" The Greek word "δυνηθῆτε" or "be able" is described by Brother Deaver as, "...'hina' with the subjunctive (Aor. subj. 2 per. pl. of dunamai) which denotes purpose" (Deaver pg. 124). The Greek word "ἀντιστῆναι" which is translated withstand here means, "to resist by actively opposing pressure or power—'to resist'" (Louw & Nida Vol. 1 pg. 494). Thus the idea here is put on the whole armor of God with the forethought of resisting evil.

"the evil day" Some have come to think Paul here is referring to a specific event. Beare wrote that he thought this evil day was "the time which the horoscope has designated as dangerous, when the unlucky star is in the ascendant" (Coffman pg. 241). Coffman would go on to call this idea ludicrous and this writer agrees. Any and every day Satan attacks that day becomes the evil day. Considering seldom the child of God is found with reprieve from temptation and sin it stands to reason why we must "be able to withstand the evil day."

"having done all, to stand firm" There are two schools of thought here. (1) This phrase is depicting the idea of being fully prepared for battle; able to properly say I am ready. (2) This phrase is depicting the idea of having valiantly fought the battle able to stand in wonderful victory.

If the first is under consideration then we notice that total preparation is required to stand firm. The entire armor is on and the mind is set for battle awaiting Satan and his demons.

If the second is to be agreed upon then what wonderful encouragement is found here by Paul expounding upon a truth taught many times in the Scriptures, that if we are faithful and fight the good fight of faith (I Timothy 6:12) we will be victorious and receive our crown of life (Revelation 2:10). Brother Deaver wrote, "On the basis of the nature of the warfare and the strength of the enemy, christian soldiers are admonished to take up the complete armor which God supplies, thus making proper preparation for battles, and then to engage in the battles, successfully withstanding and defeating all the forces of evil, and to remain standing when the battles are over, having conquered all" (Deaver pg. 125).

This writer prefers the second to the first for if one looks at the following verses it appears Paul is going to explain how that victorious child of God was able to stand. It was because they put on the whole armor of God.

Ephesians 6:14 "Stand therefore, having fastened on the belt of truth, and having put on the breastplate of righteousness." Paul now begins to explain why the child of God was able to stand firm against Satan and his demons and be victorious.

"belt of truth" Roman soldiers, more precisely legionary, used a belt for two basic reasons. (1) To give him confidence and strength to move around freely. (2) To keep all the other armor in its proper place. The Christian soldier uses truth for the same purpose. It is what gives the Christian confidence to stand in the truth anywhere and everywhere knowing he has the truth on his side. It is also that which keeps Christians in their proper place because truth is not subject to objection nor can be relegated to relativity.

Some have, over the years, proclaimed that truth is relative trying to establish that we can know nothing for certain. I'm reminded of what Brother Robert Stapleton said one time when he heard a man teach such, "I wanted to go over there and slap him on the back of the head and say, are you certain or not that you felt that?" This simple illustration shows the ignorance of those that would profess such falsehoods and proclaim such ridiculous babblings. God's Word is truth (John 8:32; 17:17) and this is why it has stood the test of time and should be sought after and never relinquished (Proverbs 23:23).

I would also like, at this time, to point out that the phrase in verse seventeen "which is the word of God" applies to more armor than the "sword of the Spirit." Each of the six pieces of armor could, and in the readers mind should, have this phrase mentally placed at the end of each piece.

"breastplate of righteousness" The Roman soldier's breastplate covered his chest and back wholly keeping his vital organs protected from his enemies. The heart has always been used symbolically by God to represent either purity or sin within man (Matthew 15:10-20). The breastplate is meant to protect the heart of Christians against the fight of Satan and his demons.

"righteousness" To be considered righteous one must be just and to be just one must be made just by the Justifier (Romans 3:26). God, the Justifier, justifies man through His plan of salvation and His plan only. God's plan includes understanding what you are doing by studying His Word (Romans 10:17). God's plan includes building upon that understanding by one putting their faith in Jesus. Putting one's faith in Jesus is not only believing Jesus is the Son of God (John 3:16) but that He is our Master and as such we must obey Him (John 14:15; Hebrews 11:6). God's plan includes building upon that faith by repenting or turning one's life from being opposed to Christ to following after Christ (Acts 17:30). This is putting ones old sinful self to death (Romans 6:6). God's plan includes building upon that repentance by confessing Jesus as the Son of God your Savior before witnesses (Matthew 10:32; Romans 10:9-10). If one has truly repented and turned toward Christ this proves such. God's plan includes one building upon that great confession by obeying the gospel (I Thessalonians 1:8). The gospel is the death, burial, and resurrection of Jesus Christ (I Corinthians 15:1-4). How can one obey a historical event? Paul tells us in his letter, inspired by God, to the Romans. It is by being baptized/immersed in water and into Christ (Romans 6:3-5). Once one has been justified and made righteous by God through faith (obedience to God's plan) then one stays righteous by remaining obedient to God through His Word (I John 1:7). The righteous breastplate therefore is steadfast obedience to God which gives every Christian the intestinal fortitude to withstand the onslaught of Satan's attacks.

Ephesians 6:15 "and, as shoes for your feet, having put on the readiness given by the gospel of peace." Here we have yet another fascinating and thought provoking verse that begs certain questions. How can putting shoes on really help a soldier and how can conflicting ideas, peace and battle, be harmonious?

"shoes for your feet" Roman soldiers wore an open toe boots called caligae. These boots were secured to the soldier's feet with straps. On the bottom of the boots the sole of the shoe was covered with hobnails. These hobnails were used to help the soldier keep his footing during marching and battles. These were not running shoes these were fighting shoes. Christians today are to put their battle shoes on so they can make a stand against the attack of Satan and his demons.

"readiness" The word readiness is the Greek word "ἑτοιμασίᾳ" and means preparation, readiness, alacrity, etc. The idea is that one is in preparation for the battle because they have the gospel of peace.

"gospel of peace" The shoes represent battle ready, and yet they are the gospel of peace as well. These two terms are conflicting in nature nevertheless when one examines the Scriptures one will see clearly how the two go hand and hand. A consequence of becoming justified is peace (Romans 5:1). We are promised that peace will continue in our lives if we stay true to the Word of God (Philippians 4:9). However we are in a constant battle with Satan (I Peter 5:8) and as such we only keep the peace of God in our lives if we win those battles. Thus "peace with God and self demands constant battle against the forces of evil" (Deaver 129).

Ephesians 6:16 "In all circumstances take up the shield of faith, with which you can extinguish all the flaming darts of the evil one." Satan is able to attack in a variety of ways. He devours like a lion (I Peter 5:8), he disguises himself like as righteous (II Corinthians 11:14), and here we see he can shoot from a distance flaming darts. He is quite the foe.

"the shield of faith" Roman soldier's had several different shields. The Greek word here is "θυρεὸν" which was the scutum. This shield was, give or take, four feet tall and two and a half feet wide. They were made of wood or brass, and were covered with leather that was saturated in water. It was worn on the left arm by the soldiers. They were a marvel of protection for the soldier who could hide behind it from those throwing spears or shooting arrows. In fact when soldier stood side by side they made a virtual wall of protection. Christians are to take up this "faith shield." Faith is a word that is, more often than not, misused. You hear people say all the time "you go so far then the rest of the way is by faith." This usage is foreign to the Scriptures for the faith found therein is not some "leap in the dark" but that which is based on evidence and substance (Hebrews 11:1). Therefore when Christians have faith it is that which they "know" to be true (I John 5:13) and have put that knowledge into practice becoming wise. Brother Lipscomb had some powerful and timeless thoughts on faith. He wrote, "To increase our faith it is necessary to study regularly the word of God...(Rom. 10:17) But in order that our faith may be strengthened and fixed as a part of our being, it is necessary that we give expression to our convictions in our daily life. No thought or feeling enters into the formation of our characters or becomes permanent until it controls the actions of our bodies and becomes a part of our being. Faith itself is accepted by God only when it has molded the actions of the body and made the body subject to its control. The conviction of the heart becomes a part of our being and enters into our character only when it prompts the body to action" (Lipscomb 132).

"extinguish all the flaming darts of the evil one" There are numerous thoughts that are apparent from this section of the verse. (1) The evil one is real and someone to be reckoned with. The world considers Satan some mythical being made up to scare people. The Bible on the other hand makes it clear Satan is not only real but he is evil. (2) The evil one is dangerous and has caused havoc since the time of Adam and Eve in the Garden of Eden. The Bible has nothing kind to say about Satan but rather, because of his danger, calls him the "father of lies," a "murderer from the beginning" (John 8:44), an "adversary (I Peter 5:8), and even a "dragon" (Revelation 12-13). (3) The evil one has darts that he hurls towards man. These darts are meant to cause the Christian soldier to drop his shield opening himself up to attack. Notice the devil doesn't have but one dart and is simply out of luck if he misses, no he has plenty of backups ready at his disposal. Though Christians are not ignorant of his devices and the flaming darts he hurls, the majority of the world has been unaware of the fact they have been pierced and are on fire.

Ephesians 6:17 "and take the helmet of salvation, and the sword of the Spirit, which is the word of God." Here we find the last two armor pieces mentioned by Paul.

"helmet of salvation" The Roman soldier's helmet, galea, was made of either very thick leather or brass. On the top of it, it usually had a plume for decoration. This helmet helped protect the soldier from a blow by the enemy's sword, club, or battle axe. This helmet for the Christian is made up of salvation. Salvation protects the Christian in three basic ways. (1) He has salvation from all of his sins at baptism (Mark 16:16; Acts 22:16). (2) He has salvation as a continual present state in Christ (II Timothy 1:10; I John 1:7). (3) He has been promised an eternal inheritance that he can hope in never becoming discouraged (I Peter 1:3-5; I Thessalonians 5:8).

"sword of the Spirit, which is the word of God" The Roman soldier's sword, gladius, was a very powerful weapon in the hands of a skilled soldier. It was anywhere in size from dagger to short sword and it was two edged and sharp. During battle is was very effective at slashing and piercing the enemy. The Christian's sword is the "inspired, the infallible, the inerrant, the all-sufficient word of God" (Deaver 130). This is the Christian's lone offensive weapon. Every piece of armor up to this point has been defensive and has had a purposed designed to stand firm and unmovable against Satan's attacks. Now Paul is telling every Christian don't just hold the line but push forward now. The sword of the Spirit is all any Christian needs to drive Satan backwards and thrust him back we must (James 4:7).

As a side note, some have concluded that it is the Spirit that wields the sword. However when one examines the context it becomes evident that this cannot be. Each armor piece, up to this point, has had the Christian "put it on" and there is nothing to suggest this sword is any different. As Foy Wallace once remarked, "if we do not wield it, then it will not be wielded" (Wacaster pg. 490). The Bible left to gather dust on the shelf is no more powerful for its owner than the knick-knack next to it. It is only when that Bible is "picked up" and used does it become "…living and active, sharper than any two-edged sword, piercing to the division of soul and of spirit, of joints and of marrow, and discerning the thoughts and intentions of the heart" (Hebrews 4:12).

Ephesians 6:18 "praying at all times in the Spirit, with all prayer and supplication. To that end keep alert with all perseverance, making supplication for all the saints." Though prayer is not associated with any armor pieces there can be no doubt that it plays an intrical part in the Christian soldier's battles and victories. Matthew Henry wrote, "Prayer must buckle on all the other parts of our Christian armour."[55] One other interesting note is the fact that the word all is found four times in this particular verse. Brother Coffman wrote, "ALL kinds of prayers and supplications are to be used: public prayers, private prayers, intercessory prayers, prayers of thanksgiving, every kind! ALL seasons are the season of prayer: all times of the day, all conditions and circumstances, all occasions, all states of mind, etc. ALL perseverance: through times of discouragement or defeat when it seems that all is lost, when victory has smiled or when it has failed.... let nothing hinder the prayer life" (Coffman PC Study Bible V5)

"praying at all times" The Greek word for praying is "προσευχόμενοι" and is a present participle verb. This is significant because "The present participle denotes action contemporary with that of the leading verb" (Deaver pg. 131). The leading verb of this Greek section is "take" found in verse seventeen. Therefore the praying mentioned here is to take place at the time of the taking.

Paul's intention in writing this verse is not to suggest we must be on bended knee at all times. In fact there are two potential thoughts here. (1) Paul could be suggesting we pray at every opportunity we have and in every circumstance, thus there is never a bad time to pray. (2) Paul could also be proposing the different kinds of prayers such as public prayers verse private prayers. This writer leans more closely to the idea that Paul is suggesting we pray at every opportunity and in every circumstance (I Thessalonians 5:17).

"in the Spirit" Paul plainly points out that proper Christian prayer is one done with the Holy Spirit's help. Jude makes this same observation, "But you, beloved, building yourselves up in your most holy faith and praying in the Holy Spirit" (Jude 20). Paul in the letter to the Romans gives more insight into this when he wrote, "Likewise the Spirit helps us in our weakness. For we do not know what to pray for as we ought, but the Spirit himself intercedes for us with groanings too deep for words. 27 And he who searches hearts knows what is the mind of the Spirit, because the Spirit intercedes for the saints according to the will of God" (Romans 8:26-27). The point is the Holy Spirit helps the Christian in his prayers by counteracting our weaknesses and helping us.

"prayer and supplication" The Greek word for prayer here is "προσευχῆς" and is the general usage of prayer meaning it is not limited in its scope. The Greek word for supplication is "δεήσεως" and means "that which is asked with urgency based on presumed need" (Louw & Nida Vol. 1 pg. 407).

"keep alert with all perseverance" The Greek word for keep alert is "ἀγρυπνοῦντες" and it is a present participle meaning it is action taking place at the same time of the "taking" in verse 17. See the earlier note on "praying at all times" for more details. The Greek word for perseverance is "προσκαρτερήσει" and is only found here in this verse. It is defined as continuation, steadfastness, unremitting and thusly translated perseverance. When a Christian takes up salvation he ought to simultaneously pray at every opportunity being constantly alert.

"making supplication for all the saints" Here we have a most important role for every Christian which is making requests and pleas on behalf of their brothers and sisters. I would venture to say there is not much more encouraging for the child of God than to know others are praying for them specifically.

Ephesians 6:19 "and also for me, that words may be given to me in opening my mouth boldly to proclaim the mystery of the gospel" Paul not only was requesting that supplications be made for the saints in general but also for him specifically. It could not be easy going through all that he had been through (II Corinthians 11:16ff) for the gospel's sake. Here we are given a glimpse into one of the avenues by which Paul stayed strong and bold in proclaiming the gospel. He relied on the strength and encouragement of knowing his brethren were praying for him. This is not to say he did not rely on God, he did (Philippians 4:13), but that he also gained much from the prayers of others. If Paul an apostle of Jesus Christ asked for the prayers of others how much more do you think you and I need the prayers of others?

"that the words may be given to me" This is the promise that was given to every apostle as they proclaimed God's Word, "When they deliver you over, do not be anxious how you are to speak or what you are to say, for what you are to say will be given to you in that hour" (Matthew 10:19).

"in opening my mouth boldly" "Though one of the most courageous men who ever lived, Paul recognized that there would be a time when he would not posses the proper courage, but for the prayers of others" (Deaver pg. 133). This is why he requested prayers and disciplined his body daily (I Corinthians 9:27). The Scriptures are replete with expectations of boldness for its gospel preachers (Acts 4:13; 29, 31; II Corinthians 3:12; 7:4; I Thessalonians 2:2).

The Greek word for boldly is "παρρησίᾳ" and literally means "all speech." Thus one is willing to speak on every subject no matter the consequences. Preachers are to preach the whole counsel of God (Acts 20:27). They are to do so in season and out of season (II Timothy 4:2). As I heard one preacher say "preachers are to proclaim the truth whether they like it or not." Those that bathe themselves in sin and darkness are not ones that like to have light shown on them yet that is exactly what boldly proclaiming the mystery of the gospel is. Gospel preachers, preach the Word!!!

Ephesians 6:20 "for which I am an ambassador in chains, that I may declare it boldly, as I ought to speak." Ambassadors were representatives of their kings. As such they were considered, by civilized countries, to be inviolable. Thus we have here a paradox; Paul a sacrosanct ambassador in chains.

"ambassador" This Greek word is "πρεσβεύω" and is an old word for the word "πρεσβυς" i.e. ambassador. This word is only found here and in II Corinthians 5:20. Thus Paul understood he was an older ambassador of Christ his King.

Some have tried to say all the saints are ambassadors of Christ however, to this writer, this appears to be wanting. Ambassadors are appointed men. Christians are called, no doubt, but not appointed. It was only the apostles that found themselves appointed by Christ and as such only apostles were ambassadors of Christ.

"chains" This Greek word is "ἁλύσει" and means a "particular word for the *coupling-chain* by which he was bound to the hand of his guard" (Wacaster pg. 493). Here we see Paul had a captive audience. It was not Paul that was captive but rather those chained to him. This is why Paul could write to the church in Philippi, "so that it has become known throughout the whole imperial guard and to all the rest that my imprisonment is for Christ" (Philippians 1:13).

"that I may declare it boldly, as I ought to speak" It would appear here that Paul is talking about his impending court date with Nero. No wonder Paul was asking for prayers. He, as Christ's ambassador, was expected to proclaim Christ boldly to Nero the emperor of Rome.

## Ephesians 6:21-24: Final Remarks

Ephesians 6:21 "So that you also may know how I am and what I am doing, Tychicus the beloved brother and faithful minister in the Lord will tell you everything." It would appear that the brethren at Ephesus were very concerned with Paul. Paul, realizing this, made plans to send Tychicus to give them a report on his state.

"Tychicus" is mentioned four other times in the in the Bible (Acts 20:4; Colossians 4:7; II Timothy 4:12; Titus 3:12). There is little known about this companion of Paul's. We know he was from Asian Minor wherein Ephesus was the capital (Acts 20:4). Paul mentioning his name to the Ephesians shows he could very well have been from there and well known to the church there as well. Paul must have trusted him greatly for it is Tychicus that was sent to Colossia (Colossians 4:7) to give them a report. Paul had plans to send him to Crete to relieve Titus (Titus 3:12) and possibly it was Tychicus that took the second letter to Timothy (II Timothy 4:12).

Ephesians 6:22 "I have sent him to you for this very purpose, that you may know how we are, and that he may encourage your hearts." Paul cared deeply for the church in Ephesus (Acts 20:37) where he had spent three years preaching (Acts 20:31) and he sent Tychicus to give his physical report so as to encourage those that were concerned about Paul.

Ephesians 6:23 "Peace be to the brothers, and love with faith, from God the Father and the Lord Jesus Christ." The common salutation "peace be to…" was used as an expression meaning happiness and prosperity in all that one does and is. One writer wrote it, "as if he had said 'I wish the continuance and increase of all happiness to you'" (Wacaster pg. 494).

"love with faith" Notice this does not say love "and" faith but rather love with faith. Paul desired that their faith was genuinely produced with love. One cannot help but think of what would later be written about this great congregation, "But I have this against you, that you have abandoned the love you had at first" (Revelation 2:4).

Ephesians 6:24 “Grace be with all who love our Lord Jesus Christ with love incorruptible.” Paul ends this fantastic letter to the church at Ephesus by reminding them that the grace of God is enjoyed by those that love the Lord with incorruptibility. In other words if these brethren wanted to stay in God’s grace they must have a never fading love for Christ. This verse clearly points to the fact that a Christian can fall from grace. Those that teach the false doctrine “once saved always saved” find themselves having to jump through imaginary hoops to get around such stark contrasting verses like Galatians 5:4 and Galatians 6:1.

## Notes


1 WORDsearch Outlines

2 New Oxford American Dictionary, “saint”

3 Coffman, Burton M. Coffman Commentaries on the NT, Ephesians, Eph.1:1 (Online) http://classic.studylight.org/com/bcc/view.cgi?book=eph&chapter=001

4 Lanier, Roy Jr “Lesson 2 Basic Precepts in Ephesians” (Online) http://www.oldpathspulpit.org/pdfs%5CEPHESIANS-YOUCANPERCEIVE.pdf

5 Thayer, Joseph H. Greek-English Lexicon of the New Testament. Accordance electronic edition, version 1.6. Altamonte Springs: OakTree Software, 2004, Eph.1:4 “chose” [ἐκλέγομαι]

6 Preacher’s Periodical “An Expository and Homiletical Treatment of Ephesians” by Eddie Cloer, Vol.II, 81, 1981, p.2

7 ApologeticsPress, “The Biblical Doctrine of Predestination, Foreordination, and Election” by F. Furman Kearley, p.3 (Online) http://www.apologeticspress.org/rr/reprints/Biblical-Doctrine-of-Predestina.pdf

8 Bauer, W., F. W. Danker, F. Arndt, and F. W. Gingrich, eds. A Greek-English Lexicon of the New Testament and other Early Christian Literature. 3d, Accordance electronic edition, version 1.6. Chicago: University of Chicago Press, 2000, Eph.1:5, “foreordained” {ASV} [προορίζω], p.873

9 ApologeticsPress, “The Biblical Doctrine of Predestination, Foreordination, and Election” by Furman Kearley, p.57 (Online) http://www.apologeticspress.org/rr/reprints/Biblical-Doctrine-of-Predestina.pdf

10 “Unconditional Election” by David Servant (Online) http://www.shepherdserve.org/calvinism/calvin_two.htm

11 The Westminster Confession of Faith and Catechisms “Chapter III Of God’s Eternal Decree” Para. III and IV (Online) http://files.wts.edu/uploads/pdf/about/WCF_30.pdf

12 Barclay, William. The Letters to the Galatians and Ephesians. The New Daily Study Bible. 3d; Accordance electronic edition, version 1.2. Louisville: Westminster John Knox Press, 2002, p.92

13 Bauer, W., F. W. Danker, F. Arndt, and F. W. Gingrich, eds. A Greek-English Lexicon of the New Testament and other Early Christian Literature. 3d, Accordance electronic edition, version 1.6. Chicago: University of Chicago Press, 2000, Eph.1:7, "redemption" [ἀπολύτρωσις]

14 Classic Ireland (Vol.3, 1996) "Slavery in the Roman Empire Numbers and Origins" by John Madden (Online) http://www.classicsireland.com/1996/Madden96.html

15 Bauer, W., F. W. Danker, F. Arndt, and F. W. Gingrich, eds. A Greek-English Lexicon of the New Testament and other Early Christian Literature. 3d, Accordance electronic edition, version 1.6. Chicago: University of Chicago Press, 2000, Eph.1:7, "trespasses" [παράπτωμα]

16 Patzia, Arthur G. Ephesians, Colossians, Philemon. New International Biblical Commentary 10. Accordance electronic edition, version 2.5. 18 vols. Peabody: Hendrickson Publishers, 1990, p.155

17 Orr, James, ed. International Standard Bible Encyclopedia. Accordance electronic edition, version 2.2. Grand Rapids: Eerdmans, 1915, "Mystery"

18 Wood, D. R. W., ed. New Bible Dictionary. 3d, Accordance electronic edition, version 2.1. Downers Grove: InterVarsity Press, 1996, Eph.1:9 "mystery" [μυστήριον]

19 Martin, Ralph P. and Peter H. Davids, eds. Dictionary of the Later New Testament and Its Developments. Accordance electronic edition, version 1.2. Downers Grove: InterVarsity Press, 1997, Eph.1:9, "mystery" [μυστήριον]

20 Bauer, W., F. W. Danker, F. Arndt, and F. W. Gingrich, eds. A Greek-English Lexicon of the New Testament and other Early Christian Literature. 3d, Accordance electronic edition, version 1.6. Chicago: University of Chicago Press, 2000, Eph.1:9, "good pleasure" [εὐδοκία]

21 Patzia, Arthur G. Ephesians, Colossians, Philemon. New International Biblical Commentary 10. Accordance electronic edition, version 2.5. 18 vols. Peabody: Hendrickson Publishers, 1990, p.155

22 Bauer, W., F. W. Danker, F. Arndt, and F. W. Gingrich, eds. A Greek-English Lexicon of the New Testament and other Early Christian Literature. 3d, Accordance electronic edition, version 1.6. Chicago: University of Chicago Press, 2000, Eph.1:10, "dispensation" [οἰκονομία]

23 The Living Word Commentary The Letters of Paul to the Ephesians, the Colossians, and Philemon edited by Everett Ferguson (Sweet Pub. Co: Austin, TX 1971), p.126

24 Barclay, William. The Letters to the Galatians and Ephesians. The New Daily Study Bible. 3d; Accordance electronic edition, version 1.2. Louisville: Westminster John Knox Press, 2002, p.100

25 Ibid, p.101.
26 The 66th Annual Bible Lectureship Freed-Hardeman University Exalting Christ in the Church edited by David Lipe and Ralph Gilmore, "The Spirit Within: A Seal and Guarantee-Ephesians 1:13-14; 3:16" by George Goldman (FHU: Henderson, TN 2000), pp.127-128
27 Robertson, A. T. Word Pictures in the New Testament. Accordance electronic edition, version 1.8. Altamonte Springs: OakTree Software, 2001, Eph.1:17, "Father of glory"
28 Ibid, 1 Cor.2:8, "Lord of glory"
29 Coffman, Burton M. Coffman Commentaries on the NT, Ephesians, Eph.1:17 (Online) http://classic.studylight.org/com/bcc/view.cgi?book=eph&chapter=001
30 Spiritual Sword Lectureship The Book of Ephesians edited by Garlan Elkins and Thomas B. Warren "Paul's Prayer (Eph.1:15-23)" by Gary Workman (Sain Pub. Co.: Lebanon, TN 1984), p.18
31 Bauer, W., F. W. Danker, F. Arndt, and F. W. Gingrich, eds. A Greek-English Lexicon of the New Testament and other Early Christian Literature. 3d, Accordance electronic edition, version 1.6. Chicago: University of Chicago Press, 2000, Eph.1:18, "know" [οἶδα]
32 Thayer, Joseph H. Greek-English Lexicon of the New Testament. Accordance electronic edition, version 1.6. Altamonte Springs: OakTree Software, 2004, "hope [elpiv]
33 Truth for Today Commentary Ephesians and Philippians by Jay Lockhart and David L. Roper General Editor Eddie Cloer (Resource Pub.: Searcy, AR 2009), p.86
34 Hendriksen, William New Testament Commentary Galatians and Ephesians (Baker Book House: Grand Rapids, MI 1979), p.99
35 Bauer, W., F. W. Danker, F. Arndt, and F. W. Gingrich, eds. A Greek-English Lexicon of the New Testament and other Early Christian Literature. 3d, Accordance electronic edition, version 1.6. Chicago: University of Chicago Press, 2000, Eph.1:22, "hath put" [ὑποτάσσω]
36 Foulkes, Francis. Ephesians: An Introduction and Commentary. Tyndale New Testament Commentaries 10. IVP/Accordance electronic edition, version 1.4. Downers Grove: InterVarsity Press, 1989, p.73
37 Bible Study Textbook The Glorious Church A Study of Ephesians by Wilbur Fields (College Press: Joplin, MO Sixth Printing Aug., 1983), p.51
38 Robert Jamieson, A. R. Fausset, and David Brown, Commentary Critical and Explanatory on the Whole Bible (Oak Harbor, WA: Logos Research Systems, Inc., 1997), Eph 5:3.
39 Ibid
40 R. C. Sproul, The Purpose of God: Ephesians (Scotland: Christian Focus Publications, 1994), 138.

41 Studies In Ephesians by Bell, R.C. pg. 48
42 All Scriptures are taken from the ESV unless otherwise noted. If other translations are used this is not necessarily an endorsement of the translation. The ESV translation is being used with permission.
43 J. R. Dummelow, Commentary on the Holy Bible (New York: The Macmillan Company, 1937), p. 966.
44 Studies In Ephesus: A Commentary on Paul's Letter to the Church of Ephesus by Wacaster, Tom pg. 465
45 The Pulpit Commentary, Electronic Database. Copyright © 2001, 2003, 2005, 2006 by Biblesoft, Inc. All rights reserved.
46 Thayer, J. H. (1889). A Greek-English lexicon of the New Testament: being Grimm's Wilke's Clavis Novi Testamenti. New York: Harper & Brothers.
47 Kittel, G., Bromiley, G. W., & Friedrich, G. (Eds.). (1964–). Theological dictionary of the New Testament. Grand Rapids, MI: Eerdmans.
48 Vine, W. E., Unger, M. F., & White, W., Jr. (1996). Vine's Complete Expository Dictionary of Old and New Testament Words. Nashville, TN: T. Nelson.
49 Notes on Ephesians from the World Video Bible School pg. 126
50 Barnes' Notes, Electronic Database Copyright © 1997, 2003, 2005, 2006 by Biblesoft, Inc. All rights reserved.
51 Coffman's Bible Commentary, Copyright © 1971-1993 by ACU Press, Abilene Christian University. All rights reserved.
52 Notes on the Book of Ephesians by Deaver, Roy C. pg. 114
53 Adam Clarke's Commentary, Electronic Database. Copyright © 1996, 2003, 2005, 2006 by Biblesoft, Inc. All rights reserved.
54 Commentary on the Epistle to the Ephesians by Lipscomb, David pg. 127; Gospel Advocate Company Nashville, TN 1939
55 Henry, M. (1994). Matthew Henry's commentary on the whole Bible: complete and unabridged in one volume (p. 2319). Peabody: Hendrickson.

# Philippians

*by*

*Donny Weimar*

---

## Introduction

The city of Philippia was located in Thrace. It was once Called Kreenides, which means fountains. The community was near the Northern extremity of the Aegean Sea. Fortified by Philipp of Macedon, it came to be called after the man. Philippi was called a colony because of the many followers of Anthony who colonized there. Gold and silver mines mines were in the vicinity, giving a measure of wealth to the citizenry. It extended from the mountains on the North East toward the South and Southeast. Now lying in ruins, three ruined towers mark the place where the fortress once stood. There is evidence of private dwellings found by archeologists. Amid the ruins there is something of a semi-circular shape, where some scholars think Paul and Silas were beaten.

## The Founding of the Church of Christ at Philippi

"Come over into Macedonia, and help us" (Acts 16:11-15) was the cry from the one who appeared to Paul, Silas and Timothy. While on his second missionary journey, the three men answered the call and travelled into the region. There they made the first converts on European soil. Lydia and her household became Christians, as did the Philippian jailor with his household (Acts 16:16-34).

## Occasion of Writing the Letter

Paul is in prison and the Philippian brothers and sisters sent Epaphroditus to minister to his physical needs. The church has partnered with him to spread and suffer for the cause of Christ. Mean spirited brothers antagonize the church and attempt to cause Paul more pain. The apostle writes the colonial church with words of encouragement, love and thanksgiving. He impresses upon them the importance of relying on God to overcome their spiritual and physical trials. A positive spiritual attitude goes a long way.

## Time and Place of Writing

Like Ephesians, it is the general consensus that Philippians was penned during the two year imprisonment of the apostle Paul, from Rome.

## The Outline of Philippians

I. Christ, the believer's life rejoicing in spite of suffering (1:1-30)
   A. Salutation (1:1-7)
   B. Joy triumphing over suffering (1:8-30)
II. Christ the believer's pattern, rejoicing in lowly service (2:1-30)
   A. Exhortation to unity and meekness (2:1-4)
   B. The sevenfold self-humbling of Christ (2:5-8)
   C. The exaltation of Jesus (2:9-11)
   D. The outworking of the in-working salvation (2:12-16)
   E. The apostolic example (2:17-30)
III. Christ, object of the believer's faith, desire, and expectation (3:1-21)
   A. Warning against Judaizers (3:1-3)
   B. Warning against trusting in legal righteousness (3:4-6)
   C. Christ, object of the believer's faith for righteousness (3:7-9)
   D. Christ, object of the believer's desire for fellowship in resurrection power (3:10-14)
   E. The appeal for unity in the walk (3:15-16)
   F. But truth is not to be compromised for the sake of unity (3:17-19)
   G. Christ, object of the believer's expectation (3:20-21)

IV. Christ, the believer's strength, rejoicing over anxiety (4:1-23)
    A. Exhortation to unity and joy (4:1-4)
    B. The secret of the peace of God (4:5-7)
    C. The presence of the God of peace (4:8-9)
    D. The victory over anxious care (4:10-23)[1]

## CHAPTER 1

# Philippians
## *by*
## *Donny Weimar*

ଔଓ

## Philippians One: Introduction

Paul suffers. The Philippians partner with him. From the shackles of imprisonment, Paul writes to his brethren.

## Philippians 1:1-7: Salutation

Philippians 1:1-2 "Paul and Timotheus, the servants of Jesus Christ, to all the saints in Christ Jesus which are at Philippi, with the bishops and deacons: 2 Grace be unto you, and peace, from God our Father, and from the Lord Jesus Christ." "The servants of Jesus Christ." The Greek δοῦλοι, here rendered servant, may have the meaning of slave. This is not any slave, but a bond-slave to Jesus Christ. This type of slave is one who has chosen to indenture life to his master, for life. Paul and Timotheus (Timothy) then here consider themselves to be voluntarily enslaved to the Christ. However, Jesus considers all his followers as friends. "No longer do I call you slaves, for the slave does not know what his master is doing; but I have called you friends, for all things that I have heard from My Father I have made known to you" (John 15:15 NASB). It may be understood, then that rather than viewing themselves as enslaved to self, Satan or sin the writer considers himself as a slave – a mark of humble obedience.

"To all the saints in Christ Jesus." Saint (ἅγιος) refers to a consecrated thing. The epistle, letter, is therefore written explicitly to all the sacred or holy people living in Philippi. Such people are said to be in Christ, which places a status or abiding presence where holiness is imputed. Since Christians are the only ones to have had sins forgiven in Christ, it must be they to whom the letter is penned. Implicitly, the epistle is communicated to all believers, as it is principally applicable to believers today (all people are amendable to its requirements).

"The bishops and deacons." Scriptural qualifications for bishops and deacons are given in 1st Timothy 3. Bishop is synonymous with overseer or as commonly known in churches of Christ as elder. The office is one of plurality. Elders are charged with the responsibility of seeing that things are done by the authorization of the ordinances of New Testament. These men also have the final word in matters of opinion regarding church affairs. The first century church does not have city and regional levels of government, as did the Jewish synagogue and synod. No hierarchy goes above the overseers, except to the Chief Shepherd, who is High Priest (Hebrews 7).

"Grace be unto you, and peace, from God our Father, and from the Lord Jesus Christ." The common greeting is a blessing from the preachers but is genuinely inspired by God. Unmerited favor and peace that surpasses human comprehension are received ultimately only from God and His unique Son. Peace is of a spiritual kind, as this Roman colony would endure affliction and tribulation consequent to their conversion to the Messiah.

Philippians 1:3-6 "I thank my God upon every remembrance of you, 4 Always in every prayer of mine for you all making request with joy, 5 For your fellowship in the gospel from the first day until now; 6 Being confident of this very thing, that he which hath begun a good work in you will perform it until the day of Jesus Christ" "I thank my God upon every remembrance of you." Gratitude is the attitude of the suffering apostle. This sentiment is inspired, but personally driven. Paul is grateful for the growing converts. Any preacher who is genuine in his evangelism is humbly thankful for souls won to Christ. It is the evangelist's pleasure to learn that those who first came to Christ have pressed on in the faith, even in the face of persecution and hardship.

"Always in every prayer of mine for you all making request with joy." Praying for the fortitude of his brethren's faith comes natural to one whose heart is set for the proclamation of the Gospel. The Philippi church of Christ made it easy for Paul to make supplication. He was not in the least anxious about her loyalty. There is an acronym for J.O.Y. that I don't know where originated. Jesus first. Others second. Yourself last. With certainty this epitomized Paul's spirit, as he wrote to edify and encourage the same.

"For your fellowship in the gospel from the first day until now." Many misconstrue the term fellowship as a social gather. The definition of the Greek, κοινωνία, is a partnership of joint participation between individuals.

Some modern Bible versions translate the word as partner or participation straightly. In the context of this epistle, the Philippians have blessed Paul and other imprisoned saints with earthly provisions. Their physical support, coupled with spiritual faithfulness, grants fellowship in the proclamation of the Gospel. The apostle Paul writes to exhort continued participation in the carrying out of the Great Commission to the world around them. As such, the colonial church would suffer persecution as well (1:29). The first day of their fellowship may be understood in two ways. Either it is the joint operation of evangelism in support of Paul beginning his Gentile ministry, or the initial conversion to Christ, marking the beginning of a life that would only end in the passing from the temporal world. For every end there is a new beginning. But, for every beginning there is not always an end.

"Being confident of this very thing, that he which hath begun a good work in you will perform it until the day of Jesus Christ." The good work is perpetual. The Greek text here renders a "perpetual" action on God's behalf. It is worked in the Christian. God's love brought the Messiah. His grace heals the sin sick. New growth comes to the individual soul and grows the entire body of believers. Faith works by love (Galatians 5:6). The faithful believer is alive and will not die. The work of salvation comes to its final fruition with the day of Christ. It is a day of deliverance, a day of reckoning. The Spirit of Christ works in the believer to bring spiritual stamina and refreshing hope to its full result of completion in Christ, at the day of His coming. (Compare Philippians 4:13)

Philippians 1:7 "Even as it is meet for me to think this of you all, because I have you in my heart; inasmuch as both in my bonds, and in the defence and confirmation of the gospel, ye all are partakers of my grace." "Even as it is meet for me to think this of you all." The King James Version's meet is archaic for agreeable. Also, the Greek translates from φρονέω, as "I am persuaded." The King James' rendering of think is a closer translation than some modern versions, which give the rendering feel. Actually, rendering the translation as opinion could more closely give the meaning. The reader of today's versions should not be afraid of Paul stating his opinion. It is his thoughts and emotions hold the Philippian church in high esteem. It is a valid statement because it is witnessed by God as true to the writer. The bottom line is Paul holds the Philippian brothers and sisters in high regard.

"I have you in my heart." This is a statement of emotion. The epistle to the Philippians is filled with emotion. Take this chapter alone.

## Phil. 1:4, 25 – Joy

Phil. 1:8 – Yearning (long after) Phil. 1:8 – Affection (in the bowels)
Phil. 1:14, 28 – Unafraid

Phil. 1:15 – Envy

Phil. 1:18 – Rejoice

Phil 1:20 – Unashamed and Courage

Phil. 1:23 – Desire

Paul affirms his love, both obligated ἀγάπη and affectionate φιλέω to the brethren; this is for a good reason.

"...inasmuch as both in my bonds, and in the defence and confirmation of the gospel, ye all are partakers of my grace." The saints proved their consecration by their union with Paul's suffering and preaching. Notice bonds is plural. He is bound by fetters and faith. Imprisoned in a Roman cell has not stopped God's work. Just as the Jerusalem church had been scattered by persecution, "went everywhere preaching the word" (Acts 8:4), Paul sets forth the example of one who presses on with Divine calling to carry the Gospel everywhere he went. So too, the church at Philippi set the example of imitating an apostle in perseverance. Epaphroditus brings material support, almost costing his life (Philippians 2:25f). The brothers and sisters of the local congregation were the first to come to Christ in the Macedonian region (Acts 16). From the get-go they support the apologetics and validity of the Good News found exclusively in Christ. It is in these ways that they are considered "partakers" with Paul in grace. As it has been eluded, faith works by love (Galatians 5:6). So too, Christians are saved by grace through a living faith (Ephesians 2:8-9 + James 2:26).

## Philippians 1:8-30: Joy Triumphing Over Suffering

Philippians 1:8 "For God is my record, how greatly I long after you all in the bowels of Jesus Christ." "For God is my record, how greatly I long after you all in the bowels of Jesus Christ." It is already established that Paul holds the Philippian believers in high regard. While this may be his personal opinion, it is witnessed by God's record. The apostle would not have been permitted to write a lie by the inspiration of the Holy Spirit. "Bowels" are literal translation of σπλάγχνον but have the more accurate rendering in a metaphor for affection as many contemporary versions translate.

Philippians 1:9-11 "And this I pray, that your love may abound yet more and more in knowledge and in all judgment; 10 That ye may approve things that are excellent; that ye may be sincere and without offence till the day of Christ; 11 Being filled with the fruits of righteousness, which are by Jesus Christ, unto the glory and praise of God." "And this I pray, that your love may abound yet more and more in knowledge and in all judgment." Paul is a prayer warrior. He already states afore that he prays for the church at his every remembrance. Now, he gets even more specific. For love to abound increasingly, it takes following through with what is known to be the LORD's will. This takes Bible study and adherence to the doctrines of Christ. The world is amenable and will be held accountable to the words of Christ on the last Day (John 12:48). More than that, the Bible is God's lesson manual on how to love. Learning to love as Jesus would have us, takes application of the law of faith. Read John 14:15 and John 15:14, for examples of the call to love biblically. The KJV rendering judgment, from αἴσθησις, is a teaching of perception and discernment. The context here does not connote the type of judgment that results in condemnation. It refers to spiritual insight during physical trial, a biblical wisdom. The New Testament calls for godliness and the ability to decipher between right and wrong on the basis of biblical understanding.

"That ye may approve things that are excellent; that ye may be sincere and without offence till the day of Christ." Approval here refers to that which comes after trial. While insufficient by itself, sincerity is essential to genuine faith. Many sincere people will not be approved in the day of Christ. However, sincerity wrapped with the innocence of holiness will stand unabashed. Hence, saints are to be without offence. 1st John will elucidate that any persons who claim to be without sin by their own accord make God out to be a liar. All people have sinned and must remain in the process of penitence. The day of Christ is a day to look forward to, because of the animosity ensued by fallacious brothers. The bottom line is that those who sincerely belong to Christ are to remain blameless by Gospel standards until the Judgment.

"Being filled with the fruits of righteousness, which are by Jesus Christ, unto the glory and praise of God." The Textus Receptus, the base text for the KJV has καρπwn, plural for fruits. "The Greek New Testament 4th edition," published by United Bible Societies, has καρπόn. Hence, the difference between the TR and the UBS is that the former is plural, "fruits," while the

UBS reads singular, fruit. The reason this is noteworthy is that the fruit of the Holy Spirit is one but multifaceted (see Galatians 5:22-23). There is solidarity in right living for those who walk not after the flesh, but rather according to the Spirit (Romans 8). Such fruit comes exclusively through Jesus Christ. Right living may be attained by anyone, but completion of a sincerely active faith is finalized only in Christ. The glory and praise of God is realized by those who persevere through maladies and martyrdom.

Philippians 1:12-14 "But I would ye should understand, brethren, that the things which happened unto me have fallen out rather unto the furtherance of the gospel; 13 So that my bonds in Christ are manifest in all the palace, and in all other places; 14 And many of the brethren in the Lord, waxing confident by my bonds, are much more bold to speak the word without fear." "But I would ye should understand, brethren." Advancing the Gospel is the goal. The furtherance is contextually a strong advancement of the Gospel. No matter their plight, Christians is in they must keep Jesus preeminent in life. Whether it is imprisonment like Paul, sickness like Epaphroditus, or anything else, a true believer trusts God to the point of dying in His name (see Revelation 2:10 for example). Paul wants readers to comprehend the bigger picture. Life is not about the natural life but the spiritual journey. God providentially works through an evangelist to save souls regardless of the physical welfare of the proclaiming worker of the Lord. God wins the soul who fights to the end of its temporal world. We will stand approved if we approve of that for which we stand. What happened to Paul brought about the salvation of souls. When Christians maintain the right motive, attitude and emphasis they will be assured of salvation: their own and those whom they convert.

"So that my bonds in Christ are manifest in all the palace, and in all other places." In Acts 16, Paul and Silas sing hymns of praise to God while imprisoned and in shackles. The entire dungeon is listening. God causes an earthquake but the prisoners do not flee. The jailor was stopped from suicide. He now sought his salvation with fear and trembling. The result was a new member in the congregation of believers. The Word carries on through the love of Gospel teachers, who have the joy of Christ despite the situation they are in. Providential works of God still moves in mysterious ways."

"And many of the brethren in the Lord, waxing confident by my bonds, are much more bold to speak the word without fear." Perfect love drives away fear. The Philippian brethren became emboldened by Paul's confident example. They witnessed the conversion of people in both high and low social statuses. Paul instilled a positive attitude in them. No matter the dire straits he was in, he preached. Just as he exhorted the Corinthians, "Follow me as I follow Christ" (1 Corinthians 11:1), here too his courage is contagious. The Gospel becomes known even to the whole Praetorian Guard. This apostle is a nonstop evangelizing machine. Now the local church is at work in the world around her.

Philippians 1:15-18 "Some indeed preach Christ even of envy and strife; and some also of good will: 16 The one preach Christ of contention, not sincerely, supposing to add affliction to my bonds: 17 But the other of love, knowing that I am set for the defence of the gospel. 18 What then? notwithstanding, every way, whether in pretence, or in truth, Christ is preached; and I therein do rejoice, yea, and will rejoice." "Some indeed preach Christ even of envy and strife." Admittedly not all, but some of the debates that have been conducted over the past few decades have had an air of rivalry between opposite positions. Two brothers going at one another void of love, let alone gentility does not measure up to the higher calling to defend the Gospel against false spirits (see for example 1 John 4:1). Biting one another is the curse of dogs. Envy is characteristic of those who promote themselves above the ranks of humility. Strife is the friction that runs visitors away and closes dying church's doors. Paul was willing to undergo the added stress of ambitious brethren. It is most humbling to learn to be content with life, as it is. Rejoicing in the face of strong tribulation is certainly a challenge. Those who speak the truth in love see the bigger picture. It is the picture of ultimate deliverance and salvation.

"But the other of love, knowing that I am set for the defence of the gospel." From the ancient language ἀπολογία brings with it the importance of standing strong in defending the truth against falsehood. Galatians 1:6-9 speaks of angels being cursed for leading a person into error. Romans 16:17 strongly asserts that church splitters are to be marked and avoided. John wrote in his second epistle that a Christian is not to so much as greet those who do not carry the Good News. Jude tells readers to contend for the faith. Out of love, the truth must be manifested. Paul told Timothy to be gentle, enabling him to be a better teacher (2 Timothy 2:24).

"What then? notwithstanding, every way, whether in pretence, or in truth, Christ is preached; and I therein do rejoice, yea, and will rejoice." Paul looked passed the attitude of the teacher. He rejoices that Christ is preached. He averred for the way of salvation, not matter how the knowledge thereof is acquired. There is no time to judge motives. Simply get moving at advancing the Word. Paul's bottom line is that Jesus Christ is to be proclaimed. The apostle is willing to die for the mission. Paul's attitude toward advancing the

Gospel is remarkable. Beat him and he glorifies God for counting him worthy of the suffering. Bind him in prison and he sings hymns to the Savior (Acts 16). This man learns to be content in whatever state he is in (Philippians 4:11). It behooves the Christian to emulate Paul's affectionate heart. With the attitude of Christ (Philippians 2:5), the Heavenward goal (Philippians 3:14), and the power to prevail (Philippians 4:13) Paul shines forth as a man of hope and comfort. The Philippians need him.

Philippians 1:19-21 "For I know that this shall turn to my salvation through your prayer, and the supply of the Spirit of Jesus Christ, 20 According to my earnest expectation and my hope, that in nothing I shall be ashamed, but that with all boldness, as always, so now also Christ shall be magnified in my body, whether it be by life, or by death. 21 For to me to live is Christ, and to die is gain." "I know that this shall turn to my salvation through your prayer." The Greek for salvation is σωτηρία and may also be translated deliverance. There appears to be a dual meaning in the context. Paul presents his faith as secure in the Lord. He affirms his Christian salvation. In 1 Corinthians 4, he writes that he is not willing to be his own judge, but leaves that up to the LORD's judgment. Paul explains his situation is one of life and death. Deliverance from prison would avert physical death for Paul. This seems to be the more pressing issue in the contextual flow. As has already been elucidated, Paul prayed for the Philippians brothers and sisters every time his memory took him there. Here, however, it is the prayers of the saints that he requests supplication from.

"and the supply of the Spirit of Jesus Christ." The Spirit is a life sustaining individual. Whether this supply is a miraculous endowment meant to keep Paul alive and motivated or if it refers to the supernatural providence that supplies needs through others like Epaphroditus and Timothy, is unclear. Nevertheless, the Spirit of Christ, along with the prayers of righteous people, will revive the apostle. He anticipates seeing them personally, face to face.

"According to my earnest expectation and my hope, that in nothing I shall be ashamed, but that with all boldness, as always, so now also Christ shall be magnified in my body, whether it be by life, or by death." There is no shame for the one who tells the truth. Paul expects he will glorify God – whether by martyrdom or by release from prison. Either way he is bold to say that Christ is magnified by his body. The spiritual image he presents is consistently godly. Paul's boasts never come out of self-interest. He brags not in himself but in the one who saves.

"For to me to live is Christ, and to die is gain." That's faith. Paul is so zealous for serving God that his life is completely enveloped with Christ-likeness. The statement declares the purpose of the believer. Consider this from Galatians 2:20, "I am crucified with Christ: nevertheless I live; yet not I, but Christ liveth in me: and the life which I now live in the flesh I live by the faith of the Son of God, who loved me, and gave himself for me." When the Philippian brethren come to the point of understanding that the entire purpose of life is to glorify God, all else is less important. Concerning death, it is a blessing to the faithful child of God. "And I heard a voice from heaven saying unto me, Write, Blessed are the dead which die in the Lord from henceforth: Yea, saith the Spirit, that they may rest from their labours; and their works do follow them" (Revelation 14:13).

Philippians 1:22-26 "But if I live in the flesh, this is the fruit of my labour: yet what I shall choose I wot not. 23 For I am in a strait betwixt two, having a desire to depart, and to be with Christ; which is far better: 24 Nevertheless to abide in the flesh is more needful for you. 25 And having this confidence, I know that I shall abide and continue with you all for your furtherance and joy of faith; 26 That your rejoicing may be more abundant in Jesus Christ for me by my coming to you again." "yet what I shall choose I wot not." The context seems to present Paul with having a choice between life and death. He wants to depart and be with Christ. That is the chief goal of every growing believer. It is as he states, "far better." As though reasoning within himself as he writes the letter, Paul's faith and zeal gives him the confidence to press on with life in the temporal world.

"Nevertheless to abide in the flesh is more needful for you." Paul always put other's needs ahead of his own. He is persuaded that it is for the betterment of the church of Christ at Philippi that he remains alive in the flesh.

"And having this confidence, I know that I shall abide and continue with you all for your furtherance and joy of faith." Paul's faith is that his deliverance from prison is forthcoming and the result will be the edification of the church. It may be asked whether any person is promised to be happy in this life. Perhaps, things may look quite bleak. Yet, there is a joy in Christ that surpasses human intellect. The physical trials Christians undergo may be seen as a spiritual exercise unto greater godliness. When mayhem happens a person has a choice. One may either push God away or draw near and dear to Him. The joy of faith is furthered by those among the children of God who endure opposition, adversity and tribulation.

"That your rejoicing may be more abundant in Jesus Christ for me by my coming to you again." Celebrating the release of Paul from prison is a cause for abundant rejoicing. He trusts in their prayerful petitions for his deliverance. Sometimes Christians underestimate prayer. It is true that God already knows our needs before we ask Him. Perhaps, it is God teaching us to rely on and trust Him. He expects us to petition Him.

Philippians 1:27 "Only let your conversation be as it becometh the gospel of Christ: that whether I come and see you, or else be absent, I may hear of your affairs, that ye stand fast in one spirit, with one mind striving together for the faith of the gospel." "Only let your conversation be as it becometh the gospel of Christ." The King James Version is archaic here. The issue is not conversation as though people were talking to one another. This verse refers to the manner of life. Philippians addresses the way a believer thinks, feels and behaves. As the late Johnny Ramsey would say, it comes down to attitude, motive and emphasis. "Becometh" is to be understood as worthiness. The idea is captured in Romans 6, "What shall we say then? Shall we continue in sin, that grace may abound? God forbid. How shall we, that are dead to sin, live any longer therein?" Crucifixion with Christ starts a new life in Christ (Galatians 2:20).

"whether I come and see you, or else be absent, I may hear of your affairs, that ye stand fast in one spirit, with one mind striving together for the faith of the gospel." It's possible that Paul could be hindered from going to see the Philippians, at this juncture. But, that's not the point. When there is an authority figure present, people tend to listen and heed instruction, rebuke and exhortation. Paul writes to affirm the importance of a good reputation even in his absence. He writes for them to stand fast in one spirit. Having a common attitude as that of the mind of Christ, (Philippians 2:5) is imperative to right living. Too, realizing that a Christian is not in the battle alone is promising. Striving together for the faith of the Gospel clearly demarcates a congregational effort to grow. Bear one another's burdens says Galatians 6:2. Getting through tough times is less difficult when the lesson is learned to depend upon one another.

Philippians 1:28-30 "And in nothing terrified by your adversaries: which is to them an evident token of perdition, but to you of salvation, and that of God. 29 For unto you it is given in the behalf of Christ, not only to believe on him, but also to suffer for his sake; 30 Having the same conflict which ye saw in me, and now hear to be in me." "And in nothing terrified by your adversaries." The reader will recall Jesus' words, "And fear not them which kill the body, but are not able to kill the soul: but rather fear him which is able to destroy both soul and body in hell" (Matthew 10:28). The saints have the bigger picture. Since the Christians' true citizenship is in Heaven, we are not afraid of the things people can do to us. Persecution will be unleashed against the church at Philippi, but they will endure. Paul has set the bar and these brethren will rise to the calling.

"For unto you it is given in the behalf of Christ, not only to believe on him, but also to suffer for his sake." Paul had been appointed to endure suffering. Now, the call is beckoning the local congregation. The Master teaches there are blessings for those who are persecuted (Matthew 5:10-12). He tells His disciples to count it joy when afflicted. God bragged on Job. The man of God overcame and was blessed. When the Christian faces hardship, the best remedy is to be persuaded that God is able to deliver. Why do bad things happen to good people? Why not? Jesus suffered. The martyrs suffered. Are we superior to them? Not in the slightest are Christians any better than the Captain of their salvation. By holding up under stress, Christians glorify the God of all comfort (2 Corinthians 1:3). Jesus promises rest for the forlorn soul (Matthew 11:29).

"Having the same conflict which ye saw in me, and now hear to be in me." Conflicted Christians may follow Paul's example, as he follows Christ (1 Corinthians 11:1). Acts 14:22 reads, "we must through much tribulation enter into the kingdom of God." Again, Scripture states "Yea, and all that will live godly in Christ Jesus shall suffer persecution" (2 Timothy 3:12). It practically seems innate that many righteous people will enter trials testing faith.

## Philippians: Application Summary

You and I may suffer in similar ways as did the early church. The guiding principles of finding encouragement during trial remain the same. We must encourage one another through the roughest of times. Some of us face financial ruin; some of us have illnesses; others have lost family or friends to a catastrophe. Putting the purpose of living as that of glorifying God, we have no fear of physical distress. It may cause us pains or heart ache. Yet, we press on to the high calling of God. Christians soar above mediocrity. Anybody can encounter affliction and tribulation. Only the faithful Christian may find the power to endure suffering. To live is Christ. To die is gain. Trust God.

As I sit typing this lectureship commentary, I identify with the need for encouragement. Like many others, I have encountered physical, emotional and mental battles. A part of my suffering is the major lows of depression. It is not easy to "pull yourself up by the boot straps," as they harshly say. The book of Philippians offers some special remedies for whatever we are battling. When a major crises ensues, we must do these things (based on Philippians chapter one). First, keep a positive attitude. Things could always be worst; that's true. Sister Pat Hollingsworth, of Laurel, Delaware, once said to me "We are too blessed to be depressed." That stuck with me. Second, be a source of comfort for other suffering people. There is a secret to feeling joy when in a dark dire place. God comforts us when we in turn comfort others (2 Corinthians 1). We receive comfort from brethren. We receive comfort from the Spirit of Christ (by whatever means you believe He operates). If we will come to realize that we are not alone to fight major battles, we will be all the stronger. Third, when we are tested we need to do exactly what Paul does in Philippians chapter one. That is, pray. Pray for others who are suffering. Fourth, get busy. A church that does nothing dies with nothing. Let us support our evangelists. Let us learn from them. Jesus is a great and shining Light. He illuminates those residing in the darkness of sorrow and sin. God is not dead. He still changes lives. By His strength we will make it.

## Chapter 2

# Philippians

*by*

*Gregg Knight*

## Philippians Two: Introduction

"I want to change the world." How about just a small part around you? Then be like Jesus! Did He not change the whole world? Do as Paul says here in Philippians chapter two by taking on the mind of Christ, verse 5, and see the difference you can make in all the people around you!

It is all because Paul was willing to answer "the Macedonian Call" do we have the gospel first preached in Europe. The invitation of "come over and help us" (Acts 16:9) leads to the writing of this "inspired thank you letter" (4:10, 14-15).

In this epistle, we witness Paul's heart was for all people, his countrymen (Rom. 10:1), the lost and especially for God's people. On his second mission trip he wanted to see how Christians fared. This epistle shows his love and concern for the church in Philippi. Maybe we could think of this as his church home even though it was Antioch that sent him out, Acts 14.

Put yourself into the shoes of those who anxiously listened to the reading of this epistle. With your imagination see the joy and encouragement they must have received from every verse. When he calls them, "his beloved brethren whom I long to see, my joy and crown…my beloved" (4:1), how it must have reminded them of the connection he made with them before! Local preachers have the same opportunity to "endear" themselves to each member of the congregation. If you don't know the names of every member, their children and grandchildren, you better get to visiting!

As chapter one concludes, verse 27 encourages us "stand fast in one spirit, with one mind striving together for the faith of the gospel." We need to ask if our efforts are to unite, to remain in fellowship, and to walk in the faith? Paul warned the brethren in Galatia of the danger of not getting along or we could turn out like dogs "bitting and devouring each other" and end up destroying each other, (Galatians 5:15).

Just think what the world could be like if we all adhered to Paul's words in Philippians 2. Just think what the church would be like if we lived by Paul's words! Do you think we could be more influential and productive than we have been in the past? Yes, and many times over could we see the fruit of our labor!

For our examination of chapter two, may we divide it into four sections:

"What It Takes to Stand United", 2:1-4.
"Think Like Jesus", 2:5-11.
"Endeavor to Please God" - 2:12-18.
"Make Me a Servant" - 2:19-30.

## Philippians 2:1-4: What It Takes to Stand United

As we think of what it takes to stand united, the old adage "easier said than done" reminds us how difficult it actually is to accomplish. Yet, with faith in God and His word, "all things are possible" so we are without excuse to not succeed in uniting with fellow believers. The stability and strength we gain from fellow Christians will help us face opponents and obstacles in life. Let us look now at some of these attributes that Paul mentions in verse one.

"consolation in Christ" (KJV) - The greek literally means "calling alongside", "exhortation" (ASV),"encouragement (NAS, ESV). We all know what it means to have someone walk by our side, being ready to support, help and defend us. This is exactly what we have in Christ! He walks beside us and is with us every step. Am I like Him in return? If my life in Christ is true then I have to be of like kind for someone else! Are you that kind of person?

"comfort of love" Similar to the first, it can mean "incentive" (RSV); . What kind of love have you received? Is what you offer to others the kind that is gentle and easy with the results of taking them "out of the snare of the devil" (2 Timothy 2:24-26)?

"fellowship of the Spirit" What is meant here? Is it the human spirit or the Holy Spirit? Since we are talking about unity and unity is the coming together of human beings to live for God and in Christ, it is the outcome we should consider here. When we are baptized, we all received God's Spirit as a gift (Acts 2:38). That act of obedience unites us together automatically when we are added to the body (1 Cor. 12:13; Acts 2:47). Notice how Paul ends his second epistle to Corinth as he mentions the action of the Godhead in our lives. He speaks of the action of the Spirit as a "communion" (2 Cor. 13:14). So the "fellowship" of human spirits is a product brought on by the work of the Holy Spirit.

"bowels and mercies" The ASV offers "tender mercies and compassions." It is very hard to treat someone unkind if they have shown us love. Loving actions produce love, friendship and fellowship. "Beloved, if God so loved us, we ought also to love one another" (1 Jn. 4:11; 21).

Paul had shown them "affection and compassion (1:8). He is now going to ask them for a specific action in return! It is not "if" but "since" these things are yours, then "fulfill" my request. Does he have the authority to command certain actions from these readers? Yes, but we realize when people are willing to respond then the result lasts much longer and has a chance to become part of their traits and characteristics! Instead of the attitude of "have to", change it to "I want to" and see the difference in results.

How are they to "fulfill" this entreaty for peace and unity? He tells them to "be likeminded." How are our minds to be alike? It happens when we concentrate on the same thing. I really like the way David Roper puts it: "The apostle wanted them united in attention (in thinking, "being of the same mind) and attitude ("united in spirit")....He also wanted them united in affection ("maintaining the same love") and aim ("intent on one purpose"). Paul wanted the Philippians to be one in heart, mind, and life." (Truth For Today Commentary: Ephesians and Philippians, David Roper, p. 435). Remember what Paul said to Corinth, that "by the name of our Lord Jesus Christ, that you speak the same thing, and that there be no divisions among you; but that you be perfectly joined together in the same mind and the same judgment" (1 Cor. 1:10). Later in the same epistle, he says that there "should be no schism in the body; but that the members should have the same care for one another" (12:25). Anywhere this does not happen, then someone is either ignorant or they are not putting effort into getting along. Is it not sad to see at least one or two old sore heads in every congregation? This kind of faction and opposition in a congregation or the brotherhood is too often seen. It certainly is a big foe to conquer, but with the spirit of "lowliness of mind" found in Jesus Christ, we can imitate and win. What a great disappoint it must be for God and His son to witness division and disharmony in the world and here in the United States. It goes completely against what our Lord prayed for in John 17. Let us "endeavor to keep the unity of the Spirit in the bond of peace" (Eph. 4:3). Surely "if a kingdom is divided against itself, that kingdom cannot stand" (Mark 3:24). What would the world be like if we carried out verse 3 and 4? Putting others first and considering them of more value will lead us to do what Paul said in 1 Corinthians 9:22: "I am become all things to all men, that I may by all means save some." The second Great Commandment says, "You shall love your neighbor as yourself" (Matt. 22:39). What would happen if we loved them "better" than ourselves? That is the point he is bringing us to. Consider the "interests" of the other fellow first and watch him faint, because that conduct is just not found in the world. But we Christians are to be "peculiar" and distinct in the world, (1 Peter 2:9).

## Philippians 2:5-11: Think Like Jesus

Where do I look to find an example, to imitate and follow? Paul challenges us to look to Jesus and to think like Him, verse 5. Do this and the result will be unity. Do this and you will walk like Jesus (1 Pet. 2:21). Paul asked his readers to "imitate me as I follow Jesus Christ" ( ).

This section easily divides into two parts: the humiliation of Christ (2:6-8) and the exaltation of Christ (2:9-11). I do not claim to know all the answers of this most difficult section as much discussion and debate has taken place and will continue into the far future. There are some very valuable lessons to be learned as well. That Jesus was willing to leave heaven and come to the earth to die for us is paramount!

As one studies this section about Christ first being in Heaven, taking the form of man, and how He "emptied" Himself, you will come to the point of realization, it is going to take much more study and then you will wonder if you ever will this side of eternity. To grasp the idea of being equal to God leads us to say "never" but Jesus could claim it, but did not. Seeing how man acts on this earth, I say he is not worth dying for, but that is the difference of being human and divine. We ought to be very glad that God and HIs Son saw value in us. As we look at the words "form" and "emptied" and "equal" we turn in circles or at least I do! What does it all mean? Maybe Paul's statement in 2 Cor. 8:9 will help: "He was rich, yet for your sake He became poor." When the image of a slave or servant is drawn before our eyes, we begin to understand what Jesus voluntarily did for mankind. He "counted it joy" to go to the cross for us (Heb. 12:2). All this leads me to ask, "Why did He do it?" The Hebrew writer says Jesus being our high priest was "touched with the feeling our infirmities" so we could come to Him (4:14-16). He did it so that we would be drawn to Him (John 12:32). By becoming a curse for us (Gal. 3:13) Christ redeemed us from the curse of the law, God's wrath (2 Thess. 1:7-9).

The cross has become His crown of glory as we see God highly exalted Jesus, verse 9. He also received a name above every other name. Just listen and notice how often this name falls from the lips of man. And I am not just talking about when they abuse it with vulgarity and vanity, but when they speak honor and praise to Him and implore of Him for help and protection. Luke reminds us "there is none other name under heaven given among men, whereby we must be saved" (Acts 4:12). Paul requires us "to do all things in the name of Jesus Christ" (Col. 3:17). God placed Jesus Christ on His right side (Eph. 1:20-21) and as head of the church (1:22). Take notice that when we honor Christ in this life that we in turn honor or glorify the Father (2:11b). You do have a knee and a tongue, so use them to glorify Jesus as the Christ.

## Philippians 2:12-18: Endeavor to Please God

Who am I aiming to please in this life? If it is only self then I will receive an undesired end. Before our becoming a Christian, we learned what it meant to be one or we may have come up out of the water only a wet sinner. Several summer camps I have been to have helped show me the need to teach a person so he does know and understand. Up at Camp LUJO near Lawton, Oklahoma, they teach the "Safety Chain" (a series of scriptures) before each baptism. I like that approach and carry it into my work with personal evangelism.

It is God's will that we work to do His good pleasure (verse 13). Jesus was obedient (Heb. 5:8-9), so then His followers should also be obedient (Acts 5:29). Paul tells us what will happen if we do not obey the gospel of Christ in 2 Thessalonians 1:8, they "will be punished with everlasting destruction from the presence of the Lord and from the glory of His power…"

It is easier to obey your mother or father when they are standing over you, but let them leave the room and notice the tendency of children. Here comes war, chaos and trouble! We always said that Mother had "eyes in the back of her head" because she knew when we were up to mischief! Paul knows human nature as well. Prove your maturity by acting the same either way, in absence or in presence! Surely God knows and sees and we can not fool Him.

There is nothing more horrible than when people are complaining. Read 1 Corinthians 10:10 and see what happens to those who murmur. Paul warns us not to be complaining, murmuring or disputing. What must have been taking place in this congregation for Paul to tell them to stop arguing and fighting? Do you know of any congregation in the brotherhood without such activity going on among its members? Satan has plenty of hold on many (Luke 22:3). Just as Jesus prayed for Peter's faith not to fail (22:32), He desires the same from us! James tells us to "resist the devil, and he will flee from you" (4:7). Remember what would happen to the church in Galatia? Act like dogs or brute, biting and devouring one another, then you will be consumed one of another, (5:15). Paul calls for us to reach a Christian character, that of being "blameless." Have you lived in such a way that no one is able to "point a finger" at you to criticize? Jesus wants us to be "innocent as doves" (Matt. 10:16). The only way you and I will ever be blameless is through our repentance, (1 John 1:8-10). Peter tells us to live in such a way that even if men speak evil of us, that no one believes them, because we have lived differently by having a "good conversation" (1 Peter 3:16-17).

This passage closes with Paul's request to "rejoice with me" (v. 18). Can you be cheerful no matter the circumstances? James tells us to "count it all joy when you fall into manifold temptations" (1:2). Did Paul know what was going to happen to him? Surely he had some idea because of all the persecution that came his way. He could say to Timothy, "endure afflictions" (2 Tim. 4:5) because of what he endured. May we stand strong so we can say with confidence "I have fought a good fight, I have finished my course, I have kept the faith" (4:7). "Be thou faithful to the end of life" may mean my dying. It might mean you have to take a stand and be willing to pay the ultimate price. We can rejoice in that!

## Philippians 2:19-30: Make Me a Servant

People who are volunteers inspire society. What makes them serve? Do I have the ability and desire to be like these two examples Paul writes about? In 2:19-30 we read about Timothy and Epaphroditus.

Paul had no man like Timothy that cared for them like he cared. He had faith in Timothy to love them the same as he. Earned trust needs to be protected with consistent action and service! Every preacher needs such a "co-laborer" to fall upon in difficult times. Do you have such a one? Are you such a one?

David had his Jonathan, (1 Sam. 18:1). We love to read about their relationship. We can learn so much from them. We can learn to serve people, but how about through Jesus Christ? Is it a position, a job or a passion for souls? Timothy had proved himself. Those at Philippi knew him and trusted him because he had been with them several times. When we spend time with people, a connection is made and they learn that we care about them. They then will care about what we say and preach. Paul sending Timothy was like going himself. When we "go into all the world" we are to be Jesus!

Do you have a need for a worker? Then find yourself a servant! An elder is a person that has already proven himself in service. That's who we are talking about now as Paul calls Epaphroditus a "servant of God."

Now throw in the picture the handling of money. Who do you ask to fill the position now? Paul knew what the "love of money" could do to a person. He still wants Epaphroditus to serve! That is an amazing compliment about the character of this man. Another compliment is that he knew how to go beyond the call of duty. He stayed in Rome with Paul to serve him instead of returning home after the assignment was finished. He also was the type to be unconcerned for his own welfare as he nearly died serving Paul. Will I die on a foreign field? Will you die in the service of the Lord? Paul would have enjoyed continued visitation from him but knew the need for his return! What would the brethren think of him for returning so soon? Would they label him a "John Mark?" Paul is careful to describe Epaphroditus' actions and service so they would be able to "receive him in the Lord."

**CHAPTER 3**

# Philippians
## *by*
## *Paul Delgado*

ꕥ

## Philippians 3:1-3: Warning Against Judaizers

Philippians 3:1 "Finally, my brothers, rejoice in the Lord. To write the same things to you is no trouble to me and is safe for you." "rejoice in the Lord" This is Paul's central theme of the entire book. He is urging the Philippians, as the original language suggests, to have a continual joy and not let it stop. Being resilient in joy is important for the Christian walk (1 Corinthians 15:58)

Philippians 3:2 "Look out for the dogs, look out for the evildoers, look out for those who mutilate the flesh." Look out for the dogs: Paul is warning the Christians to not just keep an out for the "dogs", but is emphatically warning them to "take heed" or "beware" (KJV) of the dogs. The term dogs was a derogatory term often associated with the gentiles during this time period but was also used by the prophet Isaiah to describe false teachers (Isaiah 56:10). Paul is calling his own countrymen, the Judaizing false teachers, dogs. These were individuals that were in direct opposition to the teachings of Paul and the Gospel of Christ. Adam Clarke wrote, "The Jews, who have here the same appellative which they formerly gave to the Gentiles: because the Gentiles were not included in the covenant, they called them Dogs; and themselves, the children of the Most High. Now, they are cast out of the covenant and the Gentiles taken in; therefore they are the dogs, and the Gentiles the children." (Adam Clarke's Commentary on the Bible)

"Look out for those who mutilate the flesh." These false teachers were the Judaizing teachers that were trying to bind the teaching of circumcision on the Gentiles. (Acts 15:1; Galatians 1:6-9; Galatians 6:15)

Philippians 3:3 "For we are the circumcision, who worship by the Spirit of God and glory in Christ Jesus and put no confidence in the flesh" For we are the circumcision: Paul is delivering this blow to Judaism and those who were trying to bind it on the gentiles. When Paul was saying "we are the circumcision", he was not referring to him and his fellow Jews, he is referring to all those in Christ, emphatically including the Philippians and all gentile converts in that category. He called the Judaizing teachers, Dogs, a title used by Jews for the gentiles and he called even the Gentiles, the circumcision, a title which was exclusively and proudly herald exclusively for the Jews. The fact of the matter is this, All those is Christ are the spiritual Israel and are "inwardly" Jews (Romans 2:28-29). God was not just the God of Israel (read the book of Habakkuk for a further discussion on this). He is the God over all men and requires all men everywhere to repent (Acts 17:30). To the nationalistic, ethnocentric 1st century Jew this was a hard thing to comprehend.

## Philippians 3:4-6: Warning Against Trusting In Legal Righteousness

Philippians 3:4 "though I myself have reason for confidence in the flesh also. If anyone else thinks he has reason for confidence in the flesh, I have more." I myself have reason for confidence in the flesh also: (c.f. 2 Corinthians 11:18-22) Paul about to demonstrate to the Philippians how he understands the mind of the carnal false teachers, as he was one himself.

Philippians 3:5 "circumcised on the eighth day, of the people of Israel, of the tribe of Benjamin, a Hebrew of Hebrews; as to the law, a Pharisee." Circumcised on the eight day: He came from a family that was in strict adherence to the Old Law (Genesis 17:12; Leviticus 12:3) much like our Lord and Savior, Jesus (Luke 2:21).

Of the people of Israel: he wasn't a proselyte (a non-Jew who converted to Judaism), he was the real thing (Acts 22:3; 1 Corinthians 11:22) He could, physically, call Abraham, Isaac and Jacob his fathers. This was something Jews took great pride in (John 8:38-39).

Of the tribe of Benjamin: He was a direct descendant of Benjamin, one of the favored sons of Jacob (Israel; Genesis 42:4). The Tribe of Benjamin was also one of the more loyal tribes even during the beginning of a rebellious period during the United/Divided Kingdom history (1 Kings 12:21). Though the royal family of David was of the tribe of Judah, The first king of Israel, the first anointed by God was, Saul, a member of the tribe of Benjamin (1 Samuel 9:1,2;9;17;10:1). Paul is, just this brief, statement saying, "I come from a very rich history in Judaism."

A Hebrew of Hebrews: Paul was born in Tarsus, a Hellenistic (greek influenced) city, which held onto a very Hellenistic culture. Tarsus was one of the very few Greek cultured cities that rivaled Athens in their scholars, thinkers, and religion. Even though he was born in this very heathen city, Paul came from a strictly Hebrew and traditional upbringing, untainted by the outside heathen ways.

As to the Law, a Pharisee: The Pharisees were by far the stricter sect of religious leaders in Judaism. The name Pharisee means, "Those separated, meaning separated from impurity and defilement." (Israel Abrahams, Studies in Pharisaism and the Gospels) Josephus wrote, "The Pharisees are those who are esteemed most skillful in the exact explication of their laws…" (The Wars of the Jews. Book II, chapter 8.14). Paul came from the most strict sect to the law, observing it literally and closely. Hence why he was so zealous against Christianity early in its introduction.

Philippians 3:6 "as to zeal, a persecutor of the church; as to righteousness under the law, blameless." As to zeal, a persecutor of the church: referring to his very strict jewish upbringing, and his strict Pharisaical instruction under Gamilel (Acts 22:3). Before that day on the road to Damascus, Paul (Saul) was a strict follower of Judaism. There was no wonder why he would want to thwart this new teaching taught by Jewish traitors. Though this is mere speculation, it is possible he heard of (some even believe he witnessed) the 3,000 Jewish traitors that turned from the Law on the holy day of Pentecost in Acts 2. In his mind, these rebellions were probably no different than the religious rebellions he studied in the prophets (Jeremiah 6:16,17) during the wilderness wanderings (Exodus 32:8), etc. His strict view of the law was a catalyst to why he saw the need to punish those whom he felt was in violation (Acts 8:1; Acts 9:1-2). He loved his God, He loved God's law, and would be filled with indignation when those rejected its teachings.

## Philippians 3:7-9: Christ, Object of the Believer's Faith for Righteousness

Philippians 3:7 "But whatever gain I had, I counted as loss for the sake of Christ." Paul was earning a reputation of respect during his time as a Pharisee. Having studied under the top Jewish scholar of the day, getting the okay to carry out the persecutions from the High Priest (Acts 9:1).

Verses 5-6 give all the reasons why Paul should have been herald in the jewish world. And yet he counted them all loss when became a Christian.

His education; gone
His physical ancestry; meaningless
His position in the Pharisees; no more.
Eternal glory in the sight of the Father; gained.
Which do you think mattered to Paul the most?

Philippians 3:8 "Indeed, I count everything as loss because of the surpassing worth of knowing Christ Jesus my Lord. For his sake I have suffered the loss of all things and count them as rubbish, in order that I may gain Christ." I count everything as a loss because of the surpassing worth of knowing Christ Jesus…: He now moves on to the bigger picture, no longer just talking about his Jewish heritage, but everything that was cleansed in the Blood of Christ. The word "loss" is also used as the word "damaged". Paul considered everything damaged goods compared to Christ. They were worthless and had no profit. Everything without Christ is meaningless (Matthew 6:19; Ecclesiastes 1:2; 12:13). Paul considered even the pain, the suffering, the chastisement he received for rejecting the Law as nothing compared to the glory of Christ (Romans 8:18)

Philippians 3:9 "and be found in him, not having a righteousness of my own that comes from the law, but that which comes through faith in Christ, the righteousness from God that depends on faith." Justification in the eyes of God comes through faithful obedience to God's New Covenant (Romans 5:1; James 2:14-26).

## Philippians 3:10-14: Christ, Object of the Believer's Desire for Fellowship In Resurrection Power

Philippians 3:10 "that I may know him and the power of his resurrection, and may share his sufferings, becoming like him in his death." How many of us in Christ can say this is what we want? This is how much Paul loved his Lord. He wanted to understand what Christ had gone through by understanding what it meant to suffer, and to be humble. Paul was just being all talk (c.f. 2 Corinthians 11:23-28)

Philippians 3:11 "that by any means possible I may attain the resurrection from the dead." He had the hope of being raised to eternal life even if it meant going to death. He had this same hope even on trial (Acts 23:6).

Philippians 3:12 "Not that I have already obtained this or am already perfect, but I press on to make it my own, because Christ Jesus has made me his own." The joy of heaven is what was able to help the apostle press forward. The language in this passage means that even in persecution, he was going to force his way through it all to see the glory of heaven.

Philippians 3:13 Brothers, I do not consider that I have made it my own. But one thing I do: forgetting what lies behind and straining forward to what lies ahead." Brothers I do not consider that I have made it my own: Paul is saying that regardless of what he had received from Christ, he would not stop until he finished his course. Unfortunately, many individuals have gone to their graves thinking that all they simply had to do was believe, and not have to do anything towards the efforts of the Cross. Paul was active in his faith from the day he came in contact with the blood of Christ (Acts 22:16) to his very last words (2 Timothy 4:7-8).

But one thing I do: forgetting what lies behind and straining forward to what lies ahead: This is such a refreshing statement to the Christian feeling fatigued. The word "forgetting" is key to the Christian's walk. Paul's not saying he had some sort of amnesia and did not remember what he had done before, but because God had chosen to forget what Paul had done, he had no reason to cling to it anymore. Earlier on in the chapter we read of Paul's Jewish heritage and how it no longer mattered to him because he was part of the spiritual heritage (Ephesians 1:5). To forget, in the language here, is to toss out of mind by neglecting it. It's as though losing something because it wasn't secured tight enough, and yet it wasn't important to begin with. The word "straining" is like one reaching for something so precious, as if nothing else matters. It's a strong exertion. Every spiritual muscle is being used to its max, but Paul is determined and will not give up to reach "what lies ahead," Heaven.

Philippians 3:14 "I press on toward the goal for the prize of the upward call of God in Christ Jesus." There is nothing on this earth, no greater race, no greater ambition, and nothing holds any weight compared to the goal of the Christian. Why? Because there is no greater prize. Paul, living in the 1st century, was using the illustration of the footrace. From the starting point of the race, the runner is determined to reach the end. He's trained for so long, and has endured many obstacles, that to not run with all his might would be foolish.

It was the summer Olympics of 1968, held in Mexico City. John Stephen Akhwari, a Tanzanian marathon runner, had trained his whole life to see the Olympics. During the race body cramped up due to the high altitude of Mexico city, which was very different from where he trained back home. He fell hard, wounding and dislocating and his knee joint and injuring his shoulder from the high impact of a runner hitting the pavement. Mexico City, his fellow Olympians, and the entire civilized World watched as Akhwari, stood up in complete pain, and continued running, finishing in 57th place. 57 was the number total of those who completed the race, because 18 others had given up before finishing. Akhwari could have joined the 18 who had given up; because being noted in history as last place isn't something you want. The stadium was nearly empty by the time Akwhari had reached the finish line, with a small cheering section waiting for him. When he was interviewed later and asked why did he continue running, he said, "My country did not send me 5,000 miles to start the race; they sent me 5,000 miles to finish the race."

Paul's motivation for pressing on was the love of Christ, who endured the humiliation and torment of the Cross (2 Corinthians 5:14,15; Hebrews 12:1,2)

Anyone can start the race (Acts 2:38), but how many of us will finish it?

## Philippians 3:15-16: The Appeal for Unity in the Walk

Philippians 3:15 "Let those of us who are mature think this way, and if in anything you think otherwise, God will reveal that also to you." o T h i s mindset of total commitment to the cross is a mature thought pattern. It is of those who view and take seriously their spiritual well-being.

When you go to the gym, There are several different kinds of people you will see. (1) The person who comes in once in a while since they keep forgetting to cancel their membership and might as well put it to good use. But you only see them once every so often and haven't changed very much since they've started. (2) The person who comes in and basically messes with a few weights, but has no knowledge as to what they are actually doing and refuses to take any advice, for fear of seeming like a novice (even though it's obvious they are). (3) The people who seem extremely fit, but want everyone to know they're there. They yell loud, slam their heavy weights on the floor, and wait for people to notice how strong they are. (4) Then there's the person who came into the gym, overweight, but with a determination to get healthy. They come in, oblivious to most of the equipment, but refuse to back down and be intimidated, They learn, they listen to the wise advice of those who've been in their situation, and they develop self-discipline. They don't care what people think of them in regards to how silly they look as novices. They become regulars and are determined to reach their fitness goal. Soon that same portly looking fellow, because leaner and leaner and leaner as the months go by. The simple cardio workouts they couldn't endure in the past, they push through with endurance now and have even increased. Those are the successful individuals. (5) The successful Christian is the one who never gives up. He/She presses on till they reach their goal.

Philippians 3:16 "Only let us hold true to what we have attained." Do not lose sight of the race! Keep training and running harder (2 Timothy 1:13).

There is only one standard by which we are to follow. Paul knew it wasn't in the Old Law or traditions of men, that's why he counted those things are unprofitable. It's in the New Testament (Galatians 6:16).

## Philippians 3:17-19: Truth is Not to be Compromised for the Sake of Unity

Philippians 3:17 "Brothers, join in imitating me, and keep your eyes on those who walk according to the example you have in us." The Philippians are encouraged to follow Paul's example. Remember where Paul is writing this from; in prison! He could have thrown in the towel many a times on his journey but refused. If you want success follow those that are on the path of it. He wasn't just preaching success but living the life of a spiritual failure. He was consistent in his preaching (1 Corinthians 11:1; 1 Corinthians 9:27).

Philippians 3:18 "For many, of whom I have often told you and now tell you even with tears, walk as enemies of the cross of Christ." Paul is once again, warning of those who swerved from truth. These weren't just individuals who sinned and repented of it (Romans 3:23). These individuals who fell hard and were vehement enemies of Christ. They were militantly attempting to bring down the moral of the Church and distort the doctrine (2 Timothy 2:18).

The fact that Paul was moved to tears by these individuals actions shows Paul's deep love for lost souls (Romans 9:3; Acts 20:31)

Even though Paul was sorrowful and loved these brethren very much, he was unwilling to compromise. He detested sin and hated what it did to his loved ones, but did not have a bad disposition towards those souls who departed from truth.

Philippians 3:19 "Their end is destruction, their god is their belly, and they glory in their shame, with minds set on earthly things." Their god is their belly: they don't think of eternal glory like those mentioned above. they are only content when their wants and desires are met.

Spiritual people think on Spiritual things; Worldly people think Worldly things.

## Philippians 3:20-21: Christ, Object of the Believer's Expectation

Philippians 3:20 "But our citizenship is in heaven, and from it we await a Savior, the Lord Jesus Christ." The direct contrast of these false teachers and those who are true to the Race is that the mature Christian views life on an eternal basis not on a temporal one. They're not striving to live simply in the now, but realize that every moment is one step further into eternity. The Church is not some earthly organization, it is a spiritual eternal kingdom that spans the globe and time (Daniel 2:44; Ephesians 2:19). It's citizens are those who are totally in submission to Christ and His Will. We may be American (or whatever nationality) by physical birth, but the things of this nation and this earth are meaningless when compared to Christ's Kingdom.

### Colossians 3:1-3

The Christian awaits the Savior. It is a deep longing and desire to be with Him and to hear "Well done, good and faithful servant," (Matthew 25:23)

Philippians 3:21 "who will transform our lowly body to be like his glorious body, by the power that enables him even to subject all things to himself." The faithful Christian looks for the coming of His Lord and the resurrection and transformation of his body prior to entering heaven (1 Corinthians 15:51-53).

**CHAPTER 4**

# Philippians
## *by*
## *Kenny Gardner*

## Philippians 4:1-4: The Exhortation to Unity and Joy

Despite his being a prisoner at the time, the apostle Paul's epistle to his brethren at Philippi exudes with love and joy and confidence. He began the last chapter by twice referring to them as his "dearly beloved," in addition to calling them his "joy and crown." Furthermore, he was anxious to see them—he "longed for" them. He hoped they would have both the "peace of God" and the "grace" of Christ; he concluded the chapter and the epistle by expressing his desire that the "grace of our Lord Jesus Christ" would be with all of them.

The church at Philippi was a source of joy to Paul. He called them his "joy and crown," and told them how he rejoiced "greatly" because of their "care" for him. He likewise was pleased when Epaphroditus arrived with assistance for him from the Philippian brethren, which he described as a "sweet smell" and as a "sacrifice" both "acceptable" and "well-pleasing" to God. He reminded them of the joy he experienced even in the midst of harsh adversity, joy which should have refreshed their spirits and brought joy to them. He held himself up as an example of an individual who had "learned to be content" despite his circumstances: "I have learned, in whatsoever state I am, therewith to be content. I know both how to be abased, and I know how to abound: every where and in all things I am instructed both to be full and to be hungry, both to abound and to suffer need." Furthermore, Paul simply told them to rejoice: "Rejoice in the Lord always; and again I say, Rejoice."

## Philippians 4:5-9: The Secret of the Peace of God & The Presence of the God of Peace

Even by his giving them guidance and instruction, Paul was expressing his love for and confidence in the brethren there. Twice he expressed his desire that they would have the "peace of God"; if the brethren would accept and follow his instructions (and he was obviously confident they would), then the "God of peace" would be "with them," and they would have the "peace of God, which passeth all understanding" and which would "keep" their "hearts and minds through Christ Jesus." The fact that Paul hardly said anything in this final chapter in the way of rebuke shows that he had confidence that the brethren would accept his encouragements and grow spiritually.

He was, of course, concerned about Euodias and Syntyche, encouraging them to "be of the same mind in the Lord." When Paul spoke in the next verse of the women he wanted his "true yokefellow" to "help," he apparently was referring to Euodias and Syntyche; in which case they were women who had "labored" with him "in the gospel," along with Clement and others, "whose names are in the book of life."

Paul's concern for the spiritual well-being of his brother and sisters in Philippi is evident in all of his imperatives. He urged them to "stand fast in the Lord." He told them to be moderate; at least, that is what the King James Version says: "Let your moderation be known unto all men." The original Greek word here, epieikes (e)pieikh/$), means "mild" (Strong), "gracious and forbearing" (Louw and Nida), and "equitable, fair, mild, gentle" (Thayer). Vine points out that this word comes from a Greek word meaning "reasonable" and the English Standard Version renders it "reasonableness." In this passage it is translated "moderation" (KJV), "gentleness" (NKJ, NIV, NRSV), "forbearance" (ASV, RSV), "forbearing spirit" (NAS), and "graciousness" (HCSB). Many paraphrases indicate that Christians are to be unselfish, considerate, and kind.

He also told them to pray and be grateful and not worry: "Be careful for nothing; but in every thing by prayer and supplication with thanksgiving let your requests be made known unto God" (KJV). In other words, they ought not to have any "cares" (BBE) or to be "anxious" (most translation) or to "worry" (many translations and paraphrases) about anything. According to the Amplified Version, God's people should not "fret or have anxiety about anything, but in every circumstance" make their "wants know to God." They should not be "over-anxious about anything" (Weymouth). Wuest has Paul saying, "Stop worrying about even one thing." Clearly, gratitude and prayer triumph over worry.

Paul also instructs the Philippians to meditate: "Finally, brethren, whatsoever things are true, whatsoever things are honest, whatsoever things are just, whatsoever things are pure, whatsoever things are lovely, whatsoever things are of good report; if there be any virtue, and if there be any praise, think on these things" (KJV).

Things that are "honest" (KJV; Gr. semnos, semno/$) are "honorable" (ASV, NAS, RSV, MLB) or "noble" (NKJ, NIV, NEB). Vine and Thayer say they are "august, venerable," and Matthew Arnold says they are "nobly serious." They are "worthy of praise" (NCV) "reverence" (Amp) and "have honor" (BBE).

Things that are "just" (KJV, et al.) are "right" (NAS, NIV) or "upright" (BBE). The Greek adjective dikaios (di/kaio$), in its eighty-one occurrences in the New Testament, is nearly always rendered "righteous" or "just."

Things that are "pure" (nearly all English translations and paraphrases) are "holy" (BBE, D-R). The English word "holy" does come from this Greek word, hagnos, (a(gno/$).

"Lovely" things are pleasing, agreeable, and acceptable (Vine, Thayer).

Things that are "of good report" (KJV, ASV) or "of good repute" (NKJ, NAS) are "gracious" (RSV, ASV footnote), "admirable" (NIV), "commendable" (NRSV, HCSB), and "kind and winsome and gracious" (Amp). They are things that are "spoken in a kindly spirit, with good-will to others" (Thayer). The Greek word euphemos (eu&fhmo$) comes from two words, eu (eu), good, and pheme (fh/mh), a saying or report.

"Virtue" (KJV, NKJ, ASV) is "excellence" (NAS, RSV, ESV, NIV, NRSV, "moral excellence" HCSB). "Praise" (KJV) refers to anything "praiseworthy" (NKJ). "If there be" suggests that these last two qualities are "summary concepts which include whatever else should be on the list" (Barnes).

All these things Christians are told to "think on" (KJV), or "think about" (RSV ESV NIV), "meditate on" (NKJ), "let your mind dwell on" (NAS), "dwell on" (HCSB), "ponder" (NAS footnote), "cherish the thought of" (Wey), "weigh" and "fix your minds on" (Amp), and "fill your thoughts with" (NEB). The Philippians were instructed: "Don't ever stop thinking about what is truly worthwhile and worthy of praise" (CEV). "Let them be the object of your careful attention and study, so as to practise them" (Barnes). "Ponder them well and practice them faithfully. We grow like our thoughts"

(J. W. Shepherd). "Consider them seriously and shape conduct by them" (Ferguson).

Paul also expected the Philippian brethren to be learners and putting into practice what they had learned. They were to "do" what they had "learned, and received, and heard, and seen" in Paul.

In the midst of all these directives, Paul reminded the Philippians, in a rather stern way, that they were going to be held accountable for their response to his admonitions and for their conduct in general. That is the significance of his bluntly stating, "The Lord is at hand." He is "near" (NAS, NIV, NRSV, HCSB). "The expectation that the Lord Jesus will 'come,' ought to be allowed to produce moderation of our passions, in our manner of living, in our expectations of what this world can furnish, and in our desire of earthly good" (Barnes). "The Lord is Judge, and is at hand to punish" (Clarke). Matthew Henry wrote, "The consideration of our Master's approach, and our final account, should keep us from smiting our fellow-servants, support us under present sufferings, and moderate our affections to outward good. 'He will take vengeance on your enemies, and reward your patience.'"

## Philippians 4:10-23: The Victory Over Anxious Care

Finally, after these various instructions were given, Paul devoted a large portion of this chapter to a discussion of giving. He encouraged their generosity by his own example (his willingness to suffer deprivation for the cause of the gospel), and by expressing his gratitude for their concern and for their material assistance. He "rejoiced" that their "care" for him had "flourished," adding that they had "done well" by "communicating" with his afflictions, that is, by "sharing" in his "distress" (NKJ) and "affliction" (NAS). He commended them, "It was kind of you to share my trouble" (ESV). They had "contributed" to his "needs" (Amp). They had "helped" him when he "needed it" (NCV) and "had care for" him (BBE). They were the only ones who "communicated" with him "concerning giving and receiving" (KJV), sending "once and again unto [his] necessity" (KJV).

As much as Paul appreciated their assistance, and as much as he commended them, he nonetheless was willing to make whatever sacrifice was needed to spread the gospel. He had learned to accept hardship as a part of serving God as an evangelist; he had "learned" to be "content" regardless of his circumstances. He knew what it was like to "be abased" and to "abound," to be "full and to be hungry," and to "abound and to suffer need." He was certain that Christ strengthened him, and that with that strength he could handle any adversity. "I can do all things through Christ which strengtheneth me," was his calm resolve.

Accordingly, Paul explained that he encouraged their giving for their own good. He wanted them to give, not because he "desired a gift," but because, as he said, "I desire fruit that may abound to your account." According to the various English translations and paraphrases, Paul wanted "fruit" or "profit" that would "increase" or "accumulate to" their "credit" or "account." "I am looking for what may be credited to your account," he explained (NIV). He knew that by giving they would receive a "harvest of blessing" (Amp), a "reward" they would receive for their "kindness" (TLB, NLT). He wanted them to have "the good that comes from giving" (NCV), the "blessing that issues from generosity" (Mes).

Paul also pointed out that no matter what sacrifices his brethren made, God would provide for them. "My God shall supply all your need according to his riches in glory by Christ Jesus," he stressed. God would "meet" and "fully satisfy" all their "needs" (NIV, NRSV). "God takes care of me, and He will take care of you," Paul was in effect saying (NLT).

Paul's concluding remarks displayed his love for both his God and his brethren. After prompting the Philippian Christians to "salute every saint in Christ Jesus," the apostle mentioned that the brethren who were with him, and all the saints, and even some from "Caesar's household," saluted their Philippian brethren.

Paul, after praising God ("Now unto God and our Father be glory for ever and ever. Amen."), blessed his beloved Philippian brethren with his final remark: "The grace of our Lord Jesus Christ be with you all. Amen."

## Notes

1 WORDseach Outlines

# Colossians

*by*

*Donny Weimar*

## The City of Colossae

A city in Asia Minor, Colossae was in Prhyrigia Pacatiana. It was near the place where the river Lycas goes underground for about ¾ of a mile and then reemerges to join the Meander. The river has been renamed today, Gorduk. The city was about half way between Laodicea and Hieropolis. In the tenth year of the reign of Nero (66 A.D.) an earthquake destroyed Colossae along with Laodicea and Hieropolis). The community was reconstructed and named Chronos.

## Founding of the Church at Colossae

Apparently many of the saints in Colossae had not met Paul in person (Colossians 2:1). Plausibly, Epapphrus, a Gentile convert by Paul's teaching, evangelized the region to establish the Colossae church (Colossians 1:7; 4:12).

## Time and Place of Writing the Letter

It may be estimated that the letter was written about the same time as the epistle to the Philippians. In the salutation, Timothy is mentioned in the book of Colossians and in Philippians 2:19 Paul said he was hoping to send Timothy to them, as though still with the apostle. The date therefore is approximately 62 A.D., just four years before the great earthquake.

## Occasion of Writing to the Colossians

The epistle is largely a refutation of false doctrines, described by some as "Syncrestitic Philosophy." This is a convenient phrase to describe a mixture of Gnosticism, Theosophy, Materialism, and Mysticism. First and second century philosophers combined the doctrines of men like Pythagoras with Persian Mysticism and Essenic Judaism, hence the name Syncretistic.

Paul, by the Holy Spirit, expounds Christ as the Son of God and logically reveals Christ's true relation to the cosmos. He is both the head in the physical and spiritual realms. While the Gnostics taught that Christ did not have a real body, Paul made the affirmation of the Divine Nature (Godhead, KJV) and the body of Christ (Colossians 2:9).

## The Outline of Colossians

I. Introduction: The Apostolic Greeting (1:1-8)
II. The Apostle's Sevenfold Prayer (1:9-14)
III. The Exaltation of Christ (1:15-29)
    A. The Seven Superiorities of Christ (1:15-19)
    B. The Reconciling Work of Christ (1:0-3)
    C. The Mystery of the Indwelling Christ (1:24-29)
IV. The Godhead Incarnate in Christ, in whom the Believer is Complete (2:1-23)
    A. The Danger from Enticing Words (2:4-7)
    B. The Twofold Warning Against (a) Philosophy, (b) Legality (2:8)
    C. Nothing can be Added to Completeness (2:9-13)
    D. Law Observances were Abolished in Christ (2:14-17)
    E. Warning Against False Mysticism (2:18-19)
    F. Warning Against Asceticism (2:20-23)
V. The Believer's Union with Christ, Now and Hereafter (3:1-4)
VI. Christian Living, the Fruit of Union with Christ (3:5-4:6)
VII. Christian Fellowship (4:7-18)[1]

**Chapter 1**

# Colossians
## *by*
## *Andy Kizer*

௸

## Colossians One: Introduction

In an age of uncertainty, the book of Colossians speaks with clarity about the One who matters most. We live in a day when religious toleration is interpreted to mean, "One religion is as good as another." To many people, Jesus is only one of several great religious teachers with no more authority than the others. He may be prominent but He is not preeminent. There seems to be an increasing tendency to relegate Christianity to the realm of personal preferences and opinions. Facing such syncretism the church desperately needs the message of Colossians.

By the time the apostle Paul was in his first Roman incarceration, the church had been established in the Phrygian city of Colossae. While it is possible that Paul passed through Colossae in A.D. 54, traveling from Antioch in Syria to Ephesus in Asia Minor (now Turkey), the book of Acts gives no hint that he established any congregation on the trip. Though Paul was familiar with the brethren there, someone else established the church in Colossae. That someone else must have been Epaphras, who, at the time of the writing of this letter, was a fellow prisoner with Paul (Philemon 23).

Though once a large and populous city, Colossae had suffered a serious decline. Historians tell us that its influence and importance had waned when Paul wrote to the small congregation that met in the house of Philemon (cf. Philemon 1, 2). Yet, the message to the church in Colossae contains the inspired apostle's greatest teaching about the Christ, especially in the first chapter.

Paul began his letter to the brothers by exalting the name of Jesus from whom some in Colossae had departed: "an apostle of Christ Jesus". (v. 1), "faithful brothers in Christ" (v. 2), "God, the father of our Lord Jesus Christ"

(v. 3). In the first division of the letter, as we have it today, the writer mentions Jesus by name or pronoun some thirty-one times. Colossians one is a beautiful portrait of the Christ, the Object of the Christian's faith. It is explained that Jesus is such, because He is God's Son (vv. 3, 13), because He is the Redeemer (v. 14), because He is the image of God (v. 15), because He is the Creator (v. 16), because He is the head of the church (v. 18), because He is the fullness of God (v. 19), and because He is the peacemaker (v. 20).

The first chapter of this letter about the Christ of the church has the greeting from Paul (vv. 1, 2), the gratitude of Paul (vv. 3-8), the growth of the Colossians (vv. 9-14), the greatness of the Christ (vv. 15-20), the gospel of reconciliation (vv. 21-23), and the growing of the church (vv. 24-29).

## Colossians One: The Greeting from Paul

Though we sign our correspondence when we are finished, two thousand years ago, people were beginning their letters with their identities. Therefore, Paul began this letter with his name and his authority. He verified his authority as "an apostle of Christ Jesus" (v. 1). He was then, "one commissioned—sent as an ambassador to act in the name of, on behalf of, and with the authority of the one who sent him,"[2] i.e. Christ Jesus. The Colossians who were teaching error were immediately put on notice that they were to accept this letter as Christ's message to them.

The customary salutation included the writer's name, the name of a person or the persons with the writer, and a reference to the recipients of the correspondence. With Paul was Timothy, Paul's "child in the Lord" (cf. 1 Corinthians 4:17; 1 Timothy 1:2). Timothy had been with Paul in some of his travels and was with him in Rome as he penned this letter.

Those addressed were "saints and faithful brothers in Christ" who lived and worshiped God in Colossae. The use of the word "saints" indicates their calling. Called out of the world, they were separated from the world for service to God. Therefore, they were sanctified (cf. 1 Corinthians 1:2; 6:11). "Saints" are also "faithful brothers in Christ" (v. 2). The term translated "brothers" in the English Standard Version includes sisters in Christ as well. "Brothers" and "sisters" obviously suggest the familial relationship that God's children enjoy (cf. Galatians 3:26), but these were also "faithful." The original word so translated comes from the same root as the noun, "faith," and the verb, "believe." Thus, the recipients were baptized believers (2:11, 12), and

Timothy was one as well (cf. "our brother," v. 1). Being baptized into Christ (Romans 6:3), they were "in Christ" (v. 2). Being "in Christ" they were in the same spiritual sphere as He. Jesus introduced the idea using symbolic language in John 6:56, "Whoever feeds on my flesh and drinks my blood abides in me, and I in him."

Though addressed specifically to the members of the church in Colossae, the letter was meant for others as well (cf. 4:16). We, too, get great benefit from it.

Paul's greeting contained a familiar invocation, "Grace to you and peace" (cf. Romans 1:7; 1 Corinthians 1:3). His wish for the Colossians was continual abundant living and freedom from troubled hearts in a troubled world.

## Colossians One: The Gratitude of Paul

Paul was a praying man who mentioned people and congregations by name to God. His prayers included "supplications, prayers, intercessions, and thanksgivings" (1 Timothy 2:1). Whenever he prayed for the Colossians, he was thankful to God from Whom all blessings flow (v. 3; cf. Ephesians 1:3). Beginning his emphasis on the preeminence of Christ, Paul calls Jesus the "Lord Jesus Christ" and says that God is His father affirming the deity of Christ as Jesus had done (cf. John 8:54; 10:30). A son is of the same nature as his father. If the Father is God, then the Son is also divine. This point was clearly understood by the Jews who persecuted Jesus because he was "making himself equal with God" (John 5:18). Paul addressed his prayers to God, the Father, just as Jesus instructed His disciples always to do (Matthew 6:9; Luke 11:2).

The writer was thankful for three things the Colossians possessed: faith, hope, and love. It is interesting that the same apostle had written, "So now faith, hope, and love abide, these three; but the greatest of these is love" (1 Corinthians 13:13). Their faith was in Jesus (v. 4). Their love was for their brethren, the saints (v. 4), and their hope was awaiting them in heaven (v. 5).

The Colossians' faith in Christ was something that could be witnessed. Paul had heard about it. The report is what caused his thankfulness to be expressed to God. So, the Colossians who were "in Christ" had been expressing their faith. Faith and love go together. When one walks by faith in Christ, love for all is a natural product. This love does not create exclusive groups within the church, so the love the Colossians had was "for all the saints" (v. 4). The "love" possessed was "the love" (agape) described in 1 Corinthians 13:4-7.

Paul said that the faith and love of the Colossians was "because of the hope laid up for you in heaven" (v. 5, ESV). The rest of the Bible's teaching makes us think this is upside down, for hope would seem to be based on faith and love instead of the reverse. However, the Hebrews writer partially defined faith as, "the assurance of things hoped for" (Hebrews 11:1) using a genitive plural present passive participle translated, "hoped for," indicating that faith is acting upon hope. Moreover, the Colossian text has "hope" in the accusative case which is "used of causation which is not direct and immediate in the production of a result, on account of, because of, for the sake of, with a view to...."[3] A similar use is found in Mark 2:27 where Jesus said, "The Sabbath was made for man, not man for the Sabbath." Thus, man came first, and God made the Sabbath for him, and in the case of faith, hope, and love, it is because of man's hope for something better that he examines the evidence that assures him. That faith results in love for God Who makes that for which we hope possible. Faith, hope, and love are mental and moral attitudes that always act one upon another. The more there is of one, the more there will be of another.

Hope is something not yet realized. It "is laid up for you in heaven" (v. 5). "Now hope that is seen is not hope. For who hopes for what he sees?" asked Paul in Romans 8:24. "But if we hope for what we do not see, we wait for it with patience" (Romans 8:25). This fervent yearning, confident expectation, and patient waiting for the fulfillment of God's great promises sustains us. Peter agreed with Paul's encouragement to the Colossians saying that there is "an inheritance that is imperishable, undefiled, and unfading, kept in heaven for you" (1 Peter 1:4). The "heaven" of the English Standard Version in Colossians 1:5 is a translation of the Greek plural which involves a Hebrew concept that includes the sphere of the unseen world.

This was not something new to the Colossians. They had heard it before (v. 5). The hope of heaven is a part of the gospel, "the word of truth," along with much other truth, e.g. the plan of salvation (Romans 1:16), the death, burial and resurrection of Jesus (1 Corinthians 15:1-4), Gentiles are fellow-heirs with Jews (Galatians 2:5, 14; 3:8), the manner of life Christians are to live (Philippians 1:27), and avoiding sinful behavior (1 Timothy 1:10, 11). In fact, the gospel would include all "the word of truth" the Holy Spirit has revealed.

The truth had come to the Colossians through verbal communication of "the word of truth." Their faith, hope, and love were not based on written documents but upon what they had "heard" (vv. 5, 6, 23). Not only had they heard the truth, but so had every nation "in the whole world" (v. 6). Many preachers had scattered throughout the Roman Empire taking the good news to various parts of the world (cf. Acts 8:4; 11:19). Evidently, the one who had taken the truth to Colossae was Epaphras. "You learned it from Epaphras our beloved fellow servant" (v. 7).

Epaphras was a native of Colossae, or "one of you" (4:12), who was probably the first to take the gospel to Colossae. He was with Paul in Rome when he wrote this letter (4:12). The apostle had learned from him about the condition of the church there (vv. 8, 9). Paul thought very highly of this evangelist, describing him as "my fellow prisoner in Christ Jesus" (Philemon 23), "our beloved fellow servant" (v. 7), "a faithful minister of Christ" (v. 7), and "a servant of Christ Jesus" (4:12).

Christianity is spread by the disciples' taking the gospel to other places. This is the plan we call "The Great Commission" that was given by the Lord (cf. Matthew 28:19, 20). The world doesn't come to the disciple. The Christian goes to the world and teaches. The "word of truth" is not attained through human reason or meditation. It must be taught. Jesus said, "It is written in the Prophets, 'And they will all be taught by God.' Everyone who has heard and learned from the Father comes to me" (John 6:45). Thus, the gospel had come to Colossae where it had been "bearing fruit and growing" from the very time "the grace of God in truth" had first been heard and understood (v. 6). Luke explained how, through the ministry of Paul and other preachers, the gospel was bearing fruit and growing: "…all the residents of Asia heard the word of the Lord, both Jews and Greeks….So the word of the Lord continued to increase and prevail mightily" (Acts 19:10, 20). The word of God is the source of productivity (cf. Luke 8:11; Matthew 13:19). The early church was "bearing fruit and growing" because it was continually sowing the seed. The numerical and spiritual fruits that are borne are in direct correlation to the life in the seed, those who plant the seed, the soil into which the seed is planted, and how the soil is cultivated.

Not only had Epaphras talked to the Colossians, he had also talked about them. He made a trip to Rome to tell Paul of their love in spirit (vv. 4, 8). Since there is no article nor qualifying terms such as "holy" before the word for "spirit," the writer was referring to a love that came from the depth of the human spirit. This implies a sincere Christian love that was for Paul as well as "for all the saints" (v. 4).

## Colossians One: The Growth of the Colossians

Paul and his companions, Aristarchus, Mark, Justus, Epaphras, Luke, and Demas (4:10-14) were often heard praying for the Colossians. It was

Epaphras' report that produced the petitions. "And so, from the day we heard, we have not ceased to pray for you" (v. 9). Though the wording of such prayers is not given, the content is. The lesson from this concerns our own prayers to God. Jesus' model prayers of Matthew 6:9-13 and Luke 11:2-4 are not necessarily followed "to the letter." When you don't know how or what to pray, "Pray then like this" (Matthew 6:9), remembering that the Holy Spirit helps God's children with their prayers (cf. Romans 8:26). Inspired men prayed in additional ways and with different words (cf. Ephesians 1:16-21; 2 Thessalonians 1:11). Involved in those prayers were supplications, intercessions, and thanksgivings (1 Timothy 2:1). Paul and his coworkers were continually asking for the moral discernment that would enable the Colossians to please God and the strength that would give them endurance. Requests were being made that the Colossians would grow which would then lead them to even greater things.

May "you be filled with the knowledge of his will in all spiritual wisdom and understanding," Paul wished (v. 9). "You be filled" is the action to which four other actions relate. This is indicated by the writer's use of nominative, present participles. Being present participles means the actions are to be continuous. Being filled involves bearing fruit (v. 10), increasing in knowledge (v. 10), being strengthened (v. 11), and thanking God (v. 12).

Paul and his friends wanted the Colossians to be saturated with spiritual insight. Though the facts must be known, this involves more than a knowledge of the facts of God's word. It requires a proper application of those facts, i.e. wisdom. Understanding comes from a study of God's revealed will (2 Timothy 3:16, 17), praying (James 1:5), and obeying God's commandments (cf. Psalm 19:7; 119:98). Praying for wisdom and understanding is helpful, because they come by the grace of God as well as by human effort.

A saturated spiritual insight should result in a godly life (or walking worthily, v. 10). "In a manner worthy" (ESV) is from a Greek adverb meaning, "worthily." The "walk" so described is not a physical one, but a spiritual one. Paul frequently used "walk" as a metaphor for living as a Christian should (cf. 2 Corinthians 5:7). The "walk" is with a view toward "fully pleasing" God. "Pleasing" is in the Greek accusative case making it the object of the Christian's life. It is introduced by the Greek preposition, εἰς (eis), which is "into" or "with a view toward." The English Standard Version describes pleasing God as involving "bearing fruit in every good work and increasing in the knowledge of God" (v. 10). However, Paul's style is that of a run-on sentence that is somewhat rambling with "bearing fruit" and "increasing in knowledge" being part and partial to the wish for a filling in verse nine (i.e.

"be filled"). "Bearing fruit" reminds us of the Lord's demands of discipleship: "By this my Father is glorified, that you bear much fruit and so prove to be my disciples" (John 15:8).

Chapter 1, verse 12, as we have the letter divided, does not begin a new sentence in Paul's construction, though it appears as such in the English Standard Version. Instead, in a more literal translation, Paul continues, "Walk worthily of the Lord into fully pleasing, bearing fruit in every good work and increasing in the knowledge of the God, being strengthened in all power..." (vv. 10, 11). Again, this comes under the heading, "you may be filled," which appeared at the beginning of the prayer. "Being strengthened" is from a present participle that implies not just a one-time strengthening, but a continual strengthening that comes from "increasing in the knowledge of God" (v. 10). Growing in knowledge of God's will would provide greater strength. The strength will come from God's "glorious might" (v. 11). In saying, "You will be powered with power" (the word translated, "strengthened" in verse 11 comes from the root word for "power"), Paul used a play on words. Christians are given power from God's power. That power is for the purpose of or "into" (again, the preposition εἰς is used) "all endurance and patience with joy" (v. 11). The word translated, "endurance" means, more literally, "patient endurance of evil, fortitude."[4] We might call that which is indicated by that word, "patience," while the original word translated by the ESV, "patience," is from the word that means, literally, "holding up under." Therefore, the ever-increasing strength that comes from an ever-increasing knowledge of God's will gives the power to deal with the mistreatment that comes from persecution and the power to carry on (or hold up) under the burdens of life. Being able to do that gives one joy. That joy goes along with patience and endurance. It is a byproduct of the power of God that comes from a knowledge of God's will and wisdom from the application of that knowledge. The Christian is happy that with God's help he can overcome evil and bear up under the trials of life.

Thankfulness comes to the heart of the knowledgeable child of God. The "giving thanks" with which verse 12 begins is the final one of those four present participles that relate to "you be filled" in verse 9, and, again, being present tense indicates that this is something that is continually done. Thanks are offered to God, the Father, as Paul mentioned in verse 3. The reason for the thanks is because of what God has done. He has "qualified you to share in the inheritance of the saints of light" (v. 12). The Father "qualifies" one since one cannot qualify himself. The idea is from a term meaning, "to make sufficient or competent."[5] It is found only one other time in the New Testament. In 2

Corinthians 3:5, 6, Paul said, "Not that we are sufficient in ourselves to claim anything as coming from us, but our sufficiency is from God, who has made us competent to be ministers of a new covenant...." The King James Version says, "made us able." People are not able to qualify themselves for such an inheritance as that which is "imperishable, undefiled, and unfading, kept in heaven for you" (1 Peter 1:4). Brothers (and sisters) of Christ are qualified by God and Christ to "share in the inheritance," because they are children of God. "And if children, then heirs – heirs of God and fellow heirs with Christ, provided we suffer with him in order that we may also be glorified with him" (Romans 8:17). "For in Christ Jesus you are all sons of God, through faith. For as many of you as were baptized into Christ have put on Christ....And if you are Christ's, then you are Abraham's offspring, heirs according to promise" (Galatians 3:26, 27, 29). Paul called those who share the inheritance, "the saints in the light" (v. 12). "Light" is compared to knowledge in God's word. Light dispels darkness. Light guides (cf. Psalm 119:105). Paul uses the term in this letter where he is talking about growing in the knowledge of God and the benefit of that growth. "The saints in the light" are the holy ones who are being filled with knowledge and walking worthily of the Lord. Paul's prayer for the Ephesian church must have been the same, for he said to the Ephesian elders, "And now I commend you to God and to the word of his grace, which is able to build you up and to give you the inheritance among all those who are sanctified" (Acts 20:32).

Continuing to give reason for Christian joy, Paul uses the contrast of light and darkness concerning the new place or condition of those who share the inheritance of the saints in light. When we are in Christ, we praise God and thank Him because we have been delivered! Those who enter the kingdom of God's Son are "qualified" (v. 12), "delivered" (v. 13), and "transferred" (v. 13). Paul included himself with those who have been delivered (or rescued). They have been "dragged out of danger," and God is the One Who did it. That from which He dragged the saints is the domain, rule, dominion, or authority of darkness. Darkness is the very antithesis of light, and they cannot possibly exist together or be together in the same realm. "Or what fellowship has light with darkness?" asked Paul (2 Corinthians 6:14). Yet, one must be in some realm, therefore, God takes one whom He qualifies from under the dominion of Satan (cf. 2 Corinthians 4:4) and transfers him into another realm, i.e. "the kingdom of his beloved Son" (v. 13). A change of kingdoms is indicated. One moves from the kingdom of Satan into the kingdom of God. A new condition or state of being is enjoyed! The qualified is taken from under the rule of the devil and placed under the rule of the Savior. This is the very thing Paul was chosen to help do. When the Lord confronted him, Jesus said, "I have appeared to you…delivering you from your people and from the Gentiles – to whom I am sending you (much of the church in Colossae was Gentile in ethnicity, A.K.) to open their eyes, so that they may turn from darkness to light and from the power of Satan to God, that they may receive forgiveness of sins and a place among those who are sanctified by faith in me" (Acts 26:16-18).

Paul said of God that He "has delivered" and "has transferred." Both verbs are in the tense that indicates completed action in past time, meaning that when one is delivered and transferred, he stays delivered and transferred. Moreover, that into which one is transferred is the kingdom. The kingdom exists! It is not something yet to come in our future. It has existed on this earth since the Lord established it upon His arrival in heaven (cf. Mark 9:1; Luke 24:49; Acts 2:1-4, 32, 33). Paul called it "the kingdom of Christ and God" in Ephesians 5:5. Thus, the Ephesians were in it. John was in it (Revelation 1:9). And the Colossians were in it. The kingdom is the church Jesus promised to build (Matthew 16:18, 19), and the Ruler over it is Jesus Himself, the "King of kings and Lord of lords" (cf. Revelation 19:16; John 18:36).

"The kingdom of his beloved Son" (v. 13) is a phrase that tells us to Whom the kingdom belongs. It belongs to "the Son of God's love." And only in Him do we have "redemption, the forgiveness of sins" (v. 14). This verse is a parallel to Ephesians 1:7, "In him we have redemption through his blood, the forgiveness of our trespasses, according to the riches of his grace." If we are in Christ, then we have our deliverance in Him. The price (ransom) has been paid for our redemption, i.e. His blood, and if we are redeemed, then our sins are forgiven. This is a beautiful way for Paul to set up a brief but powerful description of the greatness of the Christ.

## Colossians One: The Greatness of the Christ

In the next section of Colossians 1, Paul gives no less than eight descriptive terms to illustrate the greatness of the Christ: He is 1) "the image of the invisible God" (v. 15), 2) "the firstborn of all creation" (v. 15), 3) the Creator of "all things" (v. 16), 4) "before all things" (v. 17), 5) the Holder-Together of "all things" (v. 17), 6) the "head of the body, the church" (v. 18), 7) "the beginning" (v. 18), and 8) "the firstborn from the dead" (v. 18). Why? So that, "in everything he might be preeminent" (v. 19). Jesus Christ is supreme in the universe, the physical creation (vv. 15-17) and supreme in the church, the spiritual creation (vv. 18-20). We may develop the paragraph that is Colossians 1:15-20 under those two supreme thoughts.

## Colossians One: The Preeminence of Jesus in the Universe

The "Son of God's love" (v. 13) is the "image of the invisible God" (v. 15). The original word for "image" sounds like the English word, "icon." It means, "similitude, representation, exact image...."[6] Jesus is not just an image of God. He is the exact image. Man was made in the image of God (Genesis 1:26), but Jesus is "the exact imprint of his nature" (Heb. 1:3). The Hebrews writer described God the Son as the same substance, nature, glory, and "character" as God the Father. The Lord told Philip, "Whoever has seen me has seen the Father" (John 14:9). Owen Olbricht said, "He has made the invisible God visible and understandable. Through Him the fullness of God has been revealed."[7] Were He not God Himself, Jesus would not have been able to show God the Father to men.

Christ's being "firstborn" has to do with creation. Yet, Jesus is not "firstborn" because He was created first. When Paul said that "by him all things were created" (v. 16), he affirmed that Jesus was not a part of creation but existed before all creation. Indeed, "by him all things were created" (v. 16). Neither is He "firstborn" because He was Mary's first child. Even though the term was used in the Old Testament to refer to the child born first, it was also used to mean one who was highly esteemed. The nation of Israel was called God's firstborn (Exodus 4:22), but Israel was not born first among all nations. David is referred to as the firstborn in Psalm 89:27, but he was number eight in his family (cf. 1 Samuel 16:10, 11). "Firstborn" in these passages cannot mean those who were born first. Instead, the word refers to the status of the "firstborn."

Jesus is not a creature. He is the Creator (v. 16; cf. 1 Corinthians 8:6). A ground for His status of "firstborn" is that "in him all things were created." What the English Standard Version translates "by" (v. 16) is actually "in" with the case of the noun that follows indicating location. Vincent explains: In is not instrumental but local; not denying the instrumentality, but putting the fact of creation with reference to its sphere and centre [sic]. In Him, within the sphere of His personality, resides the creative will and the creative energy, and in that sphere the creative act takes place. Thus creation was dependent on Him.[8]

The "by (or in, A.K.) him all things were created" is immediately resolved into "all things were created through him and for him" in the last part of verse 16: "all things," whether they be "in heaven," the spiritual realm where created beings such as angels are, or "on earth," where material things are; "all things," whether they be visible in heaven or invisible on earth such as the souls of men; "all things," whether they be "thrones or dominions or rulers or authorities." These ranks, used both of good and evil, may possibly include earthly dignities, but the context of this letter indicates that the primary reference is to celestial orders. The passage is directed at the angel-worship of the Colossians (2:16-19). The two times "were created" is found in verse 16 are in two different verb tenses. Putting them together helps us to understand that the creation was a historical event in the past, and, having been created, it stands as such to the present.

The Lord's status is even further emphasized by Paul's identifying Him as "before all things" (v. 17). "He is" (He and no other is) emphatically above all things. The word "before" can be used of priority in time or of rank. Vincent says it means "in time,"[9] but Peter used it in reference to rank in 1 Peter 4:8. Paul's use of "before" could be for both time and rank, for the divine personality Who became "Jesus" is of eternal existence. He had glory "before the world existed" (John 17:5).

Christ not only created but He also maintains. "In him all things hold together" (v. 17). We have not chaos but order. Jesus is the power that provides the harmony. He keeps all its parts in their proper places. Without the Lord, the universe would fly to pieces! He "upholds the universe by the word of his power" (Hebrews 1:3). Something is needed to hold one together. That which holds all things together is the Word of God (cf. John 1:1-3).

## Colossians One: The Preeminence of Jesus in the Church

The One Who is before all things and in Whom all things hold together is also the head of the church. The church of the Christ is described as a body (cf. 1 Corinthians 12:12-31), and, if it is a body, then it has a head, and the head of the church is the Christ (cf. Ephesians 1:22, 23). Though He is not on earth but in heaven, still He is the head of the church on earth. The head of the church is the ruler of the church, therefore, God's children get their orders from Jesus. One body has only one head, and one head has only one body. "There is one body..." (Ephesians 4:4), and "Christ is the head of the church, his body, and is himself its Savior" (Ephesians 5:23).

In reference to the priority of Jesus in the paragraph now being studied, Paul said of Him four times, "He is." He is: 1) "...the image of the invisible God" (v. 15), 2) "...before all things..." (v. 17), 3) "...the head of the body, the church" (v. 18), and 4) "...the beginning..." (v. 18). The beginning of what? The beginning of redemption; the beginning of life. This "beginning" has to do with the Lord's place in the church. He is the beginning of the new spiritual creation, the church (Matthew 16:18) and every new spiritual creature (cf. 2 Corinthians 5:17). Quickly adding, "the firstborn from the dead," Paul ties the resurrection of Jesus to the church. "For as in Adam all die, so also in Christ shall all be made alive" (1 Corinthians 15:22). The Lord said, "Because I live, you also will live" (John 14:19). Thus, He was raised from the dead, the first never to die again, the first to be raised with an immortal body.

This is "in order that in everything he might be preeminent" (v. 18). It is reasonable that the One Who is the firstborn point of reference (i.e. beginning), sphere of creation, and sustainer of all is then above all. Now preeminent, He has no rival. "Might be preeminent" is better translated, "might become first." The verb, "become," indicates a position into which Jesus came in a course of time. He is the beginning and head of the universe by nature of His absolute and eternal being and became the head of the church by nature of His resurrection from the dead. "Although he was a son, he learned obedience through what he suffered. And being made perfect, he because the source of eternal salvation to all who obey him" (Hebrews 5:8, 9).

Jesus must have first place in life, because "in him all the fullness of God was pleased to dwell" (v. 19). "Fullness" refers to completeness. God is that with which Jesus is filled, and from that fullness we receive grace (John 1:16). Jesus is and has all that man really needs. He is Creator, Master, Teacher, Lawgiver, Mediator, Intercessor, Advocate, Leader, Helper, Authority, Power, Life, and Savior. He is "the exact imprint" of the nature of God (Hebrews 1:3). Without Christ, there is emptiness, no fullness. Without Christ, one is without God and without hope (cf. Ephesians 2:12). The power of God was not to be distributed among angels or men. It was, instead, to inhabit (or dwell) in the Son of God. This was a good thing, a pleasing thing, in the mind of God.

Reconciliation is with Christ and through Him (v. 20). To "reconcile" is "to transfer from a certain state to another which is quite different; hence, to reconcile, restore to favour [sic]...."[10] Paul said that one is through Christ reconciled into Christ. When one is "baptized into Christ" (Galatians 3:27), his status and condition have changed. He is "in Christ with every spiritual blessing" (Ephesians 1:7). The barrier of sin that stood between the sinner and God has been removed, and he/she is in favor with God again. God is reconciling the world to Himself "in Christ" (2 Corinthians 5:19). Jesus provides reconciliation for all who need reconciliation, on earth and in heaven. Paul made a distinction between the people on earth and souls in heaven. He did not refer to the earth but to people on the earth and not to heaven but to souls in the heavenly places. The original word translated "heaven" by the English Standard Version is plural. Many souls departed from this life before the Lord shed His blood for their sins, and they are now in the realm of the unseen dead or "hades." They died in need of the reconciliation that Jesus made possible for them (cf. Hebrews 9:15) on the cross. Upon reconciliation there is peace. There is no more conflict. One who is in Christ is not at war with God. On the cross, Jesus shed His blood for the forgiveness of the sins that drove man away from God (cf. Isaiah 59:1, 2; Matthew 26:28).

## Colossians One: The Gospel of Reconciliation

Being alienated from God and hostile in mind produced evil deeds (v. 21). Such was the case with the Colossians before reconciliation. "Alienated," they were strangers to God, and "hostile," they were antagonistic to God's will. And, as such, they were enemies of God. The hostility was in their minds or on account of their thoughts. Then, the state of their minds led them to sinful practices. They participated in "the evils," says the original text, but the Greek for "doing" is a noun in the case of the indirect object. Therefore, the thinking of the Colossians was on "the deeds of the evils." Such thinking leads to such actions, and such actions lead to enmity with God. Since God hates sin and rebellion, there was a need for reconciliation. Then, a great change occurred.

The Colossians were reconciled (v. 22). They were restored to favor with God! Paul referred to an action in the past that resulted in a present state of things. The past action was the death of Christ ("his death," v. 22) and the result was a new relationship, i.e. friendship with God. That reconciliation required "his body of flesh." No angel or spiritual being sufficed, but the physical body of Jesus Himself was offered. That sacrifice made the "in Christ" ones able to stand before God "holy" (separated from worldly defilements) and "blameless" (without blemish) and "above reproach" (free from the charge of sinfulness). As Paul said to the Ephesians, we should be "holy and blameless before him" (Ephesians 1:4). The Corinthians were told that Jesus "will sustain you to the end, guiltless in the day of our Lord Jesus Christ" (1 Corinthians 1:8), but whether the "before him" of Colossians 1:22 refers to the present time or future judgment is difficult to determine. However, in either case, a condition is attached.

Paul could not have been more emphatic than he was when he stressed that the right relationship with God was contingent upon continuing in "the faith" (v. 23). "If indeed," he said. The word translated "indeed" is treated as a suffix of the preceding word translated "if." This throws the accent back onto that preceding word and makes it, "IF!" There is a particular force then to what follows. A continuing friendship with God is contingent upon a continuing walk in "the faith." An article appears before the Greek word for "faith," indicating a particular body of doctrine that must be followed. Those who will not continue in that doctrine will not be presented holy, blameless, and without reproach to God. There is that possibility of falling away from the Lord and being lost. If they continued in the faith, the Colossians would be firm and unwavering (or "stable") and constant (or "steadfast"). Here are two building or construction metaphors that make the truth clear. The conditional clause continues with "not shifting," suggesting another and different metaphor of an anchored ship. One must not stir away from, or swerve from, "the faith." The gospel is the truth from which they could not swerve and still be steadfast. Saints who continue in "the faith" are building on the rock (cf. Matthew 7:24-27). Jesus Christ is the foundation that is sure (1 Corinthians 3:11; cf. 1 Corinthians 15:1-5).

The hope that is sure and steadfast, the anchor of the soul (Hebrews 6:19), is the "hope of the gospel" (v. 23). There is a certain hope that belongs to the gospel, i.e. a gospel hope. It is the hope of heaven that Paul mentioned before (vv. 5, 6). The Colossians enjoyed that hope because they responded positively to what they "heard." The gospel had been preached (or "proclaimed") to them by Epaphras. The gospel must be preached, received, held fast, and believed for there to be salvation (1 Corinthians 15:1, 2). By the time this letter was sent to the Colossians, that gospel had been preached "in all creation under heaven." It recognizes no boundaries. The use of "all creation" tells us that the message had been shared with more than Jews. The Gentiles had also been included in the gospel invitation. Jesus had commissioned His disciples to "go into all the world and proclaim the gospel to the whole creation" (Mark 16:15).

With what appears to be deep emotion by the mention of his own name, Paul concluded this section and linked it to the next by adding, "of which (gospel, A.K.) I, Paul, became a minister" (v. 25). He used the same term he had used for Epaphras in verse 7, "minister" or "servant." The message is the same, and the service is the same though Paul was an apostle. The gospel is for all to receive and to deliver. William Hendriksen said, "A minister of the gospel is one who knows the gospel, has been saved by the Christ of the gospel, and with joy of heart proclaims the gospel to others. Thus he serves the cause of the gospel."[11]

## Colossians One: The Growing of the Church

When Paul was writing this letter, he was in a prison in Rome and refers to that with the simple word, "now." "In my present condition as a prisoner, I rejoice in my sufferings" (v. 24). Instead of complaining, he is rejoicing, not because he was in pain but because of what the sufferings could bring. By a figure of speech called, "metonymy," he said that on behalf of the Colossians, his "...resolve to be true under continual danger said to others that they should and could do the same."[12] From that same prison and concerning that same subject, Paul wrote to the Philippians, "And most of the brothers, having become confident in the Lord by my imprisonment, are much more bold to speak the word without fear" (Philippians 1:14). He believed his "afflictions" by which he was "filling up" (or completing) Christ's afflictions were borne by him for the benefit of the Lord's body. This could not mean that Jesus was lacking in anything He did or in anything that was done to Him for the redemption of man. "He learned obedience through what he suffered. And being made perfect, he became the source of eternal salvation to all who obey him" (Hebrews 5:8, 9). Then what did Paul mean? Hendriksen explained: "We should bear in mind that although Christ by means of the afflictions which he endured rendered complete satisfaction to God, so that Paul is able to glory in nothing but the cross (Gal. 6:14), the enemies of Christ were not satisfied! They hated Jesus with insatiable hatred, and wanted to add to his afflictions. But since he is no longer physically present on earth, their arrows, which are meant especially for him, strike his followers. It is in that sense that all true believers are in his stead supplying what, as the enemies see it, is lacking in the afflictions which Jesus endured."[13]

Again, Paul calls himself a servant (or "minister") and calls his work of making "the word of God fully known" a "stewardship" (v. 25). He understood himself to be an officer or administrator in the house of God. He was not only a servant of the gospel but also of the church who had been entrusted with spreading the gospel, particularly through the Gentile world (cf. Acts 26:16-18). His talents were to be used to that end.

The "word of God" Paul was preaching included what was once a mystery (v. 26). A "mystery" in the New Testament sense of the word is "a matter to the knowledge of which initiation is necessary; a secret which would remain such but for revelation."[14] That revelation was being made known through the apostle in the inspired letters to members of the church though it had been "hidden for ages." Though it had been withheld from knowledge through previous generations and not historically realized, it was revealed to the apostles and prophets through the Holy Spirit (Ephesians 3:3-5), then it was recorded in words taught to them by the Holy Spirit (1 Corinthians 2:9-13). Paul mentioned it to the Ephesians seven times and explained that when one reads what he had received and written about it, he also would "perceive my insight into the mystery of Christ" (Ephesians 3:4). That mystery is, he added, "that the Gentiles are fellow heirs, members of the same body, and partakers of the promise in Christ Jesus through the gospel" (Ephesians 3:6). It had been present in the plan of God (cf. Ephesians 3:11, 12) and in prophecy though not in actuality. Predictions that the Gentiles could and one day would be a part of God's kingdom and covenant people are found throughout the Old Testament (cf. Genesis 49:10; Isaiah 60:1-3; Micah 4:1, 2; Malachi 1:11; et.al.). But the hope of Christ for the Gentiles was not revealed until Christ came.

The "riches of the glory of this mystery" is identified as "Christ in you" (v. 27). The Colossians' hope of honor, praise, and manifestation of glory was dependent on Christ's being in them. "Anyone who does not have the Spirit of Christ does not belong to him" (Romans 8:9; cf. vv. 10, 11). The Holy Spirit is the agent or means by which God the Father and God the Son dwell or live in the Christian (Romans 8:9, 11; 1 Corinthians 6:19; Ephesians 2:22; 2 Timothy 1:14).

Paul's aim and goal was to "present everyone mature in Christ" (v. 28). Thus, he preached Christ and Him crucified (cf. 1 Corinthians 2:2). The word translated "proclaim" in the ESV is not one that we would expect. It is, instead, a word that means, more literally, "announce" or "celebrate."

An "announcement" would be fitting for the revelation of a mystery, but it also included warning and teaching. The kind of preaching that helps us to grow has negative and positive aspects. Certain warnings, or, in this case, admonishments, are needful for healthy advancement. They were certainly needed by the Colossians for the false teachers they were facing. The rest of this letter is filled with content that armed the saints in Colossae to deal with certain specific error. With teaching of Christ and warning from all forms of wisdom, Christians grow up to maturity and become full grown (cf. Ephesians 4:15, 16). Therefore, using a present tense verb and a present participle, the apostle declared that he would keep on proclaiming and keep on warning.

Full-grown (mature) Christians are a must! Many problems are avoided by maturity. Perhaps the apostle could give to God ("present") souls who were "mature in Christ" by way of the revelation of the mystery. "Mature" is from the word for "complete," thus those whom he desired to present would be fully accomplished in Christian enlightenment. God expects His people to be mature and not childish. He has provided what is needed for that, which is "the unity of the faith" and "the truth in love" "so that we may no longer be children, tossed to and fro by the waves and carried about by every wind of doctrine…" (Ephesians 4:13-16). The gospel is for all and to emphasize that, three times Paul applied the need for food for maturity to "everyone": 1) "warning everyone," 2) "teaching everyone," and 3) "that we may present everyone." His words oppose any exclusiveness. Everyone is to grow up.

Paul meant to convert people to Christ and to bring them to maturity. He would "toil," laboring even to the point of weariness, "struggling with all his energy that he powerfully works within me" (v. 29). "Struggling" is a translation of the Greek word from which we get our English word, "agony," which refers to a painful effort (cf. 1 Timothy 6:12). The toil refers to physical labor while the struggle was within. So, Paul was consumed with his efforts, without and within, but he had the power he needed to achieve his purpose. His words at the end of the first chapter of Colossians may be more literally translated, "For this I work to the point of exhaustion, agonizing according to His energy that is energizing me with power."

## Colossians One: Summary

Rejoicing in his God-given stewardship, the apostle Paul wrote to the Colossian church about the sovereign Christ. He reminded them of their hope and thanked God for their faith and love. To face the challenges of Christian living and the errors of false teachers, the brothers would need to be mature in Christ. That which ceased to be a mystery held the power that enabled them to be true even in danger, but they had to continue in the faith, stable and steadfast. It is a toilsome and weary task, but the power of Christ is in us.

## Chapter 2

# Colossians

## *by*

## *Larry Jones*

ଓଃ

## Colossians Two: Introduction

The book of Colossians emphasizes the all-sufficiency and supremacy of Christ. From His role in the creation (1:16-17) to His authority as the Head of His Church (1:18), Paul shows Jesus as the image of God (1:15) and as the fullness of the Godhead bodily (2:9). Throughout time many false teachings have come forward concerning the adequacy of Christ to perform all the functions which the New Testament attributes to Him. Some challenge His deity, while others question His true humanity. If Christ was not God then His ability to save us would be in doubt. As Deity, if He came to this earth not truly in a fleshly body and did not experience human life as we experience it then His ability to be our advocate and mediator would be uncertain. Others portray Jesus as a demigod like personage, God-like but less than the God whose Son He is (Greek mythology's Hercules, Zeus's son – powerful but diluted in power by having an earthly mother). All such teachings casts doubt upon Jesus as our Savior and the Bible as God's inspired Word. Paul answers these doctrinal problems in the first century and understands that, "there is no new thing under the sun" (Eccl. 1:9). His same answers respond and retort the similar false teachings of the twenty first century. The following outline breaks down Colossians chapter two as it will be presented.

## Colossians 2:1-10: The Completeness in Christ

Colossians 2:1 "For I want you to know what a great conflict I have for you and those in Laodicea, and for as many as have not seen my face in the flesh."[15] Colossians two continues the thoughts Paul brings forth at the end of the first chapter. He tells them that he suffers (1:24), labors, and strives (1:29) in behalf of them and for Christ. In most of Paul's epistles, he points out the work he does and the sacrifices he makes for Christianity. We see a great example of this in Paul's second (really third) letter to Corinth. Paul describes in detail the physical trials he has endured for the cause of Christ (2 Cor. 11:23-27). Showing the scope of making his life a sacrifice for Christ he then confirms the true center of his concern, the Church, "besides the other things, what comes upon me daily: my deep concern for all the churches" (2 Cor. 11:28).

The word "conflict" might better be as the ASV translates it "I strive"[16] or the NASV "how great a struggle I have."[17] The nature of these struggles may show the continual spiritual war with Satan and the forces of evil or more specifically the fact of his Roman imprisonment (Eph. 6:10-17; Col 4:3, 10). Paul expresses the hint of danger to the Colossians already in the epistle , "if indeed you continue in the faith, grounded and steadfast, and are not moved away from the hope of the gospel which you heard, which was preached to every creature under heaven, of which I, Paul, became a minister" (Col 1:23). The apostle voices his statement of trust but also his alert of the danger of falling away which foreshadows the more detailed warnings as the epistle continues.

Paul states they have "not seen my face in the flesh" leading to the conclusion that he neither converted nor even visited Colosse or Laodicea (Col. 2:1). Recognizing the importance of keeping in touch with the congregations he began, Paul also understands the importance, as the "Apostle to the Gentiles" to contact congregations which are the indirect fruits of his labors (Rom. 11:13; 1 Cor. 3:6). In other words, congregations started by the efforts of those Paul converted or that others converted. The book of Revelation makes mention of Laodicea as one of the troubled (maybe most troubled) congregations of the Seven Churches of Asia (Rev. 1:11; 3:14-22). Within just a few years Paul will meet his prophesied death at Rome. Paul conveys his plans to expand the kingdom into Europe by way of Spain (Rom. 1:24, 28). He uses this time "in chains" productively, to strengthen congregations which will face great threatening influences. Certainly physical persecutions will abound, but more hazardous and insidious are the dangers of tainted philosophy, misapplied legalism and false doctrines

Colossians 2:2 "that their hearts may be encouraged, being knit together in love, and attaining to all riches of the full assurance of understanding, to the knowledge of the mystery of God, both of the Father and of Christ." The Biblical human "heart" represents the part of the human mind which hears, understands, accepts, applies, retains or loses the word of the Bible. The New Testament speaks of these abilities of the heart in the Parables of the Sower (Matt. 13:3-9, 18-23; Mark 4:3-9, 13-20; Luke 8:4-8, 11-15). Paul writes to encourage the hearts of the Colossians in three ways:

> To Show his Personal Care and Sacrifices in the cause of Christ that they may follow his example (Col 1:3, 9; 4:2, 10; 1 Co 11:1).
>
> To Show the Fullness of a relationship with Christ in His Church (Col. 2:2-3; Eph 1:3).
>
> To Warn against the Dangers from the outside Culture which Imperils First Century Christians (Col. 2:4, 8, 18).

The idea of being "knit together" appears several times in the Prison Epistles, twice within the Colossian letter and once in Ephesians (Col. 2:2, 19; Eph. 4:16). In all these cases the idea encourages Christians to be interwoven together to achieve their maximum potential as Christians. The purpose behind this weaving together is the greatest of Christian attributes, love. We see love (agape) as the height of the Christian Graces, one of the traits of the Fruit of the Spirit, and the greatest of the attributes of Faith, Hope, and Love (2 Pet 1:5-8; Gal. 5:22-23; 1 Cor. 13:13).

The Bible expresses the knowledge of its all-sufficiency in many verses. We have all spiritual blessings in Christ (Eph. 1:3). God has given us all things pertaining to life and godliness (2 Pet. 1:3). Through His Spirit, God gives all scripture which thoroughly equips us "for every good work" (2 Tim. 3:16-17). God did His part.

It becomes our responsibility to do our part in understanding God's word. Many do so little to study the Bible. Showing up to Bible studies, attending regular worship services and listening attentively enough to take notes provides an education in the scriptures. Daily reading (and meditation on what we read) helps our knowledge and understanding to grow. We live in an age where vast amounts of Bible reference books for every level of comprehension abound. We will never understand the fullness of what God has done for us unless we spend time and effort in understanding. The word of God provides riches we must delve into heartily and the only way to know the true God of Heaven (Col. 2:2).

A "mystery" exists which God wishes us to solve. Both the letters to Ephesus and to Colosse tell of the mystery which God presents to mankind at the coming of His Son. Paul imparts the great solution to that mystery very concisely, "that the Gentiles should be fellow heirs, of the same body, and partakers of His promise in Christ through the gospel" (Eph. 3:6). This may also reference the Word itself and the fact that the most thorough revealing of our God is through His Word by His Spirit. We may know of His existence by His creation but the details of our God come through His Word and only through His Word (Psalms 19:1; Rom. 1:20).

Colossians 2:3 "in whom are hidden all the treasures of wisdom and knowledge." As the Bible assures us of its all sufficiency so to Paul assures us of the source of that sufficiency: God and Christ (and the Holy Spirit). The various "omni" qualities of the Godhead as well as superior morality show their all sufficiency as the ultimate source of all knowledge and wisdom. Within the Bible God reveals all which He deems necessary to our understanding of Himself. We have the all sufficient Word provided by the all sufficient God.

Colossians 2:4 "Now this I say lest anyone should deceive you with persuasive words." Verse four gives us the first of several warnings in Colossians two. At this point in time the giving of the entirety of the New Testament has not occurred (1 Cor. 13:10). Culture has always been the enemy of God's people. Israel's bondage in Egypt caused them to take up worshipping the golden calf (Ex. 2:4-8). Later when about to enter the promised land, God warns the Israelites to drive out or destroy the inhabitants, for cohabitation would be a snare to the Israelites because of the Canaanites false gods (De. 7:16). We see God's wisdom by Israel's failure to fully comply with God's instructions and their constant falling into idol worship during the Judges period (Judges 2:1-3, 11; 3:7, 12; 4:1; 10:6). Culture continues to endanger God's people. In the first century, the Jewish Christians attempted to bring aspects of the Jewish religion into Christianity (Acts 15). Similarly the Greek culture through its philosophies and Roman culture which will establish the leadership pattern leading to Catholicism[18] influenced Christianity away from a Bible only. "Persuasive words" (pithanologia)[19] emphasizes the power of speech. The influential words of preaching sound doctrine draw people to the gospel and the church (Titus 1:3). Likewise those speaking against the true doctrines of the Bible have swaying ability to move individuals away from truth. Some have no love for truth and will believe the lie (2 Thes. 2:10-12). Others may be deceived and lose their souls. Paul warns them to beware!

Colossians 2:5 "For though I am absent in the flesh, yet I am with you in spirit, rejoicing to see your good order and the steadfastness of your faith in Christ." Paul encourages the Christians in Colosse for their uprightness in staying steadfast in the faith so far, even as he brings warnings about the society in which they continue to live. He wishes to do what he can for

Colosse even though separated from them. All Christians should have joy in the faithfulness of good quality brethren and have a desire to be encouraging in whatever ways we can to brethren.

Colossians 2:6 "As you therefore have received Christ Jesus the Lord, so walk in Him." Our conversion to Christianity gives each of us a goal to achieve, the fullness of Christ's example. "To the measure of the stature of the fullness of Christ" provides us an aspiration to obtain and a pattern to follow, the perfect pattern (Eph. 4:13). The Christian walk ultimately means to walk as Christ walked. "Walk" represents our journey through our lives. Paul stated, "Imitate me, just as I also imitate Christ" (1 Cor. 11:1). Many times, to the new Christian, the idea of striving to be Christ-like seems intimidating and daunting. At first, the Christian may focus on mature Christians who provide good examples to emulate. "Brethren, join in following my example, and note those who so walk, as you have us for a pattern" (Phil. 3:17). Later, as Christians mature, they may look towards their Savior as the example to follow.

Colossians 2:7 "rooted and built up in Him and established in the faith, as you have been taught, abounding in it with thanksgiving." In John fifteen, the scriptures describe the Christian's relationship with Christ as a living relationship. "I am the vine, you are the branches. He who abides in Me, and I in him, bears much fruit; for without Me you can do nothing" (Jn. 15:5). First, we must be rooted in the Christ of the New Testament and not in the various versions of Christ which the world produces. As our faith comes through the word of God, so, likewise, our understanding of being Christ-like must come through the Bible (Rom. 10:17). The world distorts and twists Christ. The Bible presents the true picture of Jesus.

Being living branches of Christ we must be built up and grow also. "As newborn babes, desire the pure milk of the word, that you may grow thereby" (1 Pet. 2:2). From the beginning of conversion, we need to grow. The Bible uses word pictures describing us as living spiritually. We must maintain our spiritual life. To live we must grow and to grow involves the word of God. God gave us scripture for the maturing and completing of ourselves (2 Tim. 3:16-17). We continue to develop beyond the "babe" stage of Christianity by adding the Christian graces until we achieve spiritual maturity and establish our faith (2 Pet. 1:5-11). The growth process carries on throughout the Christian's life. To reach the maturity we seek requires diligence and a willingness to abound in the increasing of the moral attributes which we share with our God. We must possess zeal to grow.

Colossians 2:8 "Beware lest anyone cheat you through philosophy and empty deceit, according to the tradition of men, according to the basic principles of the world, and not according to Christ." Paul cautions a second time expanding on the sources of the dangers from the culture. The world cheats (literally not just "cheats" but takes us captive as if we were plunder)[20] us by teachings which provide center stones of worldly deceit. The first century had the beginnings of Gnosticism, assorted Greek philosophical teachings and the deification of "gods" with human failings. In the twenty-first century the belief systems[21] of feminism,[22] relativism, denominationalism, post modernism, as well as, the philosophies which derive from belief in evolution all capture the minds of less mature. Jesus did not condemn the traditions of man in and of itself (washing hands is not bad in and of itself) but did denounce the raising of man's tradition to the stature of God's Word and commandments and the hypocrisy and arrogance which comes with such elevation (Matt. 15:2-6).

Colossian 2:9 "For in Him dwells all the fullness of the Godhead bodily." What is the meaning of this statement and what prompts Paul to make this proclamation? Looking at the Greek words, we gain some indication of the meaning. The word "katoikeo"[23] translated "dwells" means to reside or to house. "Pas"[24] (translated as "all") refers to "all, or the whole." "Pleroma"[25] is translated "fullness" and is defined as that which is completed, that which is filled or put in to fill up. "Theotes"[26] pertains to the Godhead or Deity as a whole (the Father, the Son, and the Holy Spirit) while "somatikos"[27] concerns the corporeal or physical body. So literally we have a statement saying that in Christ, "the whole of Deity is housed and fills Him in a physical/corporeal form." He is Deity through & through! And man too!

The context of Colossians 2:9 supports this interpretation, also. Colossians 2:8 shows that some were cheated (literally "to be captured") by "philosophy and empty deceit, according to the tradition of men, according to the basic principles of the world. . . ." Though out time, many have either denied Christ's humanity or His Deity. The Essences & Gnostics both looked on flesh as evil. Therefore, some denied Christ's physical, fleshly body. The Gnostics felt Christ was a pale emanation of the one true God, a sort of phantom image. Some Greeks might also have denied Christ being totally Deity. Their gods supposedly consorted with human women to produce weaker demigods. Their view of the Deity of Christ might have been eschewed by their former beliefs. These various traditions, philosophies and beliefs caused some to lose faith.

Paul expresses and values the importance of Jesus being 100% man & 100% God in his earthly incarnation. He makes the statement to Timothy, "For there is one God and one Mediator between God and men, the Man

Christ Jesus" (1 Tim. 2:5). To Titus, Paul speaks of Jesus' deity, "looking for the blessed hope and glorious appearing of our great God and Savior Jesus Christ" (Titus 2:13). Both these statements show that this completeness of Christ is ongoing. It was, is and continues onward.[28] If Jesus was not God then what He did for us in dying on the cross would have far less meaning and no effect in our Salvation. If He is not man then He was not truly tempted and much of His example would be lost to us. Only by being God & man does Christ obtain His ability to intercede and mediate for us with God.

Colossians 2:10 "and you are complete in Him, who is the head of all principality and power." By our conversion and inclusion in the spiritual body of Christ, the Church, we have complete forgiveness of sin and an advocate to help us afterward if we sin again (Eph 1:22-23; Col. 1:18; 1 Jn. 2:1). We know that He heads the Church but His authority transcends that into the world. Of His authority, Jesus spoke saying, "All authority has been given to Me in heaven and on earth" (Matt. 28:18b). Only God, the Father's authority surpasses the authority given (by the Father) to Jesus (1 Cor. 15:27-28). Some argue concerning the meaning of "principalities and powers" (whether spiritual or secular). Since Christ has all authority in both realms these discussions seem to have little value. The fact that the world, for the most part, rebels against the authority of Christ (and God, the Father) does not do away with the reality of that authority. "Every knee shall bow" to The Father, His Son and the Spirit one day (Isa. 45:23; Rom. 14:11; Phil. 2:10).

Verse 10 acts as a bridge to the next topic: our completeness is "in Him." But how do we move into Him and become a part of the Church. Only two verses in the New Testament tell how to get "into" Christ:

> Romans 6:3 "Or do you not know that as many of us as were baptized into Christ Jesus were baptized into His death?"
>
> Galatians 3:27 "Or do you not know that as many of us as were baptized into Christ Jesus were baptized into His death?"

Both verses show that to be "into Christ" we must be baptized into his spiritual body, the Church. Acts two illustrates the deed of baptism placing the person in the church (Acts 2:38-41). Baptism represents the moment of complete conversion, the point of total remission of sins, and the instant of our addition to Christ's church. Most of the Christ based religious world understands the importance of Faith, Repentance and Confession of our faith, yet deny the last step that saves our souls, baptism.

## Colossians 2:11-17: The Circumcision in Christ

Colossians 2:11 "In Him you were also circumcised with the circumcision made without hands, by putting off the body of the sins of the flesh, by the circumcision of Christ" Physical Circumcision created much controversy in the early times of the church. The desire and demand of some Jewish Christians to compel Gentile Christians to be circumcised and indeed to make circumcision a requirement of salvation stirred up many troubles. The Great Council of Jerusalem (the only council ever with inspired Apostles and prophets) dealt with this by denying the necessity of physical circumcision. Paul speaks of a different circumcision for the Christian.

Why the Holy Spirit through the pen of the Apostle Paul would use this unique comparison is difficult to understand. Brother Owen Olbricht, in his commentary on Colossians, points out that the comparison is by no means exact.[29] Old Testament Law required only males to circumcise where the New Testament requires male and female to be baptized. Normally babes eight days old had to be circumcised but only those over an age of accountability have need of Baptism. Circumcision only confirmed or sealed the position of child of Israel, since physical birth established the family relationship. Baptism places us in the spiritual family of God, the seal being the Holy Spirit (2 Cor. 1:22). Brother Olbricht asserts in only one sense does circumcision compare with baptism. Circumcision removed the flesh of man and baptism removes "the contamination of the spirit."[30]

In Colossians chapter three we will see our putting "off" of sinful actions and attitudes (repentance) and a putting "on" of Christ-like actions and attributes. This process speaks of our life and efforts as growing and maturing Christians. Certainly the complete forgiveness of sins requires our initial repentance of our sin. But Christ executes the "putting off" of verse eleven. Our forgiveness comes through the blood of Christ (Rev. 1:5; 1 Pet. 1:18-19). He performs our spiritual circumcision through the instrument of His blood. Moses' wife described physical circumcision as bloody (Ex. 4:25). Spiritual circumcision requires blood also, the blood of the sinless Son of God (Heb. 9:22).

Colossians 2:12 "buried with Him in baptism, in which you also were raised with Him through faith in the working of God, who raised Him from the dead." The burial of the Christian in baptism parallels the burial of our Savior (Rom. 6:1-7). "Baptisma" derives from "baptizo"[31] and means "to dip, immerse, cleanse or purify by washing." We see the picture of Christian baptism in Acts eight. The baptism of the Ethiopian nobleman tells that "both Philip and the eunuch went down into the water" (Acts 8:38). Then

Philip baptized the nobleman. Scripture tells that they, they "came up out of the water" (Acts 8:39). If pouring or sprinkling were sufficient to save then there would be no need to go into the water. But to be buried as our Savior was buried does require water and much water (John 3:23). Romans 6:4 parallels the teaching of Colossians 2:12-13: "Therefore we were buried with Him through baptism into death, that just as Christ was raised from the dead by the glory of the Father, even so we also should walk in newness of life" (Rom. 6:4). Just as Christ arose from His grave to new life we, also, rise from the watery grave of baptism to a new life. Our sins forgiven, we now call ourselves children of God and have all the benefits of being in the spiritual body of Christ, the Church.

Paul stresses the magnitude of faith in the course of our salvation. The Hebrew letter teaches us the importance of a living faith: "But without faith it is impossible to please Him, for he who comes to God must believe that He is, and that He is a rewarder of those who diligently seek Him" (Heb. 11:6). We must believe God can save us and believe in the plan of salvation as the Bible states that process. We don't have to know everything in the Bible at our baptism. We do have to know and have faith in what we must do to be saved and understand why we do these things.

Colossians 2:13 "And you, being dead in your trespasses and the uncircumcision of your flesh, He has made alive together with Him, having forgiven you all trespasses." Colossians tells us, with objective reality, the certainty our fate without Christ, describing us as "being dead in your trespasses and the uncircumcision of your flesh" (Col. 2:13). The book of Romans similarly affirms: "for all have sinned and fall short of the glory of God" and "the wages of sin is death" (Rom. 3:23; 6:23). But both sets of verses have the hope of Christ. ". . . He has made alive together with Him, having forgiven you all trespasses" and "the gift of God is eternal life in Christ Jesus our Lord" (Col. 2:13b; Rom. 6:23b).

Once again we notice a small but powerful word: all. "Having forgiven all trespasses" (Col. 2:13c). "All" means the entirety, the whole, every sin. God cleanses us completely and admonishes us to stay clean. "My little children, these things I write to you, so that you may not sin. And if anyone sins, we have an Advocate with the Father, Jesus Christ the righteous" (1 Jn. 2:1). God gives us instruction to come to Him as our Father and to ask Him to forgive us. Jesus, in teaching His disciples to pray, taught to pray for forgiveness (Matt. 6:12; Luke 11:4). Because of our Savior and Advocate as we follow His commands and live the life He would have us live: "if we walk in the light as He is in the light, we have fellowship with one another, and the blood of

Jesus Christ His Son cleanses us from all sin" (1 Jn. 1:7). As in our conversion we must repent of our sin before we come to God for forgiveness (Acts 8:22).

Colossians 2:14 "having wiped out the handwriting of requirements that was against us, which was contrary to us. And He has taken it out of the way, having nailed it to the cross." Christ came not to destroy the law but to fulfill it (Matt. 5:17). And in fulfilling the law, He shows that the Law could be kept without transgression. Jesus was "in all points tempted as we are, yet without sin" (Heb. 4:15). Some might have said, "God you made the Law too hard and none can keep it!" This impugns the justice of God. If man saves himself, by any system of law keeping, then Christ's sacrifice would be unnecessary. God gave a legal system to man. The Father understood that none would be saved by law keeping. This in no way signifies that we have a sinful nature. What we have is freewill and with our freewill we choose to sin. Certainly the world (and Satan) influences us to sin, but we do not have to sin. We choose to sin because of our own desires and weaknesses (James 1:13-15).

Peter describes the Law of Moses as a yoke which, "neither our fathers nor we were able to bear" (Acts 15:10). Paul, in several verses, tell us of the Law's passing away.

> Romans 6:14-15 "For sin shall not have dominion over you, for you are not under law but under grace. 15 What then? Shall we sin because we are not under law but under grace? Certainly not!"
>
> Ephesians 2:14-16 "For He Himself is our peace, who has made both one, and has broken down the middle wall of separation, 15 having abolished in His flesh the enmity, that is, the law of commandments contained in ordinances, so as to create in Himself one new man from the two, thus making peace, 16 and that He might reconcile them both to God in one body through the cross, thereby putting to death the enmity."
>
> Galatians 2:19 "For I through the law died to the law that I might live to God."

The Cross marks the boundary line between the jurisdiction of the old Law and the establishment of the second covenant. In Jeremiah 31:31-34, God promises a new covenant and a new law. The Hebrew letter gives some requirements which had to be met.

> The Blood was shed at the Cross – Heb. 9:13-14, 20
>
> The Testator died at the cross – Heb. 9:16

The old covenant was made obsolete by Jeremiah's statement – Heb. 8:8-10, 13; Jeremiah 31:31-34

At death, Christ became our Mediator of the New Covenant – Heb. 9:15

Takes away the Law [representative of the old covenant - LEJ] to establish the second covenant – Heb. 10:9

All stood ready for the disarming of all power and authorities and the triumph of Christ.

Colossians 2:15 "Having disarmed principalities and powers, He made a public spectacle of them, triumphing over them in it." The scriptures advise that Christ is "the head of all principality and power" (Col. 2:10). Many dispute what group Paul speaks of here.[32] Whether secular earthly leaders or demonic spiritual powers one fact remains, Christ has all authority. The word, apekduomai, translated "disarmed" in the NKJV and "spoiled" in the ASV means "to despoil."[33] Webster's dictionary defines "despoil" to mean "to rob or plunder."[34] The Jewish leaders by their traditions or false doctrines attempted to take authority from God (Matt. 15:3ff). Satan always seeks to steal and usurp the authority which God possesses. By the giving of "all authority" to Christ that authority resides with Deity (as it always really had and will always). All who attempt to gain authority in and outside of religion will one day deal with God and His Son, Jesus Christ.

This triumph represents not just the winning of a skirmish or a battle. Jesus' victory wins the whole war. Most consider the book of Revelation a difficult book to understand but the most understandable lesson in that book is that Jesus wins and Christians win with Him. "And I saw something like a sea of glass mingled with fire, and those who have the victory over the beast, over his image and over his mark and over the number of his name, standing on the sea of glass, having harps of God" (Rev. 15:2). Elsewhere in the New Testament we glimpse the historic victory, "But thanks be to God, who gives us the victory through our Lord Jesus Christ" (1 Cor. 15:57). Also John speaks of our victory in his epistles "For whatever is born of God overcomes the world. And this is the victory that has overcome the world--our faith" (1 Jn. 5:4). From the Pharisees to Satan, Christ has the victory (Heb. 2:14).

Colossians 2:16 "So let no one judge you in food or in drink, or regarding a festival or a new moon or sabbaths" Because of the doing away with the Law, the various commands concerning food and drink, or the keeping of feast days , or the keeping of the Sabbath day, no longer hold dominion over Jew (not now) or Gentile (not ever). Did some Jews, even Christians, keep the

Sabbath? Paul used the Sabbath as an opportunity to teach (Acts 13:42, 44; 16:13). He did this by choice as an opportunity and not by legal obligation. The Jewish Christians, who thought the Law of Moses must also be obeyed by all Christians, judged both their Jewish brethren who no longer kept the Law and their Gentile brethren who did not keep the Law. Acts 15 solved the problem but not all accepted the ruling of that council. Paul teaches that none have the right to judge you in matters of the former law. As long as you keep the law of Christ if you want to not eat what the Law defined as "unclean" that is your right. So too is eating unclean animals, if your choice.

Colossians 2:17 "which are a shadow of things to come, but the substance is of Christ." According to the letter to the Galatians, the Law was "our tutor to bring us to Christ, that we might be justified by faith" (Gal.3:24). All the High Priests of Israel look forward to the sinless High Priest of the Royal priesthood, Jesus Christ (Heb. 4:15; 1 Pet. 2:9). The Kings of Judah picture the coming of the perfect King of Kings (1 Tim. 6:15). Moses foretells a prophet like him yet greater than him, Jesus (Deut. 18:15, 18; Heb. 3:3-6). Over three hundred prophecies attest to Jesus as the Christ, the Son of God. Some say that almost the entirety of the Old Testament points to Jesus saying, "Christ is coming!" In the New Testament, Christ comes as the substance of all the shadows of the Old Testament.

## Colossians 2:18-23: The Church, the Body of Christ

Colossians 2:18 "Let no one cheat you of your reward, taking delight in false humility and worship of angels, intruding into those things which he has not seen, vainly puffed up by his fleshly mind." Once again, Paul issues warnings to the Colossians. Though translated as "cheat" this is a different Greek word, "katabrabeuo." The word means to "to make a victim of practices, to overreach."[35] We must not allow ourselves to be victims of those delighting in the teachings of ascetic rules of self–denial or abasement which amounts to will-worship (define as "a term descriptive of such forms of adoration and service as are not prescribed in God's word, but are offensive in his sight").[36] Colossians 2:23 mentions "will-worship" as self imposed religion. In keeping all the man-made rules, we may neglect the commandments of God which might lead to the loss of our souls.

The New Testament shows that angels deserve no worship. "Now I, John, saw and heard these things. And when I heard and saw, I fell down to worship before the feet of the angel who showed me these things. Then he said to me, 'See that you do not do that. For I am your fellow servant, and of your brethren the prophets, and of those who keep the words of this book. Worship God'" (Rev. 22:8-9). Jesus states it simply, "You shall worship the LORD your God, and Him only you shall serve" (Matt. 4:10).

The New King James translation of, "intruding into those things which he has not seen" seems a better translation than "dwelling in the things which he hath seen" of the American Standard Version. The ASV does not seem to consider the Greek word "me" which is a particle of negation which translates as "not."[37] Some commentators want to ignore the negative making the translation about apparent visions these teachers might profess to see.[38] With the negative, this phrase speaks of the impertinence of these false teachers dealing with subjects ("intruding into things") they could not possibly have seen and which had not been revealed by God.

The Bible notes that, "Knowledge puffs up" even if that knowledge proves false (1 Cor. 8:1b). Many times the false teacher may become haughty in his supposedly "superior" but ultimately false knowledge.

Colossians 2:19 "and not holding fast to the Head, from whom all the body, nourished and knit together by joints and ligaments, grows with the increase that is from God." The greatest dilemma of this situation centers in the fact that through these false teachings, the person loses Christ, the Head of the Spiritual body. Back in verse seven, we pointed out John's description of our relationship with Christ, in speaking of Christ as the True Vine (John 15:1ff). As one of the branches, we must maintain contact with the True Vine. Christ nourishes the Body. "Holding fast" involves many factors:

our diligent study of the Word

attentive adherence to the commands within that Word

growth of our faith and in other attributes of Christ

our conscientious involvement in the worship activities of prayer, listening to the

preaching of God's Word, singing, giving and of course, the Lord's Supper

steadfast service to Jesus, our Head

As we walk in the way of God, the blood continually cleanses us and maintains contact in the body, the church (1 Jn. 1:7). In Ephesians, Paul makes a similar statement as in Colossians 2:19: ". . . from whom the whole body, joined and knit together by what every joint supplies, according to the effective working by which every part does its share, causes growth of the body for the edifying of itself in love" (Eph. 4:16). Colossians 2:19 and Ephesians 4:16 represent the two sides of the same spiritual body. Ephesians stresses the importance of the Church while Colossians highlights the all importance of the Head of the Church, Jesus Christ. One cannot be separated from the other. We must hold fast to Christ.

By preaching the Word, we plant and water the seed of salvation, leading to numerical growth, but God gives the increase (1 Cor. 3:6-7). In our spiritual growth as Christians, God provides the growth medium through His Word (showing us the attributes we must "put on") and through opportunities to do His work (2 Pet. 1:5-8; Matt. 25:14-30).

Colossians 2:20 "Therefore, if you died with Christ from the basic principles of the world, why, as though living in the world, do you subject yourselves to regulations." At our Baptism, we die with Christ (Rom. 6:3-8). Our Kingdom and the rules and laws of our Kingdom transcend this physical world. We obey the laws of the earthly realm because at this time we are sojourners and pilgrims in this world (1 Pet. 2:11). Obedience of the laws of this world depends on those worldly laws being in harmony with the laws of God. When they are not in harmony we must obey the higher laws of Christ. Throughout time various groups create rules and regulations not in accord with the law of Christ. In the form of traditions or the guise of law such creations attempt to usurp the authority given by Christ. Whether dead Judaism or the doctrines of the Gnostics or current false philosophies and religious teaching we must cleave to Christ and His Word, the Bible, as the only true words of God and the only Words having power over us.

Colossians 2:21 "Do not touch, do not taste, do not handle." This phrase underscores the mentality of the oppressive philosophies threatening Colosee. At first, these actions might seem helpful in limiting temptations. Eve touched, tasted and handled (Gen. 3). Even under the Law of Moses, the dietary and religious restrictions necessitated not touching, tasting or handling. However, with the passing of the Law, "touch," "taste," and "handle" lose their power. The command to not touch, or taste, or handle has no power or purpose save the resurgence of a dead law or the effort to create a new set of rules. In either case it goes beyond the authority of man and assumes the authority of God.

Colossians 2:22 "which all concern things which perish with the using—according to the commandments and doctrines of men?" In his commentary on Colossians, Brother Owen Olbricht points out, Jesus teaches that what is eaten by a man does not defile him, but what "proceeds out of man" defiles (Mark 7:18-20).[39] Paul tells the Romans that the Kingdom of God is not about food or drink and those of Corinth that God will "bring to nought"[40] concerning food and the stomach (Rom. 14:17; 1 Cor. 6:13).[41] In the Christian religion eating has little concern (other than avoiding gluttony). Actions and attitudes are of far greater import.

Jesus spoke of man's commandments and traditions. "'These people draw near to Me with their mouth, And honor Me with their lips, But their heart is far from Me. And in vain they worship Me, Teaching as doctrines the commandments of men.'" (Matt. 15:8-9; Isa. 29:13). Earlier in Matthew 15, Jesus admonishes the Pharisees for keeping their traditions at the expence of God's commands (Matt. 15:2-6; Mark 7:3-9). Colossians 2:21-22 form a question. Are no the commands of no taste, touch or handle from man or God? The answer is from men!

Colossians 2:23 "These things indeed have an appearance of wisdom in self-imposed religion, false humility, and neglect of the body, but are of no value against the indulgence of the flesh." Verse 23 gives Paul's last warning on the subject of ascetic religion. Some false religion sounds good. Paul tells the Christians in Rome to "present your bodies a living sacrifice, holy, acceptable to God, which is your reasonable service (spiritual service)"[42] (Rom. 12:1). In not using substances which harm the body (various drugs, cigarettes, alcohol) we fulfill that command. We do not need a series commands from men to "do not touch, do not taste and do not handle." God has given us already the commands and principles we need to stand acceptable in His sight (without the additions men put in place). God warns not to add to or subtract from His word (Gal. 1:6-9; Rev. 22:18-19). Men do so at their peril.

Paul lists three culprits of ascetic religion: 1) Self imposed religion 2) false humility, and 3) neglect of the body. In false religion these claim value. The idea of controlling our bodies in a way beyond what God tells us to control or in ways which God does not give credence amounts to will worship. We do what we want to do to honor and worship God rather than that which He states pleases Him.

The ascetic methods have no real value to deal with man's temptation, his indulgences. In truth all man-made religions, doctrines, and churches have no true value. We go full circle. God provides us "all things that pertain to life and godliness" through His word (2 Pet. 1:3). His word thoroughly equips "for every good work" (2 Tim.3:16-17). His Word provides protection from temptations to indulge in sin (Matt. 4:3-10). Jeremiah states it plainly. "O LORD, I know the way of man is not in himself; It is not in man who walks to direct his own steps" (Jeremiah 10:23).

## Chapter 3

# Colossians

*by*

*Tommy Haynes*

## Colossians Three: Introduction

Chapter three is the practical answer to Paul's prayers concerning the Colossians (1:9-14). Paul puts legs on the need the church had so that they could be the new man in Christ God wanted them to be. The Colossians were apparently doing quite well with the original teaching that they had received, but this chapter takes them to the next level of Christian development. The descriptions of the Christian life are exhilarating and inspirational: "hidden with Christ in God," "the new man," "elect of God," "holy," and "beloved."

## Colossians Three: Theme "The New Man"

It seems clear that the new life in Christ is the theme for this chapter. The term only appears one time (vs.10), but the contrast between the old way of life and the new is dominant in the text. Many scholars have compared the letter to the Colossians with Paul's letter to the Ephesians, and this chapter does bear a great deal of resemblance. We have the former life, following after the sons of disobedience (Col.3:6,7; compare with Eph.2:1-3). There is also the similarity of Paul's encouragement to "teach one another (and in Ephesians "speaking to one another" Eph.5:19) in psalms and hymns and spiritual songs" (Col.3:16). There is also the whole concept of the new man in both letters (Eph.2:15; 4:24; Col.3:10). The third chapter serves as one of the bits of evidence that Paul is indeed the writer of this letter.

## Colossians 3:1-4: New In Thought

"Seek those things which are above, where Christ is..." As the mind goes, so goes the life. When we set our minds on something, it will direct our steps toward the goal. The Philippians were going to be able to overcome whatever the problem between Euodia and Synteche was because they could set their mind on different things: "Finally, brethren, whatever things are true, whatever things are noble, whatever things are just, whatever things are pure, whatever things are lovely, whatever things are of good report, if there is any virtue and if there is anything praiseworthy — meditate on these things" (Phil.4:8-9 NKJV). Paul wanted the Colossians to dwell on thoughts from above, or heavenly thoughts. The person who has died to the world and been made alive in Christ must stay focused on the goal of that new life which is heaven. When I was a boy and would plow the field for my dad, I had to stay focused on a fixed point or I would get off target and plow a crooked row. The same dynamic is being emphasized here. If we set our minds on heavenly things, we will achieve heavenly things. There is again some similarity between what Paul is writing here, and what he said to the Philippians: "Brethren, I do not count myself to have apprehended; but one thing I do, forgetting those things which are behind and reaching forward to those things which are ahead, I press toward the goal for the prize of the upward call of God in Christ Jesus" (Phil.3:13-14). Keeping our minds focused on Christ is a major part of the change from old to new in this context (See also 2 Cor.5:17).

"For you died, and your life is hidden with Christ in God." Being "hidden" in Christ would mean that we are completely surrounded by Him, even immersed in Him. This would dictate the actions we pursue, the words we say, and the attitudes we possess. This term is also consistent with Jesus' teaching in the Sermon on the Mount when He said, "For where your treasure is, there your heart will be also" (Matt.6:21). We not only store up heavenly things in heaven, we go there with our whole mind. Jesus' blood blots out the sins we once committed (Acts 3:19), and are now covered and hidden in Him as our propitiation (Rom.3:25). When God looks at our lives in Christ, He sees the clean slate, not the crimson stains.

"When Christ who is our life appears, then you also will appear with Him in glory." If we become new men through the complete change of mental process, and we hide our lives in Christ, it follows that when He comes again, we will appear with Him in glory. The Spirit of God, being our seal and down-payment on the covenant (Eph.1:14,15) means that we get to be glorified with Christ "The Spirit Himself bears witness with our spirit that we are children of God, and if children, then heirs — heirs of God and joint heirs with Christ, if indeed we suffer with Him, that we may also be glorified together" (Rom.8:16-17). This section indicates to us that we become a "part of" Christ which is the literal meaning of the word "Christian" used in scripture (Acts 26:28; 1 Pet.4:16). David mentions the glorification of man through God's "visit" to us (implying Christ's coming as a man and His substitutional death for us - Psa.8:4,5).

This change from the old to the new man gives us a whole new perspective, so that we look forward, not to earthly things, but to the glorious appearing of Christ because we are one with Him. To Titus Paul wrote: "...looking for the blessed hope and glorious appearing of our great God and Savior Jesus Christ" (Titus 2:13).

## Colossians 3:5-11: New In Action

Our thought process changes as we grow closer to living like Christ. We are motivated to be like Him so our actions will also of necessity change. If they don't, we are hypocrites of the worst sort.

An unusual term is used as Paul commands, "Put to death your members upon the earth..." (vs.5). The term "member" is the Greek word "melee." In English this word means "a hand to hand fight among several people" (Dictionary.com) and in Greek it refers to the limbs of a person. Paul is not commanding that we maim the body, but that we bring it under control through Christ. Paul addresses this with a sports analogy to the Corinthians: "But I discipline my body and bring it into subjection, lest, when I have preached to others, I myself should become disqualified" (1 Cor. 9:27). In Jesus we bring the violent struggle of our lives under control. The "sons of disobedience" are those who are insolent, rebellious, and unbelieving. The word for this is the same word from which we derive our word "apathy." These men are apathetic toward spiritual matters.

The Spirit reveals two lists in this section. The first are actual actions, the second can be both emotions and motives that lead to actions: "...fornication, uncleanness, passion, evil desire, and covetousness, which is idolatry" (3:5,6). All of these can have a sexual element to them, but are not limited to that (you can covet a thing as well as a person). All of these also deal with our passions that can turn to lust. Passion is not a bad thing, but it can be if we turn it toward something God has told us to avoid.

The second list contains both actions and attitudes. "But now you yourselves are to put off all these: anger, wrath, malice, blasphemy, filthy language out of your mouth. 9 Do not lie to one another, since you have put off the old man with his deeds" (3:8,9). Can a person be angry and not take any action? Yes. In fact, we can be angry without sin (Eph.4:26). Both wrath and malice include actions, at least in the mind, which are not healthy. They are the next step after anger. Blasphemy, filthy language, and lying are all sins of the mouth that are inconsistent with the new man who is hidden in Christ (See James 3:1-12).

The contrast of new and old is brought out plainly here: "Do not lie to one another, since you have put off the old man with his deeds, and have put on the new man who is renewed in knowledge according to the image of Him who created him, where there is neither Greek nor Jew, circumcised nor uncircumcised, barbarian, Scythian, slave nor free, but Christ is all and in all" (Col. 3:9-11). Our new identity is consistent with the identity of Christ. We gain this by deep study and reflection on scripture (2 Tim.2:15) which renews our spirit and life (Rom.12:1,2). We should no longer emphasize our nationality or ethnicity, but realize we are completely Christian, and Christian only. We sing "He is my everything, He is my all..." and this passage declares this to be true.

## Colossians 3:1-17: New In Character

In order for our thoughts and actions to change permanently, these new ways must become woven into the fabric of our lives. This is character. Someone said that "Character is what we are when no one is looking." The fact of the matter is that the Christian knows that he is under the watchful eye of the Lord at all times. We are never alone (Matt.28:20; Heb.13:5; Ps.139).

Paul gives yet another list that the Colossians were to weave into their lives. Virtually all of these are attitudes that will lead to the development of character controlling our actions. Paul reminds them they are God's elect, holy, and loved. Then he gives the list: "...put on tender mercies, kindness, humility, meekness, longsuffering; bearing with one another, and forgiving one another, if anyone has a complaint against another; even as Christ forgave you, so you also must do" (Col 3:12-14). Note that the text says these are things we must "do." Changing our character is hard work. There is study, development of personal ethics, and practice of what we have learned. Character is not something we possess naturally; it is something we grow into.

"But above all these things put on love, which is the bond of perfection. And let the peace of God rule in your hearts, to which also you were called in one body; and be thankful." Love is the greatest thing God has given to man (1 Cor.13:13). It can lead us to a type of perfection in Christ. John states: "No one has seen God at any time. If we love one another, God abides in us, and His love has been perfected in us" (1 Jon...4:12). He even states that "… God is love" (1 Jon.4:8). When we are expressing the love God has shown to us by being a forgiving and helpful person in life, it becomes easier to live in peace with yourself (See also Phil.4:7). Living in peace, and being a loving person makes the goal of unity with others far simpler.

"Let the word of Christ dwell in you richly in all wisdom, teaching and admonishing one another in psalms and hymns and spiritual songs, singing with grace in your hearts to the Lord. And whatever you do in word or deed, do all in the name of the Lord Jesus, giving thanks to God the Father through Him." Paul gives us a very practical way to allow God's word to dwell in us and that is to concentrate on His word through song. Our children learn through singing great truths that will last them a lifetime.

Imagine how we can radically change everything and everyone around us if we always strive to do everything in the name of the Lord, and always being thankful (1 Thess.5:18). Our prayers are to be filled with thanks (Phil.4:6). Now Paul says our every action is to reflect it. The complaining we often do in life would be handled quickly and well if we cultivate this characteristic in our lives.

## Colossians 3:18-25: New In Life

Paul concludes this most practical chapter by being very specific about the roles we play in this life to impress upon us the thought of being new.

"Wives, submit to your own husbands, as is fitting in the Lord." Wives are to be in submission to their husbands with the attitude that they are being in submission to the Lord in so doing (Eph.5:22). When husbands are what they are supposed to be in behavior toward their wives, this is easily accomplished (Eph.5:25ff.).

"Husbands, love your wives and do not be bitter toward them." He instructs husbands to love their wives and not be bitter toward them. "Bitter" here means "harsh, exasperated, or indignant." We are reminded of Nabal (whose name means "fool") who treated David and his men harshly when they asked for provisions from him. Nabal lost his life due to this attitude, and David ended up married to Nabal's wife Abigail (1 Sam.25:3). Men who harbor anger and resentment toward their wives are opening their lives up to heartache and disappointment. Instead, Paul uses the word "agape" as the type of love a man is to have toward his wife. This goes beyond attraction or feelings. This type of love comes from the very core of our existence, and we love in spite of our surroundings and environment.

"Children, obey your parents in all things, for this is well pleasing to the Lord."

Paul now turns his attention toward children. They are encouraged to "obey" their parents. This is a complex word that means to "hear, understand, and do what is required by authority." Paul does not add, as he did in the Ephesian letter (Eph.6:1,2), that there was a promise attached to the original statement concerning children obeying (Deut.5:16). For any of us to grow in this world, we need to obey and honor authority. This is taught and learned in the home. Parents do a disservice to their children if they do not cause this attitude to be a major part of their character. Israel suffered greatly at the hands of Eli's sons who did not respect the position of the priests and live a pure life (1 Sam.2:12-17). This lack of respect for authority led to their deaths and the high priesthood being taken away from their lineage (1 Sam.3:11-14). A father, who is a Christian, in order to reflect Christ in his actions, must teach his children to be obedient.

"Fathers, do not provoke your children, lest they become discouraged." Fathers are the next subject. Paul tells them that they are not to stimulate an angry reaction from their children, or they will become "discouraged." This word means "spiritless or disheartened." Some children test the souls of their parents, but we must nevertheless strive to change their behavior without breaking their spirit. The scriptures are here teaching us a fine balance (see also Eph.6:1-4). All those who have followed God from ancient times are to take great care of their offspring by teaching them well and treating them well (Deut.6:4-9).

"Bondservants, obey in all things your masters according to the flesh, not with eyeservice, as men-pleasers, but in sincerity of heart, fearing God. And whatever you do, do it heartily, as to the Lord and not to men, knowing that from the Lord you will receive the reward of the inheritance; for you serve the Lord Christ. But he who does wrong will be repaid for what he has done, and there is no partiality." The economy of this culture sometimes crashed in on people so that they had to sell their services to others as a bondservant. There were apparently people in this position in other churches (mentioned also in Eph.6:5-8). Runaway slaves were a problem as evidenced by Onesimus (Philemon 8-16). Paul encourages these Christians to work hard and honestly. They were to possess the new attitude of working for Christ and not for men. This would revolutionize their work as they would want to work for Christ even if they did not want to work for their master. The apostle does not pull any punches when he tells the bondservant that if he does wrong, the Lord will show no partiality. God will not excuse the slave because he is in slavery for doing what is wrong. He is to serve men like he would serve the Lord.

## Colossians Three: Conclusion

Chapter three fits in very well with the overall theme of the book of Colossians as Paul emphasizes being "complete" in Christ (Col.1:9,22,28; 4:1,22) . Our change from worldly to spiritual is not complete until we do away with the "old" man and put on the "new." We are to accurately reflect Christ because our lives are hidden inside of His life. The prospect of being new is one of the draws of Christianity. We need to make it well understood to those outside of Christ that they can be made new, and enjoy all of the blessings that come with this new life. A deep study of chapter three can genuinely assist the alien sinner in making the decision to put on Christ.

## Colossians Three: References

No direct quotes were used, but these resources were invaluable in developing this material.

P.C. Study Bible (Biblesoft's New Exhaustive Strong's Numbers and Concordance with Expanded Greek-Hebrew Dictionary. Copyright © 1994, 2003 Biblesoft, Inc. and International Bible Translators, Inc.)

Thayer's Greek English Lexicon of the New Testament (17th Printing, 1976, Zondervan Publishing House, Grand Rapids, Michigan).

Truth for Today Commentary, Colossians and Philemon, Owen D. Olbricht and Bruce McLarty (2005, Resource Publications, Searcy, AR).

CHAPTER 4

# Colossians

*by*

*David Gardner*

ଓଃଧେ

---

## Colossians 4:1: Masters Must Learn a New System of Treatment

"Masters, treat your slaves justly and fairly, knowing that you also have a Master in heaven." Verse 1 concludes the context begun in 3:18ff. The tones of justice and equality in the treatment of slaves would have been startling for masters. Convincing slaves to work hard can no longer be done with harsh and inhumane prodding. Instead, masters must adapt their methods of ownership to match their new status under the sovereign Christ. They must be kind and reasonable, paying fair wages and treating their workers with dignity and respect. Whereas in past times they may have believed they were accountable to no one but themselves, they now realize their accountability under the Maker of Heaven and Earth, who sees all things (Heb. 4:13)

## Colossians 4:2-6: A Lifestyle that Adapts to the Message it Believed

With the primary emphasis so far being on new Christian lives in a world ruled by Christ, this section becomes very practical in the demonstration of that truth. Wisdom is demonstrated in how we conduct ourselves in a world of unbelievers. Self-awareness and compassion direct the tones and words of our conversations. The people of God do not grow fainthearted or purposeless in prayer. Ultimately, we re-orient every aspect of our life towards evangelism as our knowledge increases in what Christ has done for us and what he can do in our world. We are a people of hope, a people of direction and purpose with a divine mission. The world has questions. We have answers. The world is hurting—we know the source of healing. We unite under the Pre-eminent Savior who called all things into being, and is calling the world to Him through His church.

Who can accomplish the divine commission (Mt. 28:18-20) without divine help? Paul instructs: Continue steadfastly in prayer, being watchful in it with thanksgiving. These 5 verses have an outward focus on unbelievers. How we interact in our daily world (3:22-4:1) is a reflection of how much we believe God can change it. Wherever we find ourselves (whether it is under a domineering boss or around half-hearted and unethical employees, 3:22-25), they become the direct subjects of our prayer lives. We humbly serve them, embodying the heart or Christ by interceding for them. We don't lose heart in this effort, but pray as Paul did, that they would "be filled with the knowledge of his will (1:9)." We ask the Father to illuminate their heart to spiritual wisdom and understanding. What a ministry to a lost world!

At the same time: being watchful in it with thanksgiving. The church devotes itself to prayer fully convinced that God will bring something out of it (Acts 1:14, 2:42, 4:31, 7:60, 10:9, 12:5). We lose heart in our world because of injustice and immorality. Rather than embrace a defeatist, cynical outlook, we attend to our prayers knowing that God can attend to their hearts. Like Epaphras (4:12), we will struggle in our prayers when spiritual discernment opens our hearts to a hurting world. But we keep alert! Watching, expecting, and believing--realizing that through our petitions and earnest prayer, God can make his appeal to the world through us (2 Cor. 5:20).

Thanksgiving is the only appropriate response when one witnesses lives changed by the kingdom of God. It has been the continuing thread of Colossians (1:12, 2:7, 3:15, and 3:17) and is a true mark of spiritual maturity. As the 1 leper who "turned back, praising God with a loud voice; and he fell on his face at Jesus' feet, giving him thanks," may we have the wisdom to celebrate and express gratitude for changed lives.

It's hard to develop the maturity to pray for others if you don't depend on it yourself. For Paul's ministry, his dependence on prayer is unashamedly recorded (1:3, 1:9, Eph. 1:15-20, 3:14-2, 1 Thess. 1:2, Rom. 1:8, 1 Cor. 1:4, Phil. 1:3, 2 Tim. 1:3). Here, he asks, "At the same time, pray also for us, that God may open to us a door for the word, to declare the mystery of Christ, on account of which I am in prison." By this time, the "whole imperial guard" knows he is in prison for Christ (Phil. 1:13) yet he's already thinking about the opportunities beyond the guard when he is released from chains. Whose heart is God preparing for Paul to come in contact with? What audience will he be standing before a month from now? Paul requests them to start laying the groundwork for the word by praying for receptive hearts.

When the time comes, he's not going to rely on any special oratory skills or talent (1 Cor. 2:4-5), but on the word. The mystery of Christ is God's plan for the salvation of the world that has become fully realized in the man Jesus Christ. High ranking Roman officials, poor beggars on the streets, the 9,000 men of the Praetorian Guard, a woman praying by the river, and all of humanity to the ends of the earth can be reconciled to God through the word.

We often find ourselves in contexts that may not have been our first choice. But wherever we may be, let it be for the progress of the kingdom. Every wrongdoing committed against us can eventually work itself out for the advancement of the gospel if we are willing servants. The only things that can hinder the progress of the gospel are neglected prayer lives and reluctant testimonies. Willing servants, along with intentional prayers, is the Holy Spirit's method of getting the word of God into people's lives.

"that I may make it clear, which is how I ought to speak." His utmost concern is that Jesus is communicated perfectly in his preaching. To "make clear" means to reveal or make manifest. There is a vast difference between proclaiming the Jesus of culture and commentary and the Jesus of revealed truth. We misrepresent Christ when we don't proclaim him from the treasures of wisdom and knowledge found in God's word (2:2-4).

How we conduct ourselves around unbelievers reveals what we believe about the changing power of the Spirit. Continuing his outward focus, Paul writes, "Walk in wisdom toward outsiders, making the best use of time" It's startling how quickly a wrong word or a wrong look can shut the door to conversion. It might not be fair, but unbelievers are shackled by mistrust, insecurity, and often times, their only knowledge of Christians comes from negative media portrayal. Our response is not an "us versus them" mentality. Our response is learning how to walk in the steps of Christ so that we are wise enough to graciously show the world who he is, no matter how misrepresented we are in the process. We will never make progress if there is hatred and animosity in our hearts. Conducting ourselves with wisdom is the cornerstone of future conversions. A blameless life ensures that my message is not contradictory, a humble spirit is the guarantee that my message has a foundation to be built upon, and a kind heart gives the listener a reason to listen without skepticism.

"Making the best use of time" means snatching up an opportunity to show Christ as if it may be your last (James 4.13-14). Having built a foundation of wise and gracious living, your listener trusts you. As they speak, you instinctively recognize open doors to declare the hope of Christ.

In those moments, the tone and sincerity of your words is critical. "Let your speech always be gracious, seasoned with salt, so that you may know how you ought to answer each person." In this context, we are dealing with outsiders who have questions. Urgency to answer is important, but will only be effective when seized with knowledge. The urgency to answer isn't nearly as important as the urgency to be well grounded in truth! (1 Pet. 3:15-16, Col. 1:9-10).

The helpfulness of your answer has a direct correlation to how well you listened to their question. The wisdom of being quick to hear is that you increase the relevance of your answer. You hear their questions, you sense their void, and you carefully fill it with the treasures of Christ.

## Colossians 4:7-9: Two Faithful Brothers with a Positive Report

"Tychicus will tell you all about my activities. He is a beloved brother and faithful minister and fellow servant in the Lord. 8 I have sent him to you for this very purpose, that you may know how we are and that he may encourage your hearts." Tychicus might not make it on the list of the most popular baby names of 2014, but he is certainly a man to follow. Tychicus was the carrier of this letter as well as the letter of Ephesians. (Eph. 6:21-22). We meet him in Acts 20:4 as a Christian from the province of Asia who traveled with Paul to Jerusalem. He is also mentioned in Titus 3:12 and 2 Timothy 4:12.

More importantly, he was "a beloved brother and faithful minister and fellow servant." He was someone who the Colossians could immediately trust. He was worthy of their attention as a minister, and he was proving his servant mentality by faithfully delivering this letter and informing the Colossians of Paul's livelihood (building off 2:2).

Accompanying Tychichus was Onesimus, "our faithful and beloved brother, who is one of you. They will tell you of everything that has taken place here. He is the slave written about in the letter to Philemon. Paul met him in prison (Phm. 10), and grew to love him greatly (Phm. 12-16). He is described here as a "faithful and beloved brother." As a slave trusted and praised by Paul, he holds him up as solid evidence of the point he made in 3:11: "Here there is not Greek and Jew, circumcised and uncircumcised, barbarian, Scythian, slave, free; but Christ is all, and in all." "Who is one of you" either indicates that he was from Colossae or a Christian. Regardless, he has been converted and in that they can see the inclusive nature of the gospel. Paul's ultimate goal is to restore him to the household of Philemon, promising to pay whatever Onesimus might owe.

## Colossians 4:10-14: Greetings from Paul's encouraging Co-laborers

"Aristarchus my fellow prisoner greets you". In Acts 19:29 & 27:2, he is mentioned as a Macedonian from Thessalonica. During an uprising initiated in Ephesus by Demetrius, he was dragged before a large crowd but got away unharmed (Acts 19:23-41). He was also in the group that traveled with Paul and Tychicus to Jerusalem (Acts 20:4). Being in prison with Paul, at a minimum we have to infer that he was fiercely loyal both to Paul and the spread of the Kingdom.

Also sending a greeting was "Mark the cousin of Barnabas (concerning whom you have received instructions—if he comes to you, welcome him)." This is very likely the John Mark we meet in Acts (Acts 12:12, 25; 13:5, 13). Perhaps Paul's words about "instructions concerning him" were there in order for the Colossians to believe in him again after hearing some negative things about his reliability (see also Acts 15:36-41, 2 Tim. 4:11 & Phm. 24). We don't know the content of the instructions.

The "circumcision party" in all likelihood is simply referring to the fact that these men were Jews. The 3rd mentioned is Jesus who is called Justus. These are the only men of the circumcision among my fellow workers for the kingdom of God, and they have been a comfort to me. This would also illustrate his point from Colossians 3:11 if the Colossians had been battling Jewish false teachers. In other words, it would be Paul's way of saying, "Not all Jews are like that—some have genuinely converted and understand the unifying force of the gospel. They work alongside me and they send their greetings."

"Epaphras, who is one of you, a servant of Christ Jesus, greets you, always struggling on your behalf in his prayers, that you may stand mature and fully assured in all the will of God. 13 For I bear him witness that he has worked hard for you and for those in Laodicea and Hierapolis." Epaphras originally preached the gospel at Colossae (1:7). As a diligent minister, he had devoted himself to the often forgotten aspect in bearing fruit for Christ: relentless prayer. As one who may have been from Colossae, the groaning of his prayers was that they would never settle for a mediocre faith. The image we get from vs. 12 was that Epaphras took compassion from a good idea to a living reality. He had the maturity to be proactive in his prayer life. Often, we pray as a last ditch effort. Epaphras, having seen the church go through years of struggles, knows the value of seasoning his sermons with prayer before, during, and after. His heart's desire is that their hearts would be able to see what God was doing in the world through his kingdom.

"Luke the beloved physician greets you, as does Demas." The primary text we use to note that Luke was a doctor. Not only a prolific writer, but a loyal friend who did not dessert Paul in his greatest moment of trial (2 Tim. 4:11, see also Phm. 24)

Demas deserted Christ at a later time in life (2 Tim. 4:10).

## Colossians 4:15-18: Paul's Personal Greetings

"Give my greetings to the brothers at Laodicea, and to Nympha and the church in her house. 16 And when this letter has been read among you, have it also read in the church of the Laodiceans; and see that you also read the letter from Laodicea." This final greeting is perhaps Paul's way of establishing a relationship before his planned visit to the churches in that area. Nympha may have been a widow with a home and resources to support a small gathering of Christians. They were to take this letter to Laodicea and bring back a letter from Laodicea (which may have been the letter to the Ephesians or a letter to the Laodiceans that has been lost). Either way, both letters were to be read authoritatively from the mind of Paul inspired by the Holy Spirit.

The final greeting is to Archippus: And say to Archippus, "See that you fulfill the ministry that you have received in the Lord." Philemon 2 states that he was Paul's "fellow soldier." He was a member of Philemon's household and appears to be the minister of the church that met in Philemon's house. It becomes a guessing game as to the need for this charge, but any minister of the word can relate to its content when we grow weary!

I, Paul, write this greeting with my own hand. Remember my chains. Grace be with you. We know from other references that Paul often dictated his letters but would at some point sign them in his own writing (2 Thess. 3:17, 1 Cor. 16:21, Gal. 6:11). He asks them to pray for him, and he closes with a prayer for grace (Rom. 16:20, 2 Tim. 4:22, Gal. 6:18). As they receive grace more and more, they will cultivate the compassion imperative to share gospel truth. They will look at the world with entirely new eyes: Eyes that see potential, that weep for the anguish of lost souls, and have the wisdom to mourn a lost community, propelling them into a life that reveals the true and living Christ. In this, they will ignite hope, restore moral courage, and make a plea on behalf of God to the world.

## Notes

1 WORDsearch Outlines
2 Owen D. Olbricht, Truth for Today Commentary Colossians and Philemon (Searcy, AR: Resource Publications, 2005), p. 29
3 elpidα, The Analytical Greek Lexicon (Grand Rapids, MI: Zondervan, tenth printing, 1974), p. 133
4 Ibid., makroqumia
5 Ibid., ikanow
6 Ibid., eikwn
7 Olbricht, Colossians, p. 110dependent on
8 Marvin R. Vincent, Word Studies in the New Testament, Vol. III, The Epistles of Paul (Grand Rapids, MI: William B. Eerdmans Publishing Co., seventh reprinting, 1980), pp. 468, 469
9 Ibid., p. 471[si
10 apokatallassω, Greek Lexicon, p. 43
11 William Hendriksen, New Testament Commentary Exposition of Colossians and Philemon (Grand Rapids, MI: Baker Book House, 1964), p. 85
12 Olbricht, Colossians, p. 160
13 Hendriksen, Colossians p. 87
14 musthriov, Greek Lexicon, p. 273.
15 All scriptures cited in this section of this commentary (unless otherwise noted) will be from The New King James Version. Nashville: Nelson Publishing, copyright 1982.
16 American Standard Version. Camden, New York, Nashville: Thomas Nelson Publishers, copyright 1929.
17 New American Standard Version Updated Edition. Anaheim, California: Foundation Publications, copyright 1997.
18 Cox, John, Church History. Murfreesboro, Tn: Deholf Publication, copyright 1951, reprinted 2006, pgs 39-40.
19 Perschbacher, Wesley, The New Analytical Greek Lexicon. Peabody, Massachusetts: Hendrickson Publishers, copyright 1990 – seventh printing 2006, pg 327.

20 Robertson, R.T., Robertson's New Testament Word Pictures Power Bible CD. Bronson MI: Online Publishing Inc.
21 Highers, Alan, editor The Spiritual Sword: A Handy Guide to False Belief Systems. Volume 44, July 2013.
22 Tarbet, David, "*Are There Limitations on the Role of Women?*" The Spiritual Sword: What is Happening to Us? Volume 40, April 2009 – Editor Highers, Alan.
23 New Analytical Greek Lexicon, pg 233.
24 New Analytical Greek Lexicon, pg. 315
25 New Analytical Greek Lexicon, pg. 332
26 New Analytical Greek Lexicon, pg. 201
27 New Analytical Greek Lexicon, pg. 400
28 Olbright, Owen, Truth for Today Commentary: Colossians and Philemon (Philemon by McLarty, Bruce). Searcy, AR: Resource Publications, copyright 2005, pg. 211
29 Olbricht, pgs 253-255
30 Olbricht, pg 253
31 New Analytical Greek Lexicon, pg. 66
32 Coffman, James Burton, Commentary on Galatians, Ephesians, Philippians, Colossians. Austin, Tx: Firm Foundation Publishing House, Copyright 1977, pgs 383-384.
33 New Analytical Greek Lexicon, pg 38.
34 Webster's New Pocket Dictionary. Boston, New York: Houghton Mifflin Harcourt, pg 91.
35 New Analytical Greek Lexicon, pg 221.
36 American Tract Society Dictionary. Power Bible CD. Bronson MI: Online Publishing Inc.
37 New Analytical Greek Lexicon, pg. 275
38 Weed, Micheal, The Letters of Paul to the Ephesians, Colossians, and Philemon. Austin: Sweet Publishing Company, Copyright 1971, pg. 77
39 Olbricht, pg. 296.
40 American Standard Version
41 Olbricht, pg. 296

42 American Standard Version

# Philemon
## *by*
## *Carl McCann*

ᏦᏕ

## Philemon: Introduction

Imprisoned in Rome, Paul wrote four epistles, dating from 60-62 A.D. This volume of material known as the Prison Epistles, consists of 379 verses (NKJV), and addresses separate yet connected subjects. In Ephesians Paul announces, "The church, divinely purposed by God." Colossians finds Paul heralding, "Jesus Christ, divine founder of the Church." Philippians reveals "The joy that ought to characterize the Church." And lastly, Philemon emphasizes, "Forgiveness, the greatest need of the church."

Paul was often lonely, but he was not a loner. In the twenty five verses which make up the book of Philemon, 12 individuals (including Jesus and Paul) are mentioned, along with the church that met in Philemon's house. Examining the book of Colossians reveals that 8 names are repeated. Paul possessed a deep affection and interest in others (2 Cor. 11:28).

Why do we have the book of Philemon preserved? I fear that when the book of Philemon is compared with the lofty doctrinal themes of other New Testament books, that it is easily overlooked. What lesson or lessons should we glean from a study of this marvelous little book? I believe it will benefit us to reference some of the lessons to be gleaned.

- Tact
- Apostolic Authority
- Philemon's faithfulness
- Providence
- Restoration/Restitution
- Paul's expected release from prison
- Proper treatment of fellow Christians
- Slavery

However, for this writer, the main lesson to be learned is FORGIVENESS. Interestingly, the word forgiveness does not appear in the letter, yet it is understood in nearly every verse. Forgiveness is the central theme of the Bible. As we study through Philemon please do not lose sight of this fact, Paul is appealing to Philemon, encouraging him to forgive Onesimus. Forgiveness is serious business. So serious that Jesus Christ is the only means of forgiveness (Acts 4:12) and those who have been forgiven, dare not withhold forgiveness from one who seeks it (Matt. 6:15). Before we leave the introductory section I would like to spend a little space on the subject of slavery.

Whenever slavery is mentioned questions arise. Why was slavery tolerated? Why didn't Paul or some other New Testament writer speak directly against the practice of slavery? Why didn't Paul or the early church lead a revolt against slavery? The idea of slavery is extremely foreign to us in 2014, yet as we study the subject perhaps some light will be given to help us to better understand it. Denominationalist John MacArthur has some interesting material on this subject at his "Grace to You" website (www.gty.org). Please note the following excerpts taken from an article entitled, "The Apostle Paul and Slavery." "Slavery was taken for granted as a normal part of life in the ancient world. Indeed, the whole structure of Roman society was based on it. During the period of the wars of conquest, most slaves were war captives. By the time of the New Testament, however, most slaves were born into slavery. The number of slaves was enormous, making up as much as one third of the population of the Empire. Slaves were not actually considered persons under the law, but the chattel property of their owners. They could be sold, exchanged, given away, or seized to pay their master's debt. A slave had no legal right to marriage, and slave cohabitation was regulated by their masters. As already noted, masters had almost unlimited power to punish their slaves. By the New Testament era, however, slavery was changing. Treatment of slaves was improving, in part because masters came to realize that contented slaves worked better. Slaves were often better off than freemen. They were assured of food, clothing, and shelter, while poor freemen often slept in the streets, or in cheap housing. Freemen had no job security and could lose their livelihood in times of economic duress. Many slaves ate and dressed as well as freemen. Slaves could be doctors, musicians, teachers, artists, librarians, and accountants. It was not uncommon for a Roman to train a slave at his own trade. They had opportunities for education and training in almost all disciplines. It is significant that the New Testament nowhere attacks slavery directly. Had Jesus and the apostles done so, the result would have been chaos. Any slave insurrection would have been brutally crushed, and the slaves massacred. The gospel would have been swallowed up by the message of social reform. Further, right relations between slaves and masters made it a workable social institution, if not an ideal one. Christianity, however, sowed the seeds of the destruction of slavery. It would be destroyed not by social upheaval, but by changed hearts. The book of Philemon illustrates that principle. Paul does not order Philemon to free Onesimus, or teach that slavery is evil. But by ordering Philemon to treat Onesimus as a brother (Philem. 16; cf. Eph. 6:9; Col. 4:1), Paul eliminated the abuses of slavery. Marvin Vincent comments, "The principles of the gospel not only curtailed [slavery's] abuses, but destroyed the thing itself; for it could not exist without its abuses. To destroy its abuses was to destroy it" (Vincent, Philemon, p. 167)."

I would encourage everyone to visit the aforementioned website and view the entire article. I hope I have shared enough information allowing us to better understand the subject of slavery and to trust that our all knowing Father in heaven handled the menacing practice of slavery in the very best way possible. To think otherwise is to impugn the character of God, which is a path this Christian does not care to tread (Isa. 55:8-9).

As H.A. Ironside stated, "we have stood too long at the door." It is time to enter in and observe the glorious treasure, which is the book of Philemon. To aid our efforts the outline of study in the "Teacher's Annual Lesson Commentary" (1976-77) will be followed.

## Philemon 1-3: Paul's Salutation to Philemon

Technically, Paul was a prisoner of imperial Rome. However, in his mind he was a prisoner of Christ Jesus. In other words Paul was in prison because of his defense of the gospel of Christ and on behalf of Christ (Phil. 1:12-13). Timothy, was Paul's "true son in the faith" (1 Tim. 1:2), and was apparently known by Philemon, perhaps by visiting at Ephesus ( Acts 19) or through the evangelization of Phrygia, of which Colossae was an important city (Acts 16 and 18). It is believed that Apphia, was Philemon's wife and Archippus was their son. Archippus may have been the preacher at Colossae (Col. 4:17). Paul also refers to the church which met in Philemon's home. It was commonplace in this time for the church to meet in someone's home (Rom. 16:3-5). This would indicate that Philemon was a man of means, being able to own a dwelling large enough to house the church. History informs us that it was not until the 3rd century that church buildings developed as places of worship.

Philemon, the "loving one" was apparently a citizen of Colossae, who had been converted to Christ by the preaching of the apostle Paul (v. 19). We do not know in what precise ways Philemon had been a fellow worker with Paul. This introductory section closes with the familiar refrain of grace and peace. Grace is God's unmerited favor (Eph. 2:8ff; Titus 2:11ff) and peace is the result of having obeyed the gospel (Rom. 5:1-2).

## Philemon 4-19: Paul's Message to Philemon

Characteristically Paul refreshes Philemon by identifying him as a subject mentioned frequently in prayer. Paul is sincere; he is not "polishing the apples" as one writer expressed it. Paul was grateful and thankful to God for faithful brethren, such as Philemon, and so should we be! It is truly amazing how much time Paul spent praying, particularly in appreciation of others.

Since some time has passed since Paul was last with Philemon, news had to be brought to him concerning Philemon. Evidently Epaphras was the source of such information (Col. 4:12), conjoined with Onesimus. This news revealed that Philemon's love (agape) and faith (pistis) was directed toward Jesus and the brethren. Some will mention the difference in the word order, but I don't know if there is any real need in this (Eph. 1:15; Col. 1:4). The real point is – Can my friends say the same thing about me? How about you?

Paul desires that Philemon's faith become effective (active or working), but in what sense? Previously, mention has been made of Philemon's provision for the church (v.2), his love of and faithfulness to Jesus and the brethren, he is a refresher (hydrator) of the brethren – so in what sense can Paul admonish Philemon to have an active faith? In the sense of what he is about to ask of him – namely receive Onesimus.

Paul is reluctant to command Philemon's acceptance of Onesimus, even if such would have been proper. Paul appealed rather to love, knowledge and teaching as resources of conviction, instead of forcing Philemon's compliance. I remember well Brother Johnny Ramsey saying, "A man convinced against his will, is of the same opinion still." Paul reminds Philemon of his age and his situation as a prisoner on behalf of Jesus Christ. Some have speculated that Paul was approximately 60 years old at the time of this writing. Not old by our standards – but if we consider the harsh treatment received (2 Cor. 11:22ff; Gal. 6:17) and the lack of medical services, sixty years would have made Paul an aged man.

The major burden of the letter is revealed in verse 10. Paul has skillfully led up to this appeal. Now we find the great apostle imploring on behalf of Onesimus. Somehow, Onesimus had come into contact with Paul in Rome. Onesimus heard the story of Jesus and obeyed the gospel, which alone has the power to save (Rom. 1:16). Onesimus means "helpful or useful" and up to this point he had hardly lived up to his name. What a change the gospel makes in the lives of those who hear and obey its commands. Onesimus was not the same and Paul pleads with Philemon to recognize this fact. Would Philemon give Onesimus the chance to prove it?

Paul understood the doctrine of restitution. Onesimus must return to Philemon and make right to the best of his ability the wrong he had committed. No attempt is made to cover up Onesimus' wrongdoings. Certainly Paul and Onesimus are in agreement on this point for Paul could not force Onesimus to go anymore that he could force Philemon to receive Him. Philemon is admonished to receive him as freely as he would have received Paul and his reception would be an indication of his attitude toward Paul. Paul strengthens his appeal by declaring how greatly he would have desired to keep Onesimus. Onesimus was providing a tremendous service to Paul, but without Philemon's consent Paul would not do such.

In verse 15 Paul raises a possibility, perhaps Onesimus was separated from Philemon, so there reunion might be for eternity. Providence has been described as "God working behind the scenes." Certainly this is the case with Philemon and Onesimus, neither of them could envision a positive outcome of Onesimus' actions. However, God, without interfering with the choice of either could see the return of Onesimus before he ever departed. Joseph, Esther and Onesimus all serve as cases of God's providential care and superintendence of matters without having to invoke miraculous activity. How many times has providence worked in our lives? What a glorious promise and provision.

If Philemon received Onesimus properly there whole relationship would forever change. Philemon's acceptance of Onesimus was not that of a returned slave, but of a greatly beloved, dearly cherished brother in Christ. Paul reminds Philemon of the high regard in which he held Onesimus, and declares that Philemon's love must excel his own. It would be futile for Philemon to declare his love for God, while refusing to accept Onesimus (1 Jn. 4:20). Philemon was to accept Onesimus as he would Paul. Lest that point be missed, let's consider how we would respond to a person who had severely wronged us and at a later point became a Christian. Would we be able to embrace such a one as easily as whole heartedly as we would, say the apostle Paul? This is the real challenge before Philemon!

Helping to alleviate any apprehension, Paul offered to repay Philemon any amount owed to him by Onesimus. The exact manner in which Onesimus had wronged Philemon cannot be determined, however, money would surely have been involved. Money would have been essential in aiding Onesimus to escape to Rome. It is doubtful Paul ever received a "billing statement." The latter part of verse 19 would be a sobering reminder to Philemon; he has been subtly reminded that he owed Paul! Did not Jesus address this same principle in Matthew 18:22ff? Yes he did; so how could one who owed so much refuse to forgive the debt of one who owed so little?

## Philemon 20-22: Confidence in Philemon

Paul's appeal closes on a positive note. He petitions Philemon for help and encouragement. Paul returns to play on words; using the word oinemi which is the same root word as Onesimus. Paul is stating, "Philemon when you receive Oneismus you will supply great joy (lit. help) to me." Also, the example of forgiveness would serve as a wonderful example to other Christians, including us. Here is a pivotal point as to why the book of Philemon was preserved and found its way into the New Testament. The emphasis upon forgiveness in this little book is needed in every generation and in a practical way forgiveness is "fleshed out" before us. "When one has been saved by grace, it is to be expected that he will walk in grace toward others, even to those whom he feels have mistreated and deceived him." (Ironside, p.286).

Certain that Philemon would do more than the letter requested, Paul wanted a guest room prepared. Paul was expecting to be released from prison and planned a visit to Philemon and Onesimus. Once again Paul is appealing to Philemon's acceptance and forgiveness of Onesimus. Is it plausible that Philemon would be praying for Paul's release and not comply with all that he had requested?

## Philemon 23-25: Greeting to Philemon and to Others

Observing the pattern found in several epistles Paul closes by naming several individuals. All of these names are found at the close of the book of

Colossians, providing evidence that Philemon and Colossians were sent at the same time. Epaphras, was formerly the minister at Colossae who was presently imprisoned with Paul. Mark, the cousin of Barnabas, is infamous for deserting Paul on the first missionary journey, causing the dissension and ultimate split between them (Acts 15). Thankfully as years passed he became useful to Paul (2 Tim. 4:11). Sadly the story is different for Demas. He is upheld to the brethren in Colossae (Col. 4:14), and then denounced by Paul in 2 Timothy 4. Aristarchus is also listed as a fellow prisoner; he seems to be a man of extraordinary courage and devotion who was associated with Paul in several places and circumstances (Acts 19:29; 20:4; 27:2). Doctor Luke is the final individual to note. His relationship with Paul is well documented along with the books (Luke and Acts) which he wrote, aided by the Holy Spirit of course. What a source of comfort these good brethren must have been to Paul and sadly some disappointments as well.

Paul closes with words found in every Pauline document. Grace (unmerited favor) has a source and that source is Jesus Christ and His word (Acts 20:32, 2 Tim. 2:1). Certainly we would agree with Paul, "But by the grace of God I am what I am…" (1 Cor. 15:10). May we always love and appreciate all that has been done so that we may live forever with God.

## Philemon: Conclusion

The question inevitably comes to our mind: Did Philemon obey Paul's requests? We think the answer is YES! However, there is no postscript to settle the question. But to us it is unthinkable that Philemon did not fulfill Paul's request. Paul's confidence and hope in Philemon speak to his character. May God help us to so live, forgive and serve our brethren.

## Works Consulted

Michael R.Weed, The Letters of Paul to the Ephesians, the Colossians, and Philemon (Austin, TX: R.B. Sweet Co., Inc., 1971).

Annual Lesson Commentary (Nashville, TN:Gospel Advocate Co., 1950).

Annual Lesson Commentary (Nashville, TN: Gospel Advocate Co., 1957).

Annual Lesson Commentary (Nashville, TN: Gospel Advocate Co., 1976-77).

Matthew Henry's Commentary In One Volume (Grand Rapids, MI: Zondervan Publishing House, 1961.)

H.A. Ironside, A Brief Exposition of the Epistle to Philemon (New York, NY: Loizeaux Brothers, Inc. Bible Truth Depot, 1947.)

Wilbur Fields, Philippians, Colossians and Philemon (Joplin, MO: College Press, 1969.)